National Symbols in Modern Iran

Modern Intellectual and Political History of the Middle East
Fred H. Lawson, *Series Editor*

Select titles in Modern Intellectual and Political History of the Middle East

Class and Labor in Iran: Did the Revolution Matter?
Farhad Nomani and Sohrab Behdad

Ethnicity, Identity, and the Development of Nationalism in Iran
David N. Yaghoubian

God and Juggernaut: Iran's Intellectual Encounter with Modernity
Farzin Vahdat

A Guerrilla Odyssey: Modernization, Secularism, Democracy, and the Fadai Period of National Liberation in Iran, 1971–1979
Peyman Vahabzadeh

The Iranian Constitutional Revolution and the Clerical Leadership of Khurasani
Mateo Mohammad Farzaneh

The Kurds and the State: Evolving National Identity in Iraq, Turkey, and Iran
Denise Natali

Modernity, Sexuality, and Ideology in Iran: The Life and Legacy of a Popular Female Artist
Kamran Talattof

The Story of the Daughters of Quchan: Gender and National Memory in Iranian History
Afsaneh Najmabadi

For a full list of titles in this series, visit
https://press.syr.edu/supressbook-series/modern-intellectual-and-political-history-of-the-middle-east/.

National Symbols in Modern Iran

Identity, Ethnicity, and Collective Memory

Menahem Merhavy

Syracuse University Press

First Edition 2019

19 20 21 22 23 24 6 5 4 3 2 1

∞ The paper used in this publication meets the minimum requirements of the American National Standard for Information Sciences—Permanence of Paper for Printed Library Materials, ANSI Z39.48-1992.

For a listing of books published and distributed by Syracuse University Press, visit https://press.syr.edu.

ISBN: 978-0-8156-3659-5 (hardcover)
978-0-8156-3666-3 (paperback)
978-0-8156-5491-9 (e-book)

Library of Congress Control Number: 2019948321

Manufactured in the United States of America

For Yaara, Ma'ayan, Inbar, Aner, and Noga

Contents

List of Illustrations *ix*

Acknowledgments *xi*

Note on Transliteration *xiii*

Introduction: *Old Myths Revisited* *1*

1. Modern Iran Looks to History *18*

2. A Clash of Pasts *39*

3. A Lost King Rediscovered *71*

4. Persepolis Revisited *108*

5. Celebrating Iranianness in the Islamic Republic *143*

Conclusion: *The Islamic Republic and Iranian Symbols—the Taming of the Shrew* *179*

Notes *191*

Bibliography *219*

Index *243*

Illustrations

1. ‘Ali Shari‘ati, 1972 *42*

2. Ayatollah Mortaza Motahhari, 1940s *55*

3. The winged figure found at Pasargadae *97*

4. Period-costumed soldiers, Persepolis Tent City, October 1971 *124*

5. President Mohammad Khatami visits Persepolis, January 2001 *160*

6. President Mahmud Ahmadinejad and his staff inspect the Cyrus cylinder, Tehran, October 2010 *163*

Acknowledgments

This book is an entirely revised and significantly extended and updated rendition of my doctoral dissertation submitted to Tel Aviv University in 2012. During my doctoral studies there, I benefitted tremendously from the guidance of David Menashri and Meir Litvak. Like many other Israeli scholars of Iran, I am grateful to David for his consistent support of my research. The Center for Iranian Studies, which he headed at the time, was a second home to me, socially as well as academically. Meir currently heads the center, and he was and still is an insightful reader with a sharp eye and keen observations.

Beyond their academic function, the Center for Iranian Studies and the Department for African and Middle Eastern Studies at Tel Aviv University have served as venues for meeting and engaging with dear colleagues to whom I owe so much of my intellectual development. Liora Hendelman-Baavur, Ori Goldberg, and Miriam Nissimov were great listeners and friends to consult through different parts of producing this study.

At Syracuse University Press, I thank Suzanne Guiod and Kelly Balenske for their dedicated work on this book from its early stages. I also thank the two anonymous reviewers, whose comments and suggestions were invaluable to the final text of this book, and copy editor Annie Barva.

I have had the good fortune to benefit from great scholars who have contributed immensely to the slow and evasive process of my intellectual maturity. Firoozeh Kashani-Sabet and Afshin Marashi, who commented on my doctoral dissertation, instigated the journey I embarked on to reach this book. Ali Ansari has been there all along as a senior scholar, a source of inspiration, and a friend whose comments were invaluable.

The United States–Israel Educational Foundation provided me with the opportunity to spend a year at the University of Texas at Austin, which proved to be the best academic and intellectual experience I could have wished for. I had the honor to conduct research side by side with some of the leading scholars on Iran, and they have contributed to this work more than they imagine. I would like to mention, among them, Kamran Scott Aghaie, head of the Center for Middle Eastern Studies; Atwood Blake, whose classes in Persian proved to be both challenging and rewarding; as well as Uri Kolodney, who assisted me in finding treasures at the University of Texas library and beyond. David Stronach from the University of California at Berkeley has commented on and added aspects of this research that no written source could have matched. Tori Rosen and Todd Bontemps helped along the way without hesitation, and it's a pleasure to thank them here.

I am most grateful to both the Truman Institute for the Advancement of Peace at the Hebrew University and the Alliance Center for Iranian Studies at Tel Aviv University for their support of this research.

I also thank my colleagues and friends Rami Ginat, Israel Gershoni, Lior Sternfeld, and, last but not least, Jila Aharonson and Jaleh Soroui, teachers, friends, and guides into the world of the Persian language. I am most indebted to them all.

Finally, I thank my family. First and foremost Ya'ara, who has been a partner in this work in so many ways, and my children, who joined this journey along the way, albeit unwittingly.

I was lucky to benefit from the knowledge and views of all of these individuals, but I alone am responsible for any misjudgment or deficiency in this study.

Jerusalem 2018

Note on Transliteration

The transliteration system I use is a modified form of the *International Journal of Middle East Studies* scheme. The exceptions are names and proper nouns that have a conventional spelling in English (such as "Tehran" rather than "Tihran"). I do not use diacritical marks on those proper nouns and names.

National Symbols in Modern Iran

Introduction

Old Myths Revisited

In May 2002, a group of members of the Iranian Majles (Parliament), journalists, and scholars sent President Mohammad Khatami a letter notifying him of the deteriorating condition of the archaeological site of Persepolis, the Achaemenid capital, and nearby Pasargadae, the site of the tomb of Cyrus the Great, founder of the empire in the sixth century BCE.[1] Although their alarm regarding the dangers the archaeological ruins were exposed to is understandable, that the president would find the subject of any interest was far from obvious. This interest was not disconnected from his earlier visit to the site in January the previous year, one of the first publicized visits of an Iranian leader to Persepolis since the Islamic Revolution of 1979. That earlier visit was a landmark in the long and gradual movement toward coming to terms with the pre-Islamic heritage within the Islamic Republic of Iran.

Researchers of nationalism agree that the search for a common past and a shared historical consciousness, whether continuous and real or imaginary and newly invented, is a necessary part of creating a national framework. Historical consciousness is a key element in the feeling of a common fate shared by members of the nation.

Nations, Symbols, and Memory

The search for the national past serves the claim to historical continuity, which is central to many national movements. Side by side with its liberating and at times revolutionary message, the modern nation, according to nationalists, claims to give expression to an ethnic group that has existed for centuries. Anthony Smith asserts that "history, a sense of history, and an ethnic past or pasts, have all been habitually deemed to be defining characteristics or causal factors in the formation of nations."[2]

The members of the nation, according to Smith, "share a common mass culture and common historical myths and memories."[3] The theme of continuity, which is foundational for national movements, links the claim to represent the nation and embody its aspirations. Collective cultural identity refers to "a sense of continuity, shared memories and notions of collective destiny of that unit and its culture."[4] The memory transmitted from one generation to the next often includes a golden age that stands at the heart of the community's past.[5] The golden age serves as more than a mere source of pride for the members of the nation; it is an expression of the nation's essence and of a period when this essence was given full expression: "Without a golden age, it would be difficult, if not impossible, to discover the 'true self' of the people."[6] Cultivating the national sentiment is intimately linked with the quest for one's true self, "the cult of authenticity."[7] A close connection is thus established between the study of nationalism and its claim to the national past as well as between the study of memory and its transmission to the masses, the members of the national group.

Matthew Levinger and Paula Franklin Lytle have proposed a triadic structure typical of nationalist movements and their relation to the past: the glorious past, the degraded present, and the utopian future.[8]

Maurice Halbwachs, a pioneer in emphasizing the social nature of our memory, claimed that "if we examine a little more closely how we recollect things, we will surely realize that the greatest number of memories come back to us when our parents, our friends, or other persons recall them to us,"[9] a notion that has led researchers to highlight the social aspect of memory making. Halbwachs's approach to collective memory as first and foremost a social phenomenon paved the way for research on the ways collective memory is created and conveyed by different social groups. With the rising interest in nationalism and the theories regarding its appearance, that approach became a cornerstone for the study of a nation's collective memory and the development of that memory over time and space.[10] Although Halbwachs's earlier work focused on memory as a social creation, in his later writings he was more aware of the eminence of power and institutions in formal memory, challenging the boundary between memory and tradition that he had erected earlier.[11]

The institutionalization of memory making occupied Pierre Nora, who emphasized the place memory takes in the public sphere and its uniqueness in modern society. His studies on *lieux de mémoire* expressed his perception that the modern period is characterized by the erosion of authentic memory and its replacement with public, institutionalized memory.[12] Nora emphasized the central role of the modern nation-state in the public sphere of memory and thus in shaping the public space. Jay Winter and Emmanuel Sivan criticize this aspect of Nora's theory, which, they assert, is more characteristic of Nora's homeland and natural "laboratory," France, and does not necessarily apply to other countries and societies.[13] Not only is the state limited in shaping *lieux de mémoire*, but the elites who lead the state are also far from monolithic. The case I present in this book is telling because it occurs in the shadow of a major and dramatic shift of elites in Iran from the Pahlavi state (1925–79) to the Islamic Republic (1979–present).

Without overrating the state's role, as Nora's critics have suggested he does, we can say that the state has undoubtedly been deeply involved in its society's culture of memory.[14] As Philip L. Kohl, Mara Kozelsky, and Nachman Ben-Yehuda assert, "The state needs the remote past to justify its authority and to exercise its rule."[15] Despite the fact that the state's ability to shape the public's perception of history is limited, there is no doubt it does hold great resources for influencing that perception and for being a prominent, though not sole, factor in the process of identity formation and the memory that shapes it. However, even in the sphere where the state is a leading actor, it does not necessarily control the contours of the perception of the symbols it has created. Once created, symbols and their perception seem to have a life of their own.[16]

Ferdinand Braudel, who developed the idea of the *longue durée* in his studies on the Mediterranean, posed another notion that has been highly contested in the historiography of modern Iran: the question of continuity versus change in Iranian history before and after the coming of Islam in the seventh century.[17] For Iranian historians and thinkers, it was and has been very hard to relate the country's history without some reference to the "disruptive culture change"[18] it underwent in the seventh century following its conquest by Islam. Indeed, one of the fundamental bones of contention between secularists and religiously oriented thinkers from the late nineteenth century to the middle of the twentieth century in this matter was in relation to the Islamic conquest of Iran, its aftermath, and its place in the formation of Iranian identity. Whereas Iranian secularists saw the Islamic conquest as a foreign occupation with a strong negative context, religious thinkers had to apply, at the very least, a positive view of the Arab invasion that had brought the great religion of Islam to Iran. The consecration of pre-Islamic Iran by Pahlavi modernists was a challenging effort because they were latecomers to the scene of Iranian collective memory in the modern age, struggling for primacy amid a long-established body of rites and ceremonies in the Shi'ite calendar. According to Smith, "in most cases, the mythologies elaborated by nationalists have not been fabrications, but recombinations of traditional, perhaps unanalyzed, motifs and myths taken from epics, chronicles, documents of the period, and material artifacts. . . . Such novel recombinations are pre-eminently the work of intellectuals in search of their 'roots.'"[19]

Smith defines two main trends in national movements' construction of the past: the didactic and the dramatic.[20] The didactic construction describes the past as "organic" and "natural," its nature as a living, changing organism immutable, whereas the dramatic construction emphasizes the change and diversity of the national past. In Pahlavi Iran, the two constructions were used to reinforce each other. The didactic served the dramatic by lending it a scientific aura and prestige, by translating into Persian excerpts from historians of ancient Iran in a manner that supported the state's view of it. The dramatic served the didactic when, for instance, the fruits of archaeological research were exhibited using the most sophisticated means of the time to direct a megaevent in Persepolis.

Iranian Nationalism: Between the Unique and the Generic

From the middle of the nineteenth century on, philologists, historians, and art researchers' interest in Iran's pre-Islamic past and especially in the Achaemenid period (sixth to fourth centuries BCE) constituted much more than mere scientific interest. In their studies, Western researchers began to nurture a consciousness of the importance of Iran's pre-Islamic past and its great power in the centuries before the Islamic invasion.[21] Gradually but consistently, the consciousness of Iran's great and ancient past gathered momentum among Iranian intellectuals who had been exposed to Western education, attracting even a few members of the Qajar court (1789–1921).[22] At the same time, a selection process was being implemented regarding the historical episodes considered to represent the spirit of Iran—most prominently, for example, the Cyrus era, when Iran was an imperial power that had no equal.

In the period of Rezah Shah (1925–41) the first significant steps were taken in the state's initiative concerning the glorification of Iran's pre-Islamic past. Two manifestations of this trend were the dispatch of delegations to exhibitions of Iranian art and state-sponsored construction in the style that became known as "Neo-Achaemenid." Iranians with a Western "Orientalist" education were enlisted to contribute to the revival of this legacy. Reza Shah founded the Farhangestan-i Zaban-i Iran (Academy of the Persian Language), an academic project to purify the Persian language by excising Arabic words, thus limiting one of the obvious indications of the Arab conquest's influence on Iranian culture.

Iranian nationalism has drawn the interest of researchers in the past three decades, influenced by the development theories of nationalism as well as by the Islamic Republic's coming of age. Historians and social scientists who have studied the development of nationalism in Iran can be divided into two categories that overlap with the approaches to nationalism in general: instrumentalist, viewing nationalism as an instrument in the hands of a social class whose interests this ideology serves; and historicist, viewing the national movement as evolving over time and not necessarily subservient to any other social force, economic or otherwise. The latter group can be identified mainly with Anthony Smith's ethnosymbolic approach.

Richard Cottam contends in his pioneering account of Iranian nationalism that "nationalism was not a significant force in Iran prior to the 1890s," and yet "the roots of nationalism, of course, extend into the extraordinary rich Iranian civilization down to and beyond the Achaemenid period."[23] Cottam's view has paved the way for a balanced though somewhat general account of the rise of nationalism in Iran in light of the Western powers' and Russia's ongoing onslaught on Iran in the nineteenth century, together with the basic cultural ingredients for such a development. His acknowledgment of the importance of historical awareness among Iranians is also original and has been developed by others as part of the explanation for the national movement's success in taking root in Iran in the twentieth century.[24] Cottam has also stressed the problematics ingrained in the development of nationalism in Iran from the very start—namely, the ambivalence that this nationalism developed toward the West, which had brought nationalism to Iran and yet was perceived as hostile to the political aspirations that emanated from this movement.[25]

In contrast to Cottam and his historicist approach, two researchers are marked by their modernist approach: Firouzeh Kashani-Sabet and Mustafa Vaziri. Kashani-Sabet follows the process of the construction of a consciousness of the Iranian homeland's territory from the beginning of the nineteenth century (thereby predating the process, compared to Cottam). She spares no details when describing the tortuous objections that the territorial claim had to face, internally more than externally. According to Kashani-Sabet, external pressures, such as the string of confrontations with Russia, and internal social-political changes combined to create the image of a "solid" political territorial entity called "Iran." The need to protect the country from its enemies was a central incentive for the formation of a "new geography," Kashani-Sabet argues.[26] Maps were a necessary graphic element in inculcating the feeling of belonging to a territorial unit called "Iran" in the late nineteenth and early twentieth century.[27] In that sense, Kashani-Sabet's work confirms Benedict Anderson's theory of the map as a central tool of exporting national sentiment.[28] Both Cottam and Kashani-Sabet share an emphasis on the national movement in Iran as a factor that developed in the face of an external enemy in the form of foreign powers.

In his book *Iran as Imagined Nation*, Mostafa Vaziri applies, somewhat crudely, Anderson's modernist approach. In his search for the origins of Iranian nationalism, Vaziri finds it to be nothing more than mere fabrication: the "anachronistic treatment of Iran by European modern historiography gave the land's twentieth-century governments and its masses grounds to be content about their forged identity."[29] According to his analysis, Iranian nationalism was the outcome of a blind adoption of Western racist views prevalent among intellectual circles in Iran in the nineteenth century, Iranians who were educated in the West and came into contact with these theories. Vaziri's misuse of Anderson's theory in application to modern Iranian nationalism has earned criticism from others, who see it as imposed on the Iranian case rather than adapted to or analyzed in light of the Iranian people's particular historical experience. Ahmad Ashraf, for example, has noted that Vaziri "ignored the role played by the administrative language as an important element in promoting 'proto-national cohesion' in pre-modern dynastic realms."[30] A direct application of the modernist approach to Iran suffers from two main weaknesses: first, it ignores the components of cultural cohesion in Iranian society—most prominently a dominant language—that exist in spite of that society's heterogeneous collection of ethnic communities; and, second, wholesale adoption of the modernist approach, which is universal in scope, risks ignoring the unique elements or developmental circumstances of each specific national movement. It seems that the attempt to apply the instrumentalist approach in this way creates an approach that suffers from the very illnesses it claims to have identified in Iranian nationalism—that is, being "deeply affected by western research, to the degree that [it] lack[s] any independent point of view."[31] Moreover, in adopting this European-centered argument, Vaziri ignores the deep and lasting contribution to and adaptation of Western research on Iran by Iranian scholars, professionals and laypersons alike. Mohamad Tavakoli-Targhi has shown that Iranian scholars were much more than merely passive observers in the process of intellectual awakening in Iran and the growing degree of rationalism in Persian thought. His book *Refashioning Iran* aims to reclaim the texts that reveal a process of intensive debate among Iranian intellectuals, who developed ideas such as patriotism and national awareness through a widening of the bank of symbols and terminology that they regarded as embodying these ideas to Iranians.[32]

More recent scholars, such as Afshin Marashi and Talinn Grigor, have pointed to the motivation to draw inspiration from the pre-Islamic heritage that had begun already in the late Qajar period.[33] From the middle of the nineteenth century, contacts between Iranian intellectuals and Persian-speaking Indian intellectuals contributed to the growing awareness of the cultural heritage common to both communities, which rested on the Zoroastrian past.[34]

Marashi points out the process by which the state entered the cultural realm, beginning as a relatively marginal actor in that realm toward the end of the Qajar dynasty but becoming a major producer of culture in Reza Shah's reign. This process was manifest in several areas: influencing public opinion by exposing or producing information on the history of ancient Iran or, alternately, by preventing the dissemination of that information; encouraging the intellectual trend of creating a national Iranian community loyal to the state; and encouraging the creation of a "national heritage" while adopting Western research and its agents in Iran.

In her work, Talinn Grigor concentrates on tombs of poets and intellectuals who are perceived as representing the "Iranian spirit" at its best—Sa'adi, Ferdowsi, Ibn Sina, and others. According to Grigor, finding (or inventing when the need arose) the location of tombs, destroying the old structures, and building neoclassical structures (the paradoxical expression exemplifying the phenomenon) were all part of a cultural campaign intended to educate Iranians in the "good" and "correct" culture for them.[35] Grigor's work deals with the reign of Reza Shah, during which time the Anjuman-i Asar-i Melli (Society for National Heritage) operated, its purpose being the preservation of an Iranian heritage thousands of years old. The Society for National Heritage was the framework for these activities in the 1920s.

The Pahlavi state and the shah at its head were not necessarily the initiators of the process of the nationalization of Iranian politics and public space, but they did adopt a certain worldview concerning the ancient past of Iran and its desired place in the modern world. Western Orientalists, archaeologists, and art collectors, together with a group of Iranian intellectuals and politicians, were the living spirit behind this effort. The Pahlavi state was the platform through which they implemented their plans for Iran, starting from public spaces in the guise of the discovery and renovation of tombs of Iran's classical poets.[36] Grigor's research deals with the new elite that led the change in Iran's self-perception and gave it expression at the same time, leaving architectural landmarks behind. By studying the new elite who surrounded Reza Shah and used the modern nation-state to achieve their cultural objectives and shape modern Iranians' historical awareness, she has contributed to breaking the dichotomy in our view of state and society in Iran, or, to use Cyrus Schayegh's words, to help us stop seeing the state "as completely distinct from society."[37]

The two studies briefly described here were pioneering contributions to understanding the processes that Iranian society underwent during the twentieth century, extending the discourse on Iranian nationalism beyond the political process in its narrow meaning of changes of government.

Kamran Scott Aghaie and Afshin Marashi's edited collection *Rethinking Iranian Nationalism and Modernity* examines the applicability of theories of nationalism and histories of national movements elsewhere (mainly in Europe), dealing mostly with either the broad picture of nationalist currents in modern Iran or specific aspects of it, such as gender and Arab ethnicity.[38] My intellectual exploration of nationalism in Iran has led me to consider the Islamic Republic as the political expression of a "nationalist movement that uses religion as one of its core ideological and symbolic components," as Aghaie puts it.[39]

Ali Mozaffari claims in *Forming National Identity in Iran* that "during the past 150 years, the pre-Islamic and Islamic aspects of collective identity have been singled out by different intellectuals . . . as alternative bases." Mozaffari shows how "identity narratives," or people's complex stories, can reside in places that in turn can become disconnected from physical sites. Places and sites or rituals connected with them change meaning over time as competing notions of homeland promoted by different mechanisms of power struggle for predominance. Mozaffari develops the concept of *inscription*, which for him means the efforts made by a given political order (such as the Islamic Republic) to shape its identity narrative through both temporal and spatial means.[40] His research contributes to revealing the multilayered nature of identity and its relation to places, a concept he shows is more vague than would appear at first glance. In his analysis, however, he posits two identity narratives for Iran: pre-Islamic, which, according to him, "coincides" with the Achaemenids, and the Islamic. This distinction is far from coincidental, as I show in this study. Moreover, as Mozaffari's analysis indicates, over the course of the four decades since the Islamic Revolution, a period in which we would expect the Islamic identity narrative to reign supreme, that narrative has changed beyond recognition under the influence of the pre-Islamic narrative.

In a recent study, Reza Zia Ebrahimi focuses on two Iranian intellectuals of the late nineteenth century, Mirzah Fath ʿAli Akhundzadeh and Mirzah Agha Khan Kermani. Ebrahimi traces the origins of what he terms "dislocative nationalism" in these two scholars' writings, where, according to him, they sowed the seeds of Iranian acceptance of Aryanism, a sense of pride in Iran's glorious pre-Islamic past, and Iranians' feeling of superiority over Arabs and other Semites.[41] Although Akhundzadeh and Kermani's role as harbingers of national awareness and, more importantly from the point of view of this study, of the need to hearken back to a glorious past in modern Iran cannot be denied, it is far from enjoying the exclusivity Ebrahimi seems to attribute to it. Moreover, following the ethnosymbolist approach, the present study highlights the contours, struggles, and mutual borrowing that occurred in the formation and evolution of Iranian national symbols. Ebrahimi gives the Aryan, biological aspect more than its due, and the meanings and values that came to be viewed as "Iranian" can be contested even by Iranians who share a national narrative of origin.

This study prefers the ethnosymbolic approach, which perceives nationalism as the outcome of the historical evolution of older, at times even ancient, ties among members of a group. Rather than dwelling on the origins of the national narrative or its historical validity, this approach is interested in the interpretations of and meaning given to Iranian national symbols. It seeks to reveal the ways in which a historical figure and an archaeological site bore the meanings the political elite in Iran attributed to them. In addition, it explores the process whereby those very symbols could first be rejected and then appropriated by the same group. Nationalism, according to this view, is not created out of nothing (despite what instrumentalist modernists think), nor is it an unchanged continuation of some primordial community that existed from time immemorial as such. It is instead created and united around symbols (rites, ceremonies, beliefs) that do have a long history. According to Smith, "ethno-symbolists consider the cultural elements of symbol, myth, memory, value, ritual and tradition to be crucial to an analysis of ethnicity, nations and nationalisms."[42] Instead of debating whether nationalism is real, genuine, or original, ethnosymbolism tries to explore the contours of nationalism's transmission and development from a narrow circle of intellectuals to a wide public.

As an ethnosymbolist, Smith defines his research focus as "public rites, and ceremonies, as well as . . . traditions and memories of golden ages, symbols of land and myths of chosen peoples" rather than the ideological aspects driving nationalists in their intellectual endeavors.[43]

David Kertzer demonstrates the link between nation building and symbols and rituals: "politics is expressed through symbolism." It is through symbols that politicians "struggle to assert their right to rule," while "incumbent power holders seek to bolster their authority" through the use of symbols. The need for symbolism goes much deeper than the mere struggle for the right to rule: according to Kertzer, it touches the deepest needs of every human society, traditional as well as modern. Moreover, it is an element in the process of the creation of identity, which is vital for every society to distinguish itself from its neighbors: "Through symbolism we recognize who are the powerful and who are the weak, and through manipulation of symbols the powerful reinforce their authority." This is the active and dynamic aspect of myth making in the service of nationalism. In Kertzer's words, "through ritual *aspiring*, political leaders *struggle* to assert their right to rule." Political leaders "*use* rites to *create* political reality for the people around them."[44] In other words, the process of tying the ethnic group's symbols to the national cause is an ongoing, dynamic, and hence flexible process, not a rigid formula in which the group enters symbols on one end and expects nationalism to come out on the other.

This study traces the processes of selecting and sifting symbols by the "bankers" of the "spiritual currency" of memory, as Kenneth Burke named them.[45] This means that the symbols used by the propagators of nationalism are not immutable and that the choice to use them cannot be taken for granted. It should be remembered that in Iran there are two symbol systems—Islamic and pre-Islamic. Pahlavi nationalism can be seen as the attempt to assert one set of symbols, pre-Islamic symbols, at the expense of another set, Islamic symbols, which have enjoyed a long history of socialization and acceptance in wide circles of Iranian society. The most prominent of the latter symbols is the rite commemorating the death of Hassan and Husayn, 'Ali's sons, which is a central event in Shi'i history, the cornerstone of Shi'ism's very birth as a separate religious sect within Islam. The martyrdom of Husayn and his supporters at the hands of Yazid of the Umayyad dynasty near Karbala, which Shi'ites commemorate in the Ta'aziyeh rite on the tenth day of the month of Muharram, has been an effective means of socialization and of building religious identity among generations of Shi'ites. The commemoration of Karbala in turn has enhanced a worldview that was shaped by the battle there, as Aghaie has noted: "The rituals associated with the battle have historically served as a vehicle for expressing and strengthening a variety of political and social relationships, associations, and identities."[46]

The Pahlavi state's attempt to cultivate a new iconography for Iranians had to compete with this long-established socialization of most Iranians to an alternative set of icons and rites commemorating them. The Pahlavi experience demonstrates the quite contrary results of the attempt to assert power with certain symbols in the face of other symbols, especially long-standing ones. Despite the fact that symbolism can be "a potent means of gaining and keeping power,"[47] one should also bear in mind that this is not always necessarily so, and the Pahlavi case proves it. It seems that, in retrospect, the symbolism used by the state became, for at least a large part of Iranian society, counterproductive.

This study supports the opinion, however, that awareness of Iran's magnificent past was not an invention of the late twentieth century. In the first chapter, I trace the origins of the search for the wonders of ancient Iran in order to get a better view of the circumstances that awoke interest in the pre-Islamic periods and the ways these periods were imagined and used when Iranian intellectuals looked for the reasons for the weakness of their motherland and offered prescriptions to restore it to its glorious days. From the mid–nineteenth century and well into the early Pahlavi period, another phase in the process took shape: that of carving out the historical timeline, or the "temporal depth," to use Anthony Smith's terminology.[48] This timeline was defined by the state's careful and systematic selection of a set of symbols to use in its effort at promoting the national culture it considered right for Iran.

The historiography of Cyrus the Great reveals that the way this king was imagined conformed to the way Pahlavi elite saw themselves—as the paragons of modern thought and practice. This imagining went much deeper than defining him as a monarch who thought highly of himself. It was an expression of the Iranian modernizing elite's perception of themselves as advanced and served to bridge the gap between claims to authenticity on the one hand and ever-growing feelings of deracination on the other. The feeling of not belonging to the culture promoted from above caused alienation from the political reality and the ancient past it claimed to represent. This feeling of alienation was expressed creatively by some of the most popular intellectuals of the time, such as Jalal Al-e Ahmad and 'Ali Shari'ati, and was given its full expression in response to the celebrations of Persepolis in October 1971.

The present study examines the gap between the state and its subjects exhibited by the celebrations held at Persepolis in 1971 by using archival sources that relate various instances of the common people's reactions to this state initiative (most of them, but not all, opposing it). In this way, we will closely follow, as John Bodnar puts it in his study of nationalism in the United States, "the intersection of official and vernacular cultural expressions," wherein "the shaping of a past worthy of public commemoration in the present is contested and involves a struggle for supremacy between advocates of various ideas and sentiments."[49]

One of the issues this work delves into is the Pahlavi self-image and self-perception, which was revealed in the way it celebrated itself. Celebrations such as the one that took place in Persepolis were followed by a deep search for genuine "Iranianness." This search became prominent in a few ways—for instance, in the effort to shape the modern Iranian personality in a manner that would confront the old, traditional one and try to isolate that personality's true Iranian characteristics. The relationship between modern, urban Iranians and their traditional, rural compatriots is central in this regard. Representing both Iranian authenticity worthy of admiration and "primitive," "backward" qualities, the Iranians of the state's geographical periphery challenged the Pahlavi ethos of Iranian authenticity.

I treat two Iranian symbols at length as they reached their full expression in the last two decades of Pahlavi rule and evolved over the following three decades. The first is Cyrus the Great, a historical figure who was proclaimed to be the founder of Iran, thus connecting the Crown and the formation of the Iranian nation as two interdependent events. In addition, Cyrus, as he was imagined by Iranian historians with the assistance of Western colleagues, was the embodiment of the Pahlavi ethos of the modern Iranian—advanced and modern yet understanding his right place in the nation's hierarchy.

The other symbol I examine is an event that took place at a site—thus combining a point in time, a ceremony, and a locus—that came to be regarded as expressing the Iranian spirit in its most elevated form. The question of the state's role in spreading nationalism and building national identity is important here. Anthony Smith has challenged the tendency to overemphasize the state's role in the formation of nations.[50] My analysis of the Pahlavi state's efforts at promoting historical awareness of pre-Islamic Iran supports this criticism. It seems that in the Pahlavi case the state was limited in its power to gain legitimacy from the historical narrative it promulgated and encouraged.

The celebration of twenty-five hundred years of Iranian monarchy in October 1971 poses a challenge to theorists of nationalism and state celebrations because it ironically became a rallying point for opposition to the Pahlavi state and a symbol of Pahlavi arrogance, extravagance, and oppression. That celebration at Persepolis also seemed to include much more than merely a fantasy of greatness and a chance to spend lavishly the money accumulated by the petroleum industry. I offer an analysis of this event as embodying both the Pahlavi ideals and their reception by the Iranian population and thus as demonstrating conflicting readings of Iranian history and identity.

Focusing on the evolution of national symbols in Iran in the past five decades, this study tells the story of a society in its formation and the struggle between the official and the vernacular spheres over its identity. The analysis of the Pahlavi state's efforts to cultivate national awareness by relying mainly on pre-Islamic history should be understood in light of the state's wider political goals. I treat the political implications of the "social memory" to use Aby Warburg's terminology,[51] following the "afterlife" of pre-Islamic Iran and the ways in which different political currents relate to it.[52] Thus, stating that Cyrus was chosen as a national hero is not enough because this is merely stating a fact. However, trying to understand the ethos Pahlavi historians carved out of the image of Cyrus is another matter because there lies the deeper meaning behind the Pahlavi educational project and the reaction to it first by the opposition and then by the Islamic Republic later.

Yet the fact that the Islamic Revolution of 1979 did not eradicate the pre-Islamic legacy of Iran, despite an ideology that denied the existence of borders between nations and initially negated the very existence of a national state, testifies to the resilience of the Pahlavi national project as well as to the central role of nationalism even in the Islamic revival.

Because I use the terms *Persian ethnicity* and *Iranian nationalism* in this study, though the first only sparingly, a clarification of their use is necessary. I understand Persian ethnicity, with the Persian language and the claim for historical continuity as its two main pillars, as an important and even prevalent component of Iranian nationalism, the latter being the political expression of the former, although this understanding is not altogether uncontested.[53] Put differently, I see Persian ethnicity as one of a few components composing the political entity of Iran, expressing mainly, but not exclusively, its Persian-speaking population,[54] but at the same time I agree with Shahram Akbarzadeh and James Barry that, "in most instances, Iranians do not separate Islam and Iranian heritage from one another when describing their culture, seeing these as integral in many ways."[55] Ali Mozaffari concludes that "since in Iran various ethnicities have been present, when we say Iran it is not a singular ethnicity or language or cultural wave." Moreover, he adds: "For those in the provinces, there is an added layer of ethnicity."[56] Varied though Iranian identity is, few doubt its coherence: it is a contested and evolving identity (as national identities are), yet its very existence is not challenged by any significant ethnic group within it. I see it as the outcome of a long and ongoing process, whose path I am investigating.

Chapter 1 traces the usage of pre-Islamic Iranian history by nationalist thinkers and intellectuals from the last third of the nineteenth century through the abdication of Reza Shah in 1941. Chapter 2 focuses on the discourse regarding pre-Islamic Iranian history in the context of the struggle over Iranian identity and different visions for the nation's future in the twentieth century. Analyzing the heated debate over the proper balance between different components of Iranian identity, this chapter delves into the ways Iranian intellectuals and clerics dealt with the tension between ethnic and religious components of identity during the late Pahlavi period. In it, I demarcate three paths taken in the attempt to mitigate the dissonance that modern Iranian identity entails: playing down the role of Shi'ite Islamic identity, discounting the pre-Islamic Iranian past, and seeking a balance between the two. The third, more balanced way has emerged as the leading one and is given more attention. Chapters 3 and 4 draw on two examples of the struggle within Iranian identity and its relation to the past as described in the first two chapters. Each of these two chapters shows the ramifications of a national symbol: Cyrus the Great in chapter 3 and Persepolis in chapter 4.

Chapter 5 focuses on developments and changes in the period following the Islamic Revolution of 1979 from the perspective of the Islamic Republic's nearly four decades of existence. It thus tries to answer the question of change versus continuity regarding the state's and society's relationship with pre-Islamic history and its symbols.

The concluding chapter offers an analysis and further contextualization of the Iranian case with respect to other regional societies' wider encounter with the dilemma of the selection and appropriation of national symbols in their Islamo-national identity. Although the Iranian state's attitude toward the pre-Islamic past has been inconsistent throughout the past century, the important place of the symbols of this past has been relatively continuous overall, having evolved independently of the state. The use of pre-Islamic symbols by both the state and political opposition groups has vacillated between adoration and exclusion and has sometimes sought a balance between the two. Hence, it can be argued that the state's ability to control society and culture on a broad scale is limited. This book comes to the conclusion that we must rethink some of our basic assumptions about the dominant role the modern nation-state plays in shaping society. It also demonstrates how symbols, once cultivated, take on a life of their own because their content and meaning are open to both interpretation and appropriation.

A study of Iranian national symbols would have benefited greatly from a visit to the national sites in Iran as well as from the opportunity to speak to Iranians of different walks of life who visit those sites. Unfortunately, this was not possible because of the political animosity between the Islamic Republic and my homeland, Israel. I sincerely hope that this relationship will change in my lifetime to allow me and other scholars like me to visit the land of our research passion.

1

Modern Iran Looks to History

Harbingers of Historical Awareness in Modern Iran

The development of historical awareness and the cultivation of national myths in modern Iran should be studied as an integral part of the country's political and social development. I argue that the aggrandizing of such historical myths as Cyrus the Great and the archaeological site of Persepolis was both an answer to threats to the integrity of the Iranian entity as well as a way to overcome these threats. In addition, I follow a few Iranian historical myths and demonstrate how once they are cultivated and accepted in the national pantheon, they seem to have a life of their own. Whether in the hands of fans or foes, these myths continue to haunt the Iranian national debate over the country's "correct" identity and the way to attain its proper place among the nations.

By referring to these stories as "myths," I am not commenting on their historical truth or falsity as such but rather pointing to their ability to stretch beyond their time and place and exceed their historical record.[1] To understand their role in creating national identity in modern Iran, it is important to see that they are facets of a worldview, which at the same time fueled that very worldview, inspiring its thinkers and political leaders and imbuing them with a vision for Iranian society and prescriptions for what they saw as its malaises.

Historical myths have a life of their own, even if they do not always have a commonly agreed upon image or legacy. We see this in the contours of Iranian historical myths from the early twentieth century to the period following the death of Ayatollah Ruhollah Khomeini in 1989, in which the same myths appear and reappear, transgressing political orders and state ideologies. Myths are resilient; in fact, the resistance to and rejection of national myths can at times work in their favor in the long run. For example, the Pahlavi state's attempt to de-politicize religious myths during its last decade and a half (1963–79) did not hurt and even benefitted these myths' cultivation in the subaltern political culture spearheaded by Khomeini. The Islamic Republic's attempts in its early years to repress Iranian pre-Islamic symbols had much the same boomerang effect.

From the middle of the nineteenth century, in light of Iranian military setbacks, many Iranian intellectuals compensated for feelings of inferiority vis-à-vis the West with the cultivation of a deep sense of cultural and historical superiority. Iranian men of letters, although unorganized at that time, constantly reminded ordinary Iranians of past imperial glories and encouraged them to demand that their leaders restore what was widely regarded as the nation's "natural rights."[2] As the foundation for this new self-perception, Iran's role and its people's history had to be (re)considered in a wider context of world civilizations. Turning to Iran's glorious past was a way to soothe its badly injured national pride.

During the first two decades of the twentieth century, Iranian intellectuals began publishing works in this vein, which praised and glorified Iranian history, especially its remote past. These publications coupled revalorized historical myths with a modern agenda and were intended to inspire the various reforms their authors were promoting, such as democratization of the political system, purification of the Persian language, and the creation of a modern education system. Many of these writers promoted the view that Iran's ancient glory was an expression of Iranian natural ingenuity, which had been brutalized by the Arab invasion and its accompanying religion, subjugating a great majority of the population.

An important aspect of the background to this rising national awareness was a series of Iranian military defeats by Russia in the first half of the nineteenth century, in which Iran lost substantial parts of the Qajar state's territory. The treaties signed by the Qajar kings included the Golestan Treaty of 1813, in which Fath 'Ali Shah (1772–1834) handed over the northern Caucasus to Russia, and the Turkemanchay Treaty of 1828, which was even more devastating for Iran's status in the region because it required Iran to give up all future claims to influence in the Caucasus and agree to broad economic concessions that granted foreigners extensive rights to conduct trade in Iran. Turkemanchay was more than a military defeat; it can be regarded as the end of Iran's claim to regional power in both a military and a territorial sense.[3]

After these defeats, Iranian intellectuals began reflecting on the causes of both the territorial losses and the growing internal strife. Late Qajar-era intellectuals, such as Mirza Agha Khan Kermani (1855–96) and Mirza Fath 'Ali Akhundzadeh (1812–78), developed a sense of yearning for Iran's ancient past and suggested an explanation for Iranian territorial losses. Despite differences in emphasis, in particular aspects of their analysis of the Iranian malaise, the two agreed that significant lessons could be drawn from Iran's glorious pre-Islamic past in the interests of improving its situation in the present. Prominent historians in the Pahlavi period continued to develop this line of thought, including the historian and politician Hasan Pirniya (1871–1935) and the literary critic Sa'id Nafisi (1896–1966), both of whom thought that ancient Iran had been a model nation before the Arab army's conquest of it in the seventh century. This line of thought represented a significant break from the traditional Muslim historical perspective, which tended to divide history into only two periods: the Jahiliyya, or the period preceding the Prophet Mohammad and his message—a period generally viewed as negative—and the period that followed the appearance of Islam, which was obviously viewed more positively.[4]

Making things worse and driving home the fact of Iran's deterioration, its loss of territorial assets was coupled with a loss of social cohesion. European expansion conjured a vision not only of the motherland being in jeopardy but also of one regional empire making way for another. Historians have emphasized the perception of the integrity of the land of Iran and its unique qualities as the center of identification for members of the nation.[5] I focus instead on the understanding by intellectuals such as Akhundzadeh and Kermani that national feeling could function as a remedy for dangers to Iranian unity. They called for political reform as a means to attain feelings of power and viability for modern Iran.

Iranian nationalist thought at this time followed the triadic structure typical of nationalist movements, described in the model suggested by Matthew Levinger and Paula Franklin Lytle: the glorious past, the degraded present, and the utopian future. According to Levinger and Lytle, "this narrative pattern not only motivates political action, but also diagnoses the causes of national decline and prescribes the specific actions required for the community's redemption."[6] The Pahlavi state would promote an idealized view of ancient Iran as a unified and cohesive society that fell with the onslaught of the Arab invasion: "Our thousand-year-old rule that the Arab invasion put an end to . . . they [the Arabs] ruined our country beyond recognition," as Akhundzadeh put it in one of his letters.[7]

Interest in the archaeological sites in Iran grew in the course of the nineteenth century as Europe began looking for discoveries in what was known as the cradle of civilization: Mesopotamia, the Middle East, and Iran. Though restricted mainly to one archaeological site in Iran in the beginning, the competition between different archaeological missions and the struggle over the right to excavate and control the findings of some of the ancient tells in the Iranian plateau brought additional Iranian archaeological sites to the attention of European explorers. Members of the Iranian elite were not blind to these developments.[8]

One of the pioneers in the field was Henry Rawlinson (1810–95), a British officer who became deeply involved in research on the ancient Middle East while on duty in Iraq and Iran. His deciphering of the Achaemenid inscriptions at Behistun was considered a breakthrough, which brought a clearer understanding of the ancient empire to both modern Europeans and Iranians. The French archaeological missions, mainly those headed by Marcel Dieulafoy (1884–89) and Jacques de Morgan (1857–1924), which increased awareness of the remains of pre-Islamic epochs in Iran's history, inspired members of the Iranian elite to relate to the ancient dynasties as tangible objects of veneration. Notable among them was Mohammad Hasan Khan (a.k.a. I'timad al-Saltanah, 1843–96), a member of the Qajar court and man of letters. I'timad al-Saltanah composed *Durar al-tijan fi tarikh Bani Ashkan* (Pearls of the Crowns in the History of the Parthians, 1890–92), which Firoozeh Kashani-Sabet calls "the first Persian-language book on the subject and a reference guide for future historians such as Hasan Pirniya."[9] Hasan Pirniya's book *Tarikh-i Iran-i bastan* (A History of Ancient Iran, 1934) in turn became almost canonical for the next generation of Iranian nationalists as the main source on Iranian history.[10]

Durar al-tijan fi tarikh Bani Ashkan gained currency among members of the Qajar elite as a source of legitimacy for their dynasty and for themselves as leaders of a country with a great heritage. Nasir al-Din Shah (r. 1848–96) and Muzaffar al-Din Shah (r. 1896–1907) are two examples of elites who used court patronage to cultivate this national heritage.[11] Nasir al-Din commissioned Professor Jules Richard, who taught at the state seminary Dar al-Funun, to photograph the ruins and inscriptions of Persepolis. He later assigned Luigi Pesce, an Italian officer, to this mission. The Qajar monarch and other members of his court followed Richard's work closely, demonstrating the rising awareness, at least within court circles, of the significance of archaeological research.[12]

Another member of the Iranian elite in this period was 'Abd al-Baha 'Abbas (1844–1921), the son of Baha'ullah (1817–92), founder of the Baha'i religion. In his writings, 'Abbas combined contemporary political criticism with admiration of ancient Iran and especially the Achaemenid Empire. According to 'Abbas, who wrote *Maqala-yi shakhs-i sayah* (A Traveler's Narrative) in 1888, the success of the Achaemenid Empire was owing to its religious toleration and freedom of thought. Arguing for more freedom and openness in the political atmosphere, he found these qualities to be the main reasons for the Achaemenid Empire's leading role in the ancient world: "In the time when the mighty government of Persia did not interfere with [men's] consciences, diverse sects entered in and abode beneath the banner of the great king . . . [and] the extent of the empire increased from day to day."[13] In contrast to the Achaemenid policy, the Safavids (1501–1736) suppressed the non-Shi'ite minorities, which caused various rebellions among these minorities, such as the revolts in Afghanistan and Turkmenistan.[14] 'Abbas's personal experience as a member of a persecuted sect shaped his analysis of Iranian ancient history.[15]

Two of these intellectuals are of special concern here because of their contribution to nationalist thought: Mirza Fath 'Ali Akhundzadeh and Mirza Agha Khan Kermani, both of whom saw the present as bleak in contrast to the great past. The two contributed to the use of historical discourses in the service of Iranians' national yearning in the late nineteenth century.

At about the same time that intellectuals directed their criticism at the political leadership of Iran (and the court at its center), declaring them to be obstacles on Iran's road to greatness, interest in Iran's national heritage rose among members of the court itself, including the shah. Although their enthusiasm was limited to the findings of treasures underground, the shah and some of his courtiers became interested in these discoveries, which seemed to be the relics of ancient Iran, to which they wanted their names attached. This interest was rather apolitical and was just another tool for aggrandizing the monarch. More importantly, sporadic interest in archaeological findings at this time was not articulated in the kind of ideological terms that became the hallmark of the Pahlavi period.[16]

National Relics

The Iranian authorities first paid attention to archaeology during the fifty-year reign of Nasir al-Din Shah in the second half of the nineteenth century. Thrilled by European interest in archaeology, Nasir al-Din began to fund a few archaeological digs in Iran. During his reign, the state started to finance the restoration of national buildings and sites such as the bazaar centers of Shiraz and Isfahan, which were perceived to be part of an architectural legacy of which Iran should be proud.[17] His court already included those who had patriotic feelings and ascribed importance to these digs.[18] Nasir al-Din visited an exhibit at the new Persian wing of the Louvre Museum in Paris, which prompted him to grant the French government exclusive digging rights to Susa (biblical Shushan), which would last until October 1927.[19] During this time, many museums in the West exhibited recent archaeological finds, especially "exotic" ones from the far reaches of the colonial empires. These exhibits combined curiosity about the new discoveries with a show of the strength of the European powers vis-à-vis the parts of the world they controlled. Additional museums sprang up in the wake of these exhibitions and attracted even more visitors.[20]

The court initially perceived archaeology as a way to discover things of great economic value to bolster the increasingly depleted national treasury. However, exhibitions of finds from Iran's ancient sites unintentionally stimulated the court's awareness of the importance of the past and of its ability to recruit that past to establish the symbols of the state.

Nasir al-Din Shah and several of his courtiers brought about changes in the second half of the nineteenth century that formed an intermediate stage in what would become a much more coherent and consistent program in Reza Shah's time. For example, they cleared part of the public space in Tehran, ruining some of the old neighborhoods, to allow for modern parades and processions, although national ceremonies with a message of historical continuity were not held until the late 1920s.[21]

During the last quarter of the nineteenth century, a secular national pre-Islamic affiliation began forming among a relatively limited group of intellectuals, which was shaped in contradistinction to the traditional religious affiliation of the overwhelming majority of the Iranian people.[22] While these developments were occurring in Iran, European academic institutions and individuals were becoming even more eager to excavate Iranian ruins. Institutions and individuals used their political ties to pressure the Qajar court to grant them excavation rights. The most famous was the commission granted to the French archaeological mission headed by Jacques de Morgan, who excavated Susa in the years 1897–1908.[23] The French mission, the biggest one until then in terms of the number of participating staff members, unearthed hundreds of artifacts, most of which were sent to Paris for exhibition.

The scientific study of archaeology played a dual role in the development of Iranian historical self-awareness. On the one hand, reflecting Iran's complex relationship with Western powers at the time, archaeology was yet another field that exemplified Iranian weakness because Iran's power ironically lay only in its ability to choose to whom it would sell its national assets. On the other hand, the archaeologists' finds from the ancient periods in which Iran enjoyed world domination and enormous power caused the rising Iranian intelligentsia to believe that Iran had the potential to regain its power.

The archaeological discoveries made during the 1920s and 1930s added another dimension to what would become one of the hallmarks of the state-led cultural project during the early Pahlavi period—the claim to scientific objectivity. Henry Rawlinson's deciphering of the cuneiform inscriptions in 1850 had a limited effect on Iranian intellectuals, though it did not go unnoticed. But toward the end of the nineteenth century, in light of the treasures found by the French missions and the breakthroughs gained from philological research on the ancient languages of the Near East, archaeology took on a growing role in symbolizing the ancient glory of Iran in the modernist discourse because it provided a tangible connection with the ancient past, using methods that were considered to be scientific, Western, and modern. In other words, archaeology gave Iran's modernizing elite, such as Akhundzadeh and Malkum Khan (1834–1908), who had close contacts with Henry Rawlinson, the power to speak in the name of modernity and progress while aggrandizing the past, promoting their modern agenda in its name, and relying on solid and "unquestionable" facts such as monuments and inscriptions found in archaeological sites in Iran.

Texts were not only proof of Iran's greatness in the past, but also real, tangible places to which this greatness could be attached.[24] As Abbas Khalili, writer and newspaper editor of *Eqdam* (Proceedings), aptly put it, "One stone can change your whole view of history."[25]

It is clear that archaeology played a leading role in fueling nationalist symbolism even before the first three decades of the twentieth century. Iranian intellectuals had long been interested in their cultural heritage. In his book on Iranian intellectuals and their discovery of classic texts in the eighteenth and nineteenth centuries, Mohamad Tavakoli-Targhi shows the high degree of self-awareness and curiosity displayed by Iranian (and Persian-speaking Indian) men of letters concerning their cultural heritage as well as the ever-growing Western influence on their culture and politics. Though emphasizing that this process was not one of mere imitation or adoption of Western ideas, Tavakoli-Targhi admits that "modern historical writings harnessed the Iranian homeland (*vatan*) to an immemorial past beginning with Mahabad and Kayumars and pointing toward a future unison with Europe." He further claims that Iranian intellectuals were deeply interested in their ancient history and pre-Islamic heritage not simply as a reaction to Western ideas and influences but also because they saw engagement with that heritage as a positive and active process.[26]

Notwithstanding this intellectual tradition of fascination with the Iranian past, the Western influence on the field of archaeology in Iran is clear. Iranians had to rely on the results of excavations and research conducted by Western archaeologists. Their role was thus quite limited, restricted primarily to granting concessions to European missions to excavate in Iran or to finding treasures in various tells that were dug up by local antiquities dealers. So the shift in focus from the historiography of ancient Iran to the archaeology of its ruins paradoxically made Iranian nationalists even more dependent on Western knowledge because this field was completely in Western hands until well into the twentieth century.

From another perspective, developments in archaeology can serve as a litmus test for assessing changes in the worldview of the intellectuals who were involved in the national movement and at times in politics in the period after the downfall of the Qajar dynasty in the mid-1920s. The difference between the reformers of the early Pahlavi period and their predecessors in the late Qajar period has mainly to do with the role of the scientific method in shaping the "right" future for Iran, which would start with reshaping its past. Here archaeology played an important role as a gateway to the acceptance of the scientific method in defining the Iranian past and in shaping the contours of its development. The political changing of the guard with Reza Khan's rise to power in 1921 made it possible for intellectuals who were now bureaucrats in the new administration to bring these historical perceptions of Iranian history to the surface.

World War I had a great effect on the formation of Iranian nationalism owing to Muslims' disillusionment regarding the power of Islam to unite them. The Ottoman sultan's call for jihad did not prove a great success in the Middle East. The Ottoman Empire's humiliating treatment of Iranian exiles transformed this disillusionment into a deep disappointment with Islam's potential to unite Muslims of different origins. Qawam al-'Ulama-yi Kirmanshahi, an Iranian residing in Istanbul during the war, described his feelings on this matter: "An Iranian, though a Muslim, is more an Iranian. An Iranian would sacrifice himself for the sake of his belief, but would surely give his life sooner than that for the sake of his independence."[27]

The early-twentieth-century intellectuals' consciousness of the glorious past and their explicit linkage between the past and the vision of a modern and Western Iranian society connect the developments in the nineteenth century to the developments in Reza Shah's era. According to this paradigm, Iran's imperial past included the values that Iranian society needed to embrace to stride toward modernity. Most prominent in this group of intellectuals was Hasan Taqizadeh (1878–1970), an opposition publicist and later also a member of Parliament and government minister, whose activities included the publication of a journal that was widely influential among the new intellectuals, *Kaveh*.

The journal was named after the mythical Iranian hero who, according to the legend, saved Iran from Zahhak, the Arab usurper. The title choice was not coincidental: it expressed the need for a national hero to save Iran from foreign encroachment. Taqizadeh included in *Kaveh* many translated essays by selected historians of the time that praised and celebrated Iran's past as the cradle of civilization. Taqizadeh did not spare criticism of the current Iranian society in light of the superior values upon which ancient Iranian culture was based, which he believed had faded over time, mainly owing to foreign influences and their attendant superstitions. In addition to *Kaveh*, two other journals containing similar national, modern messages were published in this period, *Iranshahar* (The Land of Iran, Berlin, 1922–27) and *Ayandeh* (Future, Tehran, 1925–28).[28]

These three journals, published during the interwar years, were important media that spread modernist and secular ideas as well as a growing sense of national identity in Iran. They were part of an important step toward creating an Iranianness with specific political content that demanded radical changes both from the state and from society.

Taqizadeh, himself a product of Iranians' access to Western education, was an intellectual with overt political intentions. These intentions came from a deep belief that philosophical ideas could and should be applied to social life to deliver the happiness that they could bring society, if only applied wisely. This belief was a version of the ideas of the Enlightenment as they came to be applied to Iranian politics and life. Scientific, rational thought was the way to solve social malaise.[29]

If we read *Kaveh* through the lens of nationalist discourse promoted and developed by the expatriates in Europe and led by Taqizadeh, it becomes clear that the history recruited as inspiration for dealing with the challenges of the present included both the Islamic and the pre-Islamic periods. For example, Taqizadeh did not refrain from using historical precedents from the Islamic period to describe the dangers confronting the homeland: England and Russia are enemies of the motherland as well as enemies of Islam; Iran is an "Islamic regime," and the Central Powers' war against Russia and England is "the battle of Badr," so called after the famous battle waged by the Prophet at the dawn of Islam. The term *jihad* is also used to describe the war against these powers.[30] However, in recruiting the glorious past to deal with the present, Taqizadeh, Hosein Kazemzadeh-Iranshahr (1884–1961),[31] and other Iranian expatriate intellectuals preferred images from pre-Islamic history. The images taken from mythology and documented history, especially from the Achaemenid period, helped them express their patriotic feelings toward the Iranian homeland.

Their choice of topics was apparently deeply influenced by their reliance on Western studies dealing with various issues in pre-Islamic Iranian history. For instance, Iranian folklore was further validated by being the object of Western, "scientific" research, not just a collection of popular beliefs.[32] The scholarly work on ancient Iran, which enjoyed a scientific aura, helped the Iranian intellectuals connect the glorious past of the motherland with the new discourse of modernity.

Touraj Atabaki has pointed out that among the generation of Iranian intellectuals active in the years following World War I, the emphasis shifted from territory as a defining element of the nation to a linguistic common denominator. According to Atabaki, this shift was a result of the influence of European fascism at the time. However, it seems that this "nostalgia for a distant past and glorifying ancient Iran,"[33] which he mentions as an element that came to the fore in this brand of nationalism, was a response to the need to justify the deep change these intellectuals tried to bring about in their country and society.

In contrast to local traditional pride, handed down from one generation to the next through songs and tales of the bravery of the founding fathers, the modern consciousness of expatriate Iranians in Europe was based on archaeological findings and Western historical research and clearly aspired to scientific standards. Referring to this trend in nineteenth-century Europe, Magnus T. Bernhardsson has concluded that "the lessons of history offered both comfort and directives to those intellectuals committed to the idea of progress. The legacy of the past, they believed, could be used to ascertain a general trend in social and economic development as well as offering verification and justification of their own values and aesthetics."[34] This European mode of thinking inspired Iranian intellectuals.[35] The orientation to science determined the specific expressions of the transmission of Iranian nationalism in this period, imbuing it with the image of modernity as perceived by the new state administration, a modernity that was a vital and inherent component of the message of nationalism that the country's elite considered desirable.

Taqizadeh and his friends were the link that connected this early awareness of the need to use Iran's past with the period in which this concept was embraced by the modern state, which, in its turn, tried to monopolize the concept. After World War I and especially after the coup d'état led by Reza Khan in 1921 and his coronation as shah in April 1926 (the Majles had already declared him shah in December 1925), the institutions of the shah's modern Iranian state adopted this concept articulated by a narrow elite, and the shah portrayed himself as being at the forefront of these ideas.

The Father, the Son, and the Zeitgeist

Reza Khan's rise to power in 1921 made way for the implementation of reforms that had been brewing in the minds of Iranian intellectuals from the 1880s. Now in a position of power, officials who believed in and strived for these reforms wasted no time in putting them into practice, including rehabilitation of the military, modification of the education system, and the subjugation of tribes to central rule.[36] In addition, Reza Shah's rule also brought symbolic changes to Iran, such as the introduction of a Western dress code. To increase foreign recognition of the change, "Iran" was made the country's exclusive name, eliminating the alternative name "Persia," which some governments and their diplomats still used.[37]

Upon Reza Khan's assumption of rule in 1921 and his coronation in 1926, a group of politicians armed with a cohesive national agenda led the process of assimilating a national consciousness based on the magnificence of the pre-Islamic past. This group consisted of state officials in the second generation of Iranians educated in the West and was headed by Hasan Pirniya, Abulhusayn Taymurtash (1883–1933), and Mohammad 'Ali Foroughi (1877–1942). They instituted a number of measures whose main thrust was to foster a national Iranian heritage devoid of religious affiliations.

The process of conserving the Iranian national heritage and creating sites for secular pilgrimage began during Reza Shah's reign (1925–41). European scientific interest in such sites, which the shah and the elite surrounding him had sporadically followed, was replaced by a new motivation for excavation in Iran: the discovery of Iranians' national heritage.[38] The change that occurred from the end of the Qajar period to the Reza Shah era was more than just an addition of motifs to the national project; it constituted a significant transformation in the character of the cultural project and the state's role in bringing it about.

Reza Shah sensed the power inherent in the establishment of a national bond, uniting Iranians under the throne and creating an Iranian entity embodied by the position of the shah at its head. Though an officer with very little formal education, Reza Shah soon grasped the potential of adopting and cultivating national symbols. One testimony exists to the fact that he was deeply influenced by the poetry of the *Shahnameh* (Book of Kings) by Abul-Qasim Ferdowsi (935–1020), who articulated the centrality of the Crown as embodying Iranian ethnic identity.[39] The establishment of the Farhangestan, the shah's approval of the construction of tombs for national poets, and his reference to Iran's greatness in the remote past suggest that he was well aware of the power inherent in evoking past glory.

In Reza Shah's nationalistic view, one can already find an ambivalent and somewhat paradoxical relation to the West and its effect on Iranian nationalism. On the one hand, the West was perceived as a model of modernization and everything progressive; on the other hand, it was seen as intrusive and as threatening the loyalty of Iranian youth to their country, its people, and its culture. The Society for National Heritage (est. 1922) was led by young, modernized, and Western-educated politicians, some of whom pushed Reza Shah to the position of strength he gained later on. Among them was Mohammad 'Ali Foroughi, a graduate of Dar al-Funun, an eminent politician, and prime minister under Reza Shah and Mohammad Reza Shah (r. 1941–79).[40] He was involved in every important cultural event and initiative in the period and hence was described by one scholar as "the ultimate scholar-statesman of modern Iran."[41] Foroughi had a central role in inculcating modern Iranian nationalism within circles of power in early Pahlavi Iran. He was one of the secondary intellectuals whose role was crucial in conveying Iranian nationalism and the significance of the legacy of ancient Iran in marking the modern Iranian state's destiny. Another important voice was that of Hasan Taqizadeh, the sharp-witted editor of the Berlin-based periodical *Kaveh* during World War I and the interwar years and a member of the Majles during the 1930s and 1940s. Other influential politicians and men of letters who shaped the cultural scene of Pahlavi Iran were 'Isa Sadiq (1894–1978), minister of education and culture; professor and editor Sa'id Nafisi; and future minister of education 'Ali Asghar Hekmat (1893–1980).[42] For the members of this group as representatives of a generation of Western-educated Iranians, the cultural revival of Iran had two complementary foundations: in modernization, which in those years was tantamount to westernization, and in the cultural revival of national awareness, an important element of which was the sense of belonging to the pre-Islamic legacy of ancient Iran.

Disregard for Islamic history was somewhat strengthened during this period. The organization established at the beginning of the 1920s, the Society for National Heritage, instead concentrated on the following areas: encouraging a style of architecture termed "Neo-Achaemenid" because it used motifs from Achaemenid remains scattered around the country; conducting ceremonies and commemorating exemplary figures from Iran's cultural past; and exalting and publishing many studies of Iran's history, with the underlying theme that Iran's magnificent past portended a brilliant future. In addition, there was a dramatic change in the attitude toward archaeological sites. For example, in the 1930s the tombs of medieval poets such as Sa'adi and Hafez were rehabilitated, and Reza Shah opened the first national museum of antiquities in Iran in 1937.[43]

Iranian authorities' handling of archaeological sites was another sphere in which changes followed the overthrow of the Qajar dynasty. Rather than simply granting concessions to European excavation teams, these authorities had an ever-growing say in the work being done at archaeological tells throughout Iran. The significance of the transfer of authority to Iran signed with the French government in 1927 was enormous, and it set the scene for the national, secular cult of the Pahlavi regime later on, particularly in 1971.[44]

The series of ceremonies commemorating twenty-five hundred years of Iranian monarchy were held at a site that had been nurtured for years as expressing Iran's historical spirit, and it was not mere coincidence that this site became the center of the events in 1971. Until 1927, archaeology was firmly under Western control in Iran (as in other countries in the region), where the Antiquities Authority was headed by a European archaeologist whose role was to make sure Western interests were not harmed. For most of the reign of Reza Shah, there was tension between the Iranian administration and Western archaeologists, who tried to "borrow" artifacts from the excavations they worked on and to take them home to local museums. The nationalization of the Antiquities Authority and the cancellation of the French concession was a bold step in declaring independence over the study of the remains of Iran's ancient past. The motivation to take this step was deeply influenced by the recognition of the (by then) well-established importance of such a move, politically as well as symbolically.[45] Historians in the Pahlavi period based their research on this perception of Iranian history and contributed to its scientific aura.

At the same time that archaeology was removed from the absolute control of Europeans in the course of the 1940s, archaeological research spread to other sites beyond Susa, which had been the focal point of archaeological interest in the nineteenth century.[46] This shift in focus reflected a greater scientific interest in the ancient history of Iran and away from an emphasis on Iranian archaeological sites as a source for better understanding the Bible.[47]

In order to make sense of Iranian history and adapt it to the theme of a nation awakening with Reza Shah's rise to power, the regime characterized the periods preceding the current one, especially the Qajar period, as dominated by anarchy and slumber. This theme echoed well into the late Pahlavi period. The rise of Cyrus the Great in the sixth century BCE seemed like an early version of this theme of awakening in that Cyrus established order from the nation's state of chaos. It seems that what Yael Zerubavel has termed "commemorative density"—that is, the emphasis attached to what are perceived as positive and symbolic periods in a nation's history, while playing down the commemoration of other periods—went through a formative phase during Reza Shah's reign.[48] This process included paying limited attention to historical periods that did not contribute to the glorification of the past (or even harmed it), which is of no less importance to the act of commemoration than memory itself. What Nora terms "the dialectic of memory and forgetfulness"[49] was manifest in the attempt to erase the Qajar period as well as other Islamic periods that were not seen as contributing to the vision of Iran as an independent political unit as well as in the description of them as dark periods in Iran's history. In the studies of archaeological heritage, one may see a consistent trend across the Qajar and Pahlavi periods, which serves "commemorative density." The change is notable in the use made of the Pahlavi regime's flagship site, Persepolis.

During the Pahlavi period, the image of Iran as a beauty awakening from a long sleep became one of the central historical themes of the state and its elite. Sa'id Nafisi, one of the leading official historians of the early Pahlavi state, developed the idea in his history book *Pishraftha Iran dar 'asr-i Pahlavi* (Development of Iran during the Pahlavi Era, 1939) that the late Qajar period was a time of anarchy and chaos, which ended with Reza Khan's rise to power. This idea reappeared in various ways and posited the Pahlavi period as the only alternative to civil war and anarchy.[50] This historical narrative played on a deep fear running through the Iranian collective unconsciousness: the disintegration of Iran and the loss of independence that would ensue as a result.[51]

One should bear in mind the choice made by Pahlavi historiography to put forth the Achaemenid period rather than other periods, such as the

Sassanid and the Parthian, which were also known for the ruling dynasty's military strength. Although no clear-cut conscious ideology behind this choice has been established, several possible reasons for it present themselves. First, the search for the origins of Iranian greatness made the oldest dynasty known at the time (i.e., at the beginning of the twentieth century) the most suitable. European research on ancient Iran and the archaeological interests of the people who led that research, such as Ernst Herzfeld (1879–1948), located the Achaemenid period as the starting point of Iranian civilization. Because these people were the ones who taught the first generation of Iranians who showed interest in ancient Iran, their choice contributed greatly to that made by the Iranian political and intellectual elite in this matter. Second, the choice of the Achaemenids was also influenced by the fact that they were relatively familiar to Western historians and intellectuals owing to the Greek sources written about them (such as the famous *Cyropaedia* and the Bible), which in the eyes of believers in the monotheistic religions added an aura of greatness to the founder of the Iranian Empire. It was more problematic to put the Sassanid dynasty, which ended with the coming of Islam to Iran in the seventh century, at the center of Iranian historical identity because some saw this dynasty's swift downfall as proof of its lack of legitimacy, and hence it became the symbol of ancient Iran's collapse in the face of Islam.[52]

Cultural creations, primarily poetry, were the main components of heritage fostered in the 1920s and 1930s. Many Western experts were invited to a grand event in 1935, the commemoration of a thousand years since the birth of Abul-Qasim Ferdowsi, author of the national epic, the *Shahnameh*, in 1035.[53] Poets' tombs, which constituted physical symbols of the glorification of cultural heritage, testified to the emphasis placed on the cultural aspect of the political creation of Iranian heritage rather than on politics in the narrow sense of the word. It is significant that it was not the tombs of kings that were renovated or rediscovered, but rather those of Iranian cultural heroes. There might have been logistic and economic reasons for this emphasis on cultural heroes, but I would argue that the elite who surrounded Reza Shah did not see the monarchy as a main component of Iranian national identity but rather as a symbol that should serve the national collective memory. Hasan Pirniya, a court minister and lay historian, even warned in the late 1920s that a situation in which the religious and intellectual elites do not fulfill their role of curbing the shah's power would be extremely dangerous.[54]

During the 1920s and 1930s, two events initiated by the Pahlavi state demonstrate its perception of the heritage of Iran's past and attest to the ever-growing involvement of the Pahlavi administration in the formation of Iranian national memory. The first was Reza Shah's coronation in April 1926; the second was the millennium of the birth of the poet Ferdowsi, celebrated in October 1935.

The first event was planned largely by Mohammad 'Ali Foroughi, Reza Shah's closest ally at the time and his prime minister. Besides the somewhat exotic name the new shah chose for his dynasty, from a script of Middle Persian known to a handful of Western scholars at the time, the atmosphere surrounding the ceremony was imbued with fervor for the authentic and the romantic. At Reza Shah's coronation, orchestrated by Foroughi, the past glories of Iran appeared as a source of inspiration and even legitimacy for the newly crowned shah:

> Jamshid and Fereydun [mythological kings of the Iranians] . . . are not equal to Cyrus and Darius in terms of their elevated status. The best testimony is that of our enemies, and so we can rely on the testimony of their enemies that twenty-five centuries ago they established the grandest of all states till then, which extended from India and China on one end and Rome and Greece on the other. Merely reflecting on the rectitude and the greatness of the Iranians and the awe-striking remains of the buildings of Takht-i Jamshid [Throne of Jamshid, another name for Persepolis] and the inscriptions of Bisotun attests to the superiority of their heroism and administration.[55]

In order to add dramatic effect, Foroughi cried: "Shahenshah! The Iranian nation knows today that the Shah with whom it sympathizes is of pure breed and good stock, who is not taking this task upon himself for the sake of tangible profit or standard of living . . . but in order to fulfill his holy goal and for the sake of enhancing the tranquility and prosperity of the sons of this land."[56] Foroughi compared the shah to his predecessors, who had pulled the Iranian nation out of dark periods in its history. He concluded by quoting the famous Ferdowsi.

The intellectuals, very much creations of the previous era, which had opened up to Western education, were a bridge between Western perceptions of Iran and Iranians' rising self-awareness of the legacy of ancient Iran. The connection to and influence by the West did not end with the intellectuals' return home after a few years of studies abroad, though. The memoirs of 'Isa Sadiq, one of the people who shaped education in modern Iran, attest to the great influence Western scholars had on the development of his and other Iranian intellectuals' identity through acquaintance with research on ancient Iran. Sadiq's relationship with Western scholars of ancient Iran—for example, David Eugene Smith (1860–1944) of Columbia University—helped form his self-perception. Smith and his somewhat mystical bond with Iranian culture left a deep impression on Sadiq, who testified that he was the only Iranian among sixteen intellectuals who attended a dinner and discussion on the poetry of 'Umar Khayyam (1048–1131) in 1933 while on a visit to the United States. Smith had translated sections of the famous *Rubaiyat* and, as Reza Shah's guest, had the honor to hand it to the shah at an official interview.[57] Smith gave a lecture bearing the title "The Influence of Iranian Culture on America" to some of the leading figures in the Iranian political and cultural arena. The gist of his speech was that American society was materialistic in essence and lacked any spiritual dimension, so it needed to look to Iranian culture, which was the epitome of spirituality. Foroughi thanked the guest for his "great contribution to Iranian culture." In his book, Sadiq also tells of a mystical experience Smith underwent during his visit to the famous Lutfallah mosque in Tehran, when he purportedly said, "Nothing but the belief in God could make such a meticulous thing be created."[58]

The nationalist thinkers and political patrons used Ferdowsi in quite an anachronistic way, putting some of their views regarding state and society into his mouth and using the poet's aura of greatness to reject what they saw as dark periods in Iran's history. For example, by means of the Ferdowsi admirers' jargon, hatred toward the Arab conquest of Iran in the seventh century as well as the rejection of Turkish influence on Iranian culture made their way safely into his legacy. Although these views could be referred to as part of the poet's legacy, it was farfetched to claim that Islam is alien to Iranians' true culture. At this point, the legacy of nineteenth-century nationalists discussed at the beginning of this chapter, such as Kermani and Akhundzadeh, was given a mythological grounding in the Iranian cultural pantheon of poetry. Some nationalists even depicted the medieval poet Hafez as a worshipper of the Mithra cult.[59] By turning Ferdowsi into a political proponent of monarchism, nationalists shifted the emphasis from the poet's efforts at preventing Iranians from forgetting their origins (real or imaginary) to placing the Crown at the center of Iranians' identity. Thus, a historical poet was turned into a nationalist on behalf of Iranian monarchist tendencies.

The idea of celebrating the anniversary of Ferdowsi's birth was led, among others, by Mohammad 'Ali Foroughi and Hasan Taqizadeh. Taqizadeh contributed to the accessibility of European research on the *Shahnameh* by translating the poem into Persian in the journal *Kaveh*, which he edited. The month-long celebration was held in Tehran, Mashhad, and Tus (Ferdowsi's birthplace). There was a strong academic presence, including such leading international scholars as Arthur Christensen and Henry Masse.[60]

The fondness for Ferdowsi was also demonstrated in imitations of his monumental work, what became known as "the modern *Shahnameh*," a compilation of verses describing Iranian history from the fall of Yazdegerd III to the rise of Reza Khan (thus presumably completing the *Shahnameh*, which ends with the downfall of the Sassanid Empire and the death of its last king).[61]

Conclusion

The millennial celebration for Ferdowsi typifies the Pahlavi blend of national glorification with an aura of scientific legitimacy. The presence of the first generation of Iranian scholars on ancient history of Iran was also a novelty at the time and represented a great movement of intellectual emancipation on the part of the rising Iranian intelligentsia.[62]

Despite a certain continuity and agreement on the main tenets of Iranian historiography throughout the Pahlavi period, from the rise of Reza Shah to the downfall of his son, there was no simple unanimity in the choice of the "correct" heritage on which to educate a generation of patriotic Iranians in the twentieth century. It was, after all, a long period during which numerous figures took part in the process of nation building. There were also, as we shall see, differences in the political emphases attached to the historical heritage being transmitted.

Reza Shah's reign left a deep imprint on the fostering of a pre-Islamic heritage in Iran, which was not erased when he was deposed by the Allies in 1941. Rather, it provided the foundation for the perpetuation of this heritage later on. Nevertheless, the difference between the reign of the father and that of the son is significant, not only because of the many means at the latter regime's disposal (especially in the last decade of its existence) but also because Mohammad Reza Shah's court played a much more central role in the process and dictated a historical narrative in which the Crown was presented as a central factor in the continuity of Iranian identity throughout the ages.

2

A Clash of Pasts

Pahlavi Discourse and Its Enemies

In the previous chapter, we saw the roots of the idealization of ancient Iran and how its image and perceived legacies became relevant to modern Iranian nationalists as viable role models and sources of both national pride and emulation. The questions remain: To what degree was the ancient past of Iran relevant to modern Iranians, both laypersons and clerics? How did the seeds sown in the late nineteenth century flower in the sixth and seventh decades of the twentieth century, and who were the mediators who brought them to the wider educated youth who were the hallmark of this period, students and the professional classes?

The thought of ʿAli Shariʿati, Ayatollah Mortaza Motahhari, and Shojaeddin Shafa', a court historian and a central figure in the Pahlavi historical narrative, is central here. All three influenced and even shaped the Iranian discourse on the ancient past of Iran and its relevance to modern Iranians. Shariʿati and Motahhari were teachers, popular ones at that, who offered viable frameworks of identity and meaning. Shafa' was an establishment figure and later an active expatriate who was not satisfied with just escaping from the Islamic Republic but tried to promote the Pahlavi worldview from afar till the very end of his life. All three also grappled with young Iranians' bewilderment about their national identity and the relevance of the past, as well as the choice of the most relevant segment of it to serve as a model, to their present. And, as we will see, two of them left an indelible mark on the question of national identity in the contemporary Islamic Republic.

The question of the role of Iranians in world history, whether in an Islamic frame of reference or a Western-oriented one, was a constant theme of intellectual discourse during the late 1960s and throughout the 1970s.[1] Voices of dissent to the Pahlavi state discourse, despite disagreeing with the worldview presented by the state and its ideologues, were nevertheless deeply influenced by it. Their oppositional voices were shaped to a large degree as a counterattack to it. In this counterattack, they gave different answers to the same questions this discourse tried to respond to regarding Iranians' unique role in Islamic civilization.

ʿAli Shariʿati: Between Prophecy and Nationalism

ʿAli Shariʿati (1933–77) was one of the most influential thinkers and speakers in the Iranian public sphere from the mid-1960s until his tragic and mysterious death in 1977. Four months after his death, there was an outbreak of unrest that culminated in the downfall of the Pahlavi state. Shariʿati was arrested a few times in the course of his public activity, a fact that shows that the Sazeman-i Ettelaʿat va Amniyat-i Keshvar (SAVAK, Organization of Intelligence and Security of the State) was well aware of his popularity.[2] In fact, from as early as 1957 SAVAK agents had been monitoring the movements of the young Shariʿati, who had been seen attending meetings of revolutionary content in Mashhad, where his father had been active.[3] His charisma caused a generation of young educated Iranians to flock to his lectures at the Husayniyya Ershad, which he used as a platform—both mouthpiece and press house—to express his subversive ideas. Shariʿati's innovative ideas and radical views invited educated Iranians to reflect on their identity without turning their backs on the Marxist and leftist views many of them shared and that had an important role in reshaping their worldview.[4] By breaking the wall of suspicion that seemed to separate religious affiliation from leftist demands for social justice, Shariʿati's thought and speeches formed a bridge that a generation of Iranians was very eager to traverse.

Identity and authenticity were hotly debated topics among Iranian thinkers from the mid-1960s on.[5] Writers, religious leaders, and philosophers in Iran grappled with, debated, and reformulated Iranian identity and its connection to different cultural, religious, and historical legacies. The way ʻAli Shariʻati dealt with these topics is of great relevance to understanding another facet of the revolution that would bring down the Pahlavi order and eventually establish the Islamic Republic because he had extensive influence on a generation of young, urban, educated Iranians, the kind of people who led the revolution following his death.

Shariʻati was ambivalent toward nationalism in general and its Iranian version in particular. On the one hand, he rejected the Pahlavi version of Iranian nationalism, wherein the king is at the center and Shiʻism is relatively marginal to the history of the nation. On the other hand, he tended to define Shiʻism as a distinct Iranian religion and form of worship, thus dressing nationalism in religious garb.

To understand Shariʻati's complex approach to Iranian nationalism, we need to consider two factors that contributed greatly to its crystallization. The first is his academic work and close contact with French orientalists, mainly Louis Massignon (1883–1962) and Henry Corbin (1903–78), during the 1960s.[6] Shariʻati spent five years (1959–64) in Paris, a period that had a significant influence on some of his views on Iranians and their place in Islamic civilization. The second factor that shaped his worldview was the Pahlavi state's pretension to being the modern incarnation of ancient Iran and to shaping Iranian nationalism in its image. This pretense had far-reaching consequences in the discourse of Iranian intellectuals during the regime's last decade and a half, many of whom turned against the Pahlavi state and everything it resembled. One intellectual identified more than any other with the attack on the adoption of a Western framework of identity was Jalal Al-e Ahmad (1923–69). Best known for popularizing the term Gharbzadegi (Westoxication), Ahmad attacked the fascination with museums and relics of the past, which came, according to him, at the expense of attention to the present and the exploitation that characterizes the present: "We are to be objects of research in the museum or the laboratory, nothing more. Watch that you don't alter this raw material!"[7] Although less adamant in preaching about religious emotions, Al-e Ahmad also saw Islam as a refuge from the cultural onslaught of the West, aided by its Iranian admirers.

1. ʻAli Shariʻati, 1972. Unknown photographer, Wikimedia Commons.

Shiʻite Islam and the Spirit of Iran

The idea that Shiʻite Islam is unique to Iran and expresses its deep essence can be traced back to the Orientalist oeuvre of Count Arthur de Gobineau (1816–82), who portrayed Shiʻism as utterly alien to the spirit of original Islam.[8] Gobineau championed the view that Shiʻism was in fact the expression of an eternal Iranian spirit that continued after the fall of the Sassanid Empire. In the fashion of other Orientalist myths, this view was an invitation to an essentialist definition of both Shiʻism and the Iranian spirit.[9]

The idea that Shiʻism expresses the enduring spirit of Iran found resonance among two prominent French orientalists with whom Shariʻati was in contact during his Paris years, Louis Massignon and Henry Corbin. Shariʻati served as Massignon's research assistant and consequently was also in contact with Corbin, who was Massignon's student. Shariʻati's approach to Iranian identity was deeply influenced by these two scholars' Orientalist theories, especially Corbin's.

According to Corbin, Shiʻi Islam is a unique kind of Islam, one that embodies the Iranian spirit and uses Islam as its expression. The eternal Iranian spirit, according to this somewhat essentialist and romantic view of Shiʻism as well as of Iranians, for centuries found its expression in Zoroastrianism. With the advent of Islam, this spirit shaped Shiʿism in its own unique character, rendering it different from Sunni Islam not as a matter of historical or political necessity, but rather as an essentially different religion. Corbin saw the twelfth-century mystic and philosopher Suhrawardi as an Iranian who "tried to bring about a revival of the theosophical wisdom of the ancient Persians."[10] This analysis led Corbin to think that "to speak of Iranian Islam is in fact to speak of Shiite Islam."[11] Corbin called Shiʿism "Iranian Islam,"[12] a view that took root among many Iranian nationalists and even clerics and that exists to this day. It would later be endorsed by some politicians in the Islamic Republic.[13]

This Orientalist background is significant for understanding Shariʿati's attempts at delineating Shiʿi Islam as Iran's special and separate path, where the nation's essential traits are expressed in its worship and belief. Shariʿati was not the only Iranian intellectual of this period to adopt this view. In fact, this Orientalist notion had a deep influence on many intellectuals and on the ulema in Iran from the moment it made its way into the local discourse on Iranian identity and its relation to Shiʿism. It even entered the sensitive and authoritative field of Qur'anic exegesis.[14] Shariʿati's choice to study Persian literature and the history of Islam at Mashhad University points to his view of the inseparable nature of the two fields.[15] In fact, Shariʿati contended that any attempt to understand Iranian history in the past thirteen hundred years without delving into Islamic history or vice versa was futile.[16]

Redefining Pre-Islamic Iran

As a popular lecturer at the Husayniyya Ershad, with an ever-growing number of listeners, Shariʿati had to grapple with these questions and offer his devout listeners with a way to face the Pahlavi claim to Iranian authenticity and continuity. As was the case for other Iranian thinkers of his time, rising to the challenge of defining Iranian authenticity would have an impact on his credibility as a guide for perplexed Iranian youth facing dilemmas of identity and tradition.[17]

Shariʿati developed a theory that combined two elements of Iranian identity: the ancient pre-Islamic culture and the Shiʿite faith. He recognized the significance of the pre-Islamic culture as the first formation of Iranian identity, one that had produced a great religion and a monumental civilization. However, he rejected Iranian pre-Islamic culture as a viable source of national identity, particularly one that could endow modern Iranians with a unifying message. That greatness, he argued, was long gone by the time Iranians were introduced to Islam.[18] Just as that culture could not fend off Islam in the seventh century, it was not an adequate or relevant basis for an ideology of national liberation in the face of Western influence in the modern period. He was thus arguing against the nationalism based on pre-Islamic culture that the Pahlavi state tried to promote. To begin with, he denied the existence of a cohesive cultural and national community in pre-Islamic Iran.

Shariʿati's view arose as a reaction to Iranian nationalists' case for cultural nationalism as part of the glorification of pre-Islamic Iran from the middle of the nineteenth century. Mirza Fath ʿAli Akhundzadeh, whom we met in the previous chapter, depicted, or rather imagined, ancient Iran to be a mirror of what Shariʿati viewed as Iran's modern decadent and despotic state. It is no wonder, then, that he succumbed to the idealized vision of a society living in harmony and practicing equality and egalitarian values. Other nationalist thinkers followed suit and developed a genre that has not lost its vitality in aggrandizing and idealizing pre-Islamic Iran as a repository of modern values, where both the individual and society as a whole could realize their potential. The reign of Reza Shah (1925–41) ushered this discourse into the public sphere through the state's ever-growing involvement in education and the public sphere, to the point that this discourse eventually became the state's official discourse.[19] State ceremonies, archaeological sites, and a nascent educational system sought to serve this purpose.

As noted in chapter 1, the Iranian nationalist view of ancient Iran was that this unified and cohesive society had fallen under the onslaught of the Arab invasion: "Our thousand-year-old rule that the Arab invasion put an end to . . . they ruined our country beyond recognition," Akhundzadeh lamented in a letter.[20] This historical narrative, which glossed over hundreds of years from the Achaemenid period to the Sassanid Empire, became the semiofficial story of Iran on the part of Pahlavi intellectuals, first and foremost Shojaeddin Shafa'.[21] Ancient Iran was praised as the cradle of civilization and the source of many values, mistakenly taken to be the legacy of the Greeks.[22]

Shari'ati, in contrast, replaced this romantic picture with a totally different one, that of a caste society whose elements can hardly be seen as sharing a common fate or set of values, a society where each group—priests, the court, and the masses—was segregated from the others, with virtually no way of breaking the barriers that separated them. His analysis of late Sassanid society was probably influenced by his studies of European society during the ancien régime (which preceded the French Revolution) as well as by his criticism of the Pahlavi social order, where the few tried to legitimize their rule over the many by clinging to divine dicta. Sassanid society, he argued, was characterized by social schisms that surpassed economic realities and permeated the religious and cultural spheres, arts, and lifestyles. Even written and spoken languages created such impassable demarcations among Iranians as to make even a semblance of national unity and cultural community impossible.[23]

According to Shari'ati, then, it was hard to speak of ancient Iran as a nation because it was deeply divided along economic and social statuses. These castes were quite rigid, and in reality there was no way of crossing the lines between them. Even linguistically, he contended, it was difficult to speak of one nation at that time because the administration used Dari, whereas the clerics spoke Avesta, the ancient Indian language. They did not even use the same script to write the different languages they used. Thus, the separation between the four classes—administrators, clerics, professionals, and the masses—was virtually impregnable and hermetic.[24]

In the absence of a common spirit, a common culture, and a common conscience, what held this fragmented society together, Shari'ati concluded, was "only the principle of monarchy and worship of the king."[25] It was precisely owing to these conditions that Sassanid society was so vulnerable to outside attack, a fact that made the invasion by the Arabs and the religious conquest by Islam all the easier. In a somewhat prophetic manner, Shari'ati warned his listeners that a political entity that relies solely on the monarch is doomed to collapse when faced with social forces of unrest.[26] Hence, he asserted, it is no wonder that Zoroastrian Iranians welcomed the coming of Islam, which brought them the message of justice and equality.

Shari'ati's second argument questioned the very relevance of pre-Islamic culture to contemporary Iranian life. Mocking the cultural nationalist argument that the ancient Iranian culture constitutes "one of our deep-rooted and glorious cultural selves," Shari'ati retorted with the question: "But where is this cultural self?" His response was that this "brilliant and original culture does not exist in society but only in history: for the historian, then, ancient Iran exists forever, whereas for the sociologist it is no longer in existence because it has no presence in society."[27]

Whereas cultivation of the national pre-Islamic heritage was one of the hallmarks of intellectual activity in the service of the state during the 1930s, it became identified with Western domination in the period following the declaration of the "White Revolution" by Mohammad Reza Shah. This pivotal change in the attitude of prominent members of the Iranian intellectual elite was evident in the polemical writings of others who became hostile to everything identified with Western influence.

For Shari'ati, then, historical greatness was not the yardstick by which one could measure the value of one's past. Those who did so were trying to take Iran back in time, which was neither possible nor desirable:

> What we have now is an age-old return, the wealth of the Achaemenid period, the Sassanid period . . . and the periods before them, are we returning to those? This old and antiquated return, one that is rooted in history, is one that we are separated from by hundreds of years. This Achaemenid, archaeological, and old return is one of historians, archaeologists, scientists; they can discover and comprehend it, but our nation does not feel it is its own return.[28]

Shari'ati refers here to the Pahlavi state's evident enthusiasm for ancient sites such as Behistun, Persepolis, and Pasargadae.[29] Every inscription was recorded and analyzed as if it would tell Iranians who they are. Shari'ati felt that this attempt to cling to the greatness of the past as if it could elevate the nation in the present enjoyed no emotional resonance among the people: "What feelings do our people have toward the inscriptions and the ruins that exist here? They think that jinns have written them. This testifies to the fact that they have no connection whatsoever with them."[30]

Shari'ati's criticism of the aggrandizement of ancient Iranian symbols went well with the criticism he directed at traditional Islam, which he felt cultivates rites and preaches passive acceptance of reality, whereas Shi'ites in reality "do not accept the path chosen by history[;] . . . they negate the leadership which ruled over history."[31] Shari'ati identified the "return" that the Pahlavi state professed with all that is bad in traditions and superstitions that have accumulated over the years and that tend to lull people into ignoring their current plight. In other words, the Pahlavi historical nostalgia had the same effect as the conservative religious establishment, but with a scientific aura and modernist enthusiasm.

According to Shari'ati, the intellectual ideologue is essentially different from the historian and the archaeologist. The ideologue takes interest in the past only insofar as it helps him in understanding and shaping the present. In other words, the intellectual's commitment is to society and not to scientific inquiry as such.[32] Interestingly, Shari'ati's call for a history that is relevant to the present did not necessarily contradict the usage of history. On the contrary, it justified and demanded it. His argument with the state revolved around the specific usage it made in his time. Put differently, Shari'ati objected not to the applicability of history to national needs but rather to a specific implementation of that application. This point is important in understanding the fact that the Islamic Revolution would not bring about the erasure of the nation-state but rather fill it with new content and sanctify its doctrine, including its historical aspect (which I discuss further in chapter 5).

Persepolis as an Asset, Persepolis as a Liability

As October 1971 drew near, the need to compete with the Pahlavi historical narrative seemed ever more pressing. In a rather more graphic manner, one that resonated with many Iranians in light of the celebrations of twenty-five hundred years of Iranian monarchy, Shari'ati defined two different views of the site of the celebrations, the Achaemenid capital of Persepolis: "The sociologist will find Persepolis interesting only to the degree that he can make it relevant and living for contemporary Iranians—say, for instance, if he can let an Iranian family dwell there. For the historian studying the structures, pillars, etc., of the site, it is a reality for its own sake."[33] According to Shari'ati, the pre-Islamic culture that the Pahlavi establishment tried to promote as a hallmark of Iranian identity was a piece of "discontinued" history with little or no connection to the present. It could more easily be found in history books and museums than in Iranians' dominant beliefs and practices. The vast majority of people had no memory or knowledge of this past. "Our nation does not feel that [cultural] self as its own, and the heroes, personages, and mythologies of that period do not have life, movement, and pulsation among our people. Return to oneself does not mean [return to] an abstract self and a dead past but rather to a cultural self that existed in the soul and conscience of society."[34] Although Shari'ati did not turn his back altogether on pre-Islamic history, he maintained that it was Islam, not ancient Iran, that constituted the dominant feature of Iranian history and culture. Iran's Islamic cultural identity had deep roots in Iranian history and permeated every facet of life in Iranian society. It was as Muslims that Iranians for the first time in centuries developed sentiments of national identity in opposition to Arab attempts to dominate them in the name of Islamic universality. It was also within the framework of Islamic civilization that Iranians over the past millennium had made their greatest contributions to human advancement in the fields of science, philosophy, arts, and literature. And, more recently, it was an Islamic Iran that had contributed to Islamic resistance against Western imperialism with the spiritual leader Jamal al-Din al-Afghani (1838–97) as well the successful protest movement of the Tobacco Rebellion (1891–92).[35] Rereading Iranian history enabled Shari'ati to visualize an Iranian identity that was modern and had a selective choice of moments of greatness, while remaining loyal, indeed forging a new loyalty, to its Islamic faith.

An Iranian Islam?

From what I have presented so far, one might conclude that Shari'ati rejected the Iranian particularistic identity as a Western fallacy (which he at times claimed to do). Indeed, when it came to contemporary Iran,

Shari'ati had little trouble persuading his audience that its existence constituted the substance of Iran's history, the spirit of its culture, the mode of its life, and the determinant of individual and social behavior. However, Shi'ite Islam, for him, was not a universal religion per se but rather Iranian Islam. It was what gave Iran its distinctive character as a national community and was the only force that could effectively challenge imperialism and its consequences for Iranian society: loss of cultural identity and social cohesion. Their religious affiliation, then, had saved Iranians from national-cultural assimilation.

According to Shari'ati, the religion the Arabs had brought to Iran was separate from the Arabs as a people. In other words, the Iranian uprisings that broke out two centuries after the coming of Islam to Iran, known as the Shu'ubiyya, caused the separation of Islam in Iran from the Arabs who had brought it there. The message was stronger than the messenger. There was, he said, a tendency among Iranian nationalists to confuse the uprisings with anti-Islamic feelings, but in truth what Iranians demanded was Islam without the Arabs (*islam minhaye 'Arab*).[36]

Arabs had a negative influence on Islam, Shari'ati argued, because they contradicted the precepts of this religion with their 'Arabzadegi, "Arab-toxication"—that is, their condescending attitude to non-Arabs. Iranians, therefore, saved Islam from deteriorating to a racist religion and thus served as its true interpreters.[37]

Every Iranian intellectual who sought to be loyal to both his religion and his society at the same time had to separate Islam from the Arabs "because the Arabs ruled over the people in the name of Islam, the *khalifa*s of the Prophet, and the edicts of the Qur'an," but in fact they used these lofty concepts.[38] The great struggle over the identity of Islam took place in the first two centuries of Islam, which some misunderstood to be a time of Iranian silence in the face of Arab supremacy.[39] In fact, Shari'ati stated, "what we see during the two first centuries (the so-called 'two centuries of silence') is not an Islamic culture taking the place of an Iranian one, but rather the removal of Sassanid culture in favor of one that combines Sassanid, Semite, Islamic, Greek, Western, and even Jewish elements."[40]

In Shari'ati's essential classification of Semites versus Aryans, he considered the Semitic to have a clear set of characteristics, such as enthusiasm, carelessness, restlessness, brutality, and lack of imagination. Indians and Iranians, in contrast, possess the opposite characteristics. They tend to be mild, gentle, and imaginative and are inclined to abstract thinking. It is therefore no coincidence, according to Shari'ati, that most of what is called "Islamic art" was created not in Mecca and Medina, but rather in other centers of Islamic culture, such as Khorasan, Rayy, Isfahan, and Nishapur. On the cognitive level, Semites seem to lose the larger picture in focusing on the details, and Aryans are less careful with details.[41] Because Islam originated in the Semitic race, it had the potential to become a brutal and violent religion. However, with the influence of the Iranian population, it changed and became more mild and pragmatic. Thus, Iranians saved Islam from expressing the negative features it was bound to have because of its Semitic origins.

Shari'ati drove his point home using examples from Islamic history, such as art and poetry. For instance, he mentioned apocalyptic tendencies that are, according to him, prevalent in Arab history, in contrast to the lack of them in Indian and Iranian history: both the Semite and the Indian-Iranian expect the coming of an unseen savior, following whose arrival the world will be full of justice and truth. But the Semites have no patience to wait for long; this is why in the twelve hundred years since the disappearance of the *imam-i zaman* (i.e., the hidden imam), there have been at least a hundred pretenders to that title, but in the more than three thousand years that Iranians have waited for Saoshyant (the Zororastrian savior) and the Indians have expected the reappearance of Buddha, there have been no claimants, and there is no rush to have any either.[42]

Shari'ati juxtaposed leaders from the two civilizations to prove his point: the Egyptian president Gamal 'Abdel Nasser and the Indian leader Mahatma Gandhi. The first was brutal and cruel, whereas the latter led nonviolent resistance.[43] He even compared the Prophet Mohammad to the Buddha, who was tranquil and peaceful and hence had greater accomplishments as a prophet.[44] This comparison is remarkable because it shows the great lengths to which Shari'ati was willing to go, sacrificing the one symbol on which all Muslims supposedly agree to prove his nationalist claim.

Shari'ati's view of the characteristics of the two races served his purpose of proving that the blending of the two "races" and the creation of

Shi'ism brought out the best of both and lifted their potential to new heights. The most important point in Shari'ati's analysis of this development is that the contact of Semites and Aryans with the conversion of Iranians to Islam formed a compound, a new phenomenon, a Shi'ite-Iranian Islam. It is not the Islam of the prophet or a reincarnation of ancient Iranian religions, but rather something else. In the course of the creation of this compound, the Semitic elements in Islam were eroded, as were some of the Iranians' Aryan characteristics.[45] This view explains Shari'ati's contention that trying to return to pre-Islamic glory lacked sense. According to Shari'ati, those who seek the glories of the past do so in vain not only because historically they have very little to hang on to (even Ferdowsi in the *Shahnameh* had nothing good to say about the late Sassanid period), but also because, more than that, they are trying to get rid of a creation that cannot be put back into the bottle. It is neither possible nor desirable.[46]

Unlike Ayatollah Ruhollah Khomeini (1902–89) and his assistant Sadeq Khalkhali (1926–2003), who had nothing positive to say about nationalism, Shari'ati was infused with national pride, to the extent that his writings even occasionally reveal a condescending and racist attitude toward the Arabs. Thus, in another essay where he dealt with the question of the intricate relationship between Iranians' religious and national identity, he described pre-Islamic Iran as "our old civilization," which was "one of the most advanced, universal, and ancient civilizations in human history." In a manner reminiscent of Pahlavi historians, ostensibly his adversaries, who preached loyalty to the Pahlavi national discourse of continuity dating back to pre-Islamic periods, Shari'ati asserted that Iran is an heir of the Mesopotamian civilizations that rivaled the Greek and Roman civilizations, while contributing many elements to both Islamic and European civilizations.[47]

Shari'ati followed the Orientalists he had been in contact with when dealing with the question of the unique Iranian spirit and its relation to Shi'i Islam. As such, he felt that he belonged to a twelve-hundred-year-old civilization with magnificent art and literature that relied on Islam, the greatest religion in the world. Shari'ati called Iranian Islam "the meeting point of Aryan and Semitic spirits,"[48] a by-product of the transformative impact of Islam on the Iranian mode of thought and disposition, on the one hand, and Iranians' creative efforts to contribute to the development of Islamic ideology and culture, on the other. He cited the Iranian traditions in philosophy, mysticism, literature, and poetry as integral elements of what he called "Irano-Islamic" culture and the basic constituents of a specifically Iranian national identity.[49]

Islam's relation to the existence of ethnic divides is vague and ambivalent in this view and difficult to define in terms of rejection or adoption. Shari'ati categorically rejected the perception that confused Islam's opposition to racial discrimination and ethnic domination with opposition to the diversity of nations and nationalities in human societies. He based his assertion on the following Qur'anic verse (49:13): "People, We created you all from a single man and a single woman, and made you into races and tribes so that you should recognize one another."[50] This verse, according to Shari'ati, indicates that the existence of distinct and independent nations is not a political theory or merely a sentiment, but "a natural reality in creation," just as other divisions among humans, such as sex and culture, are natural. In addition, Shari'ati argued, there is a profound and progressive reason for the division of mankind into various nationalities. The Qur'an has substituted mutual intercourse and knowledge for conflict, pride, and domination in the relationships among nations. Equally important is the fact that the natural outcome of such relations is the growth of self-knowledge by various cultural and national groups.[51]

In Shari'ati's view, Iranian nationalism alone is not a source of comfort in and of itself. It must be coupled with its twin, its inseparable element, Shi'i Islam. Shi'ism is the basis for the anticolonialist activity and identity formation that he saw as homegrown staples of Iranian culture and identity.

Shi'i Islam and Iranian National Identity

Shari'ati divided nationalism into two phases: in the first phase, nationhood is a foundation of the community, gaining awareness and spreading among a growing number of members in society. In the second phase, nationhood becomes an assertion of unity and distinctiveness in the face of external domination and threat. In the first phase, nationalism is a natural and therefore a lasting phenomenon, surpassing time and place. However, the brand of nationalism that follows the achievement of independence and the end of colonialism tends to become a deceptive cover for the denial of social and class divisions.

Given the important place of pre-Islamic cultural tradition in Iranian nationalist thought and policy, Shari'ati could not but raise the question of the relations between Iranians' national identity and their religious one. Iran has two "historical-cultural selves," he conceded: its pre-Islamic, ancient culture and the culture formed following the conversion of Iranians to Islam. He recognized the significance of the pre-Islamic legacy as the first formation of Iranian identity, one that had produced a great religion and a monumental civilization. The deterioration of the Sassanid Empire had brought about the demise and extinction of this civilization, but not of the basic belief system it represented.

Shari'ati denounced the claim of a uniform and continuous development of a national community in pre-Islamic Iran. The case for this view of Iranian nationalism had been promoted by, among others, Ehsan Yarshater (b. 1920), a professor of Persian literature, who maintained that in pre-Islamic Iran there was "a very strong sense of nationalism, nurtured by common aspirations and ideas, a common tradition and common ethnic and linguistic background."[52] Shari'ati, in contrast, maintained that late Sassanid society was deeply divided along caste and class lines. It was therefore a society where social division encompassed the religious and cultural spheres, arts and lifestyles, separating different social strata to the degree that unity and cultural community were concepts devoid of meaning. Mirroring Pahlavi historians, Shari'ati and other oppositionists imagined ancient Iran to be a precursor of its Pahlavi descendant, reflecting social division and the alienation of the masses rather than unity, as the Pahlavis would have it.[53] In the absence of a common spirit, a common culture, and a common conscience, what held this fragmented society together was "only the principle of monarchy and worship of the king."[54] It was precisely owing to these conditions that the Iranians welcomed the coming of Islam, which brought them a message of justice and equality.

According to Shari'ati, religious ethics, presented as a set of injunctions and rituals, is a universal ideology addressed not to a particular group or community but to all men. In contrast, nation or nationality is the historically evolved collective personality of a particular group of people, manifested in its disposition, temperament, and behavior. Nationality bears the same relation to religion as personality to belief, reality to truth. To adopt or to formulate an ideology involves an active assertion of choice and will, but a person simply inherits his membership in the collectivity to which he belongs. Therefore, one could discard his own worldview and moral ideals and adopt others, but one could not do the same with his national-cultural heritage. This division, reminiscent of the one that scholars of nationalism still make between civic and ethnic nationalism, assuming the first to be based on choice and the other on birthright, played an important role in Shari'ati's thought.[55] However, in social reality the question is not so simple, Shari'ati argued, hence the source of the confusion. As an ideology, religion always gives rise to the development of culture and civilization, a process in which various people participate. In the creative effort to understand and explain the new religion, to adapt to its teachings, and to make it adaptable to its new condition, each collectivity produces cultural forms and lifestyles that have a deep and undeniable impact on the collective spirit of the nation.[56]

It is difficult to summarize 'Ali Shari'ati's thought on the relations between Iranian nationalism and Shi'ism. Ambivalence is the overriding element in his thought regarding this topic. In his view, although Islam is a universal religion, Iranians do have a unique and irreplaceable role in it. They elevated it to a height it would not have attained if not for their contribution to its evolution. Islam, however, did not eradicate a cultural world that had existed before it arrived in Iran because Iranians preserved that culture and carried it on into the new historical phase, Islamic Iran.

Although Shari'ati attacked the Sassanid Empire, which preceded the Islamic conquest, he did not cut all ties to it and avoided the sensitive issue of Zoroastrianism as a religion. A less-ambivalent and more-pronounced negation of Western nationalism was adopted by the closer circle of clerics who surrounded Ayatollah Khomeini (if not in body, because he was in exile for the last decade and a half of the Pahlavi state, then in spirit). One of the most prominent of these clerics was Ayatollah Mortaza Motahhari, to whom we now turn.

2. Ayatollah Mortaza Motahhari, 1940s. Unknown photographer, Wikimedia Commons.

Mortaza Motahhari and the New Irano-Islamic Consciousness

Mortaza Motahhari (1920–79) was an ayatollah, a *mujtahid*, Khomeini's student, and a professor of philosophy at Tehran University. A graduate of seminaries in both Mashhad and Qom, Motahhari was well aware of the collision between Reza Shah's modernization policies and the clerics. His family was in fact a victim of some of the shah's controversial steps, such as the banning of religious attire.[57] Motahhari wrote extensively on diverse topics, from Islamic economy and philosophy to politics and literature. One of his most famous compositions is a booklet titled *Dastan-i rastan* (The Story of the Virtuous), which is a compilation of short stories on Shiʿite leaders in the formative period of this faith. Combining moral messages with a social critique of late Pahlavi society and state, this book seems to have been more widely circulated than any other he wrote.[58] The wide circulation of his ideas, especially among the educated youth, attests to the importance he attached to the friendly presentation of his religious views, especially with respect to the competition he felt these ideas had with Marxist ones at the time.[59] Acknowledging the problem of the clergy's diminishing relevance to the youth, Motahhari set out to deal with it rather than sidestep it, the way Shari'ati seemed to do.[60] Even if it is not true that the assassins who killed Motahhari were inspired by Shari'ati, there is no doubt that the two had parted ways well before Motahhari's untimely death. During the years that Shari'ati became a popular speaker at Husayniyya Ershad, Motahhari, who had brought him there in the first place, received news about the fierce attacks Shari'ati leveled at large segments of the clergy. That these attacks—coming as they did from such a popular speaker as Shari'ati—had a ripple effect did not go unnoticed by Motahhari, who felt somewhat responsible for the situation and sought to curb the charismatic speaker he had brought to the Husayniyya.[61]

Motahhari's lectures on the reciprocal cultural and theological contributions between Iran and Islam were based on the feeling of crisis and disappointment in Arab nationalism and especially in what had seemed like its political zenith, Nasserism. The subservience of Islam to Arab nationalism explained, according to Motahhari, the great failure of the latter, which culminated in the major setback of 1967. Michael Fisher and Mehdi Abedi suggest that Motahhari's lectures seemed to reinforce Iranian nationalist themes.[62] Ironically, the crisis of Arab nationalism and Nasserism pushed Motahhari to reveal the weakness of Arab nationalism but not the flaws of nationalism in general. Indeed, the lectures turned into an encomium of Iranians' contribution to Islam and thus cultivated nationalist themes. He was influenced by left-wing Third Worldist ideologues, especially Egyptians.

Motahhari tried to answer the question that he saw as most relevant to Iranians during the late twentieth century and that seemed to resonate in the writings of many intellectuals of the time: Should we Iranians count Islam as ours or as something foreign and external? According to national criteria, should Islam be part and parcel of Iranian nationalist feelings or outside them?[63]

Like Shari'ati, Motahhari was ambivalent toward nationalism. Despite Mahmood Davari's impression that Motahhari denounced "pan-Iranianism and Iranian nationalism,"[64] it is more easily argued that although averse to the first tendency, he showed more flexibility toward the second. On the one hand, like other Islamic scholars, he saw nationalism as a means used by the West to control colonized societies. According to this view, nationalism was an ideology invented to divide and rule the Third World, creating rivalries and wars between neighboring societies and thus preventing any potential for unity among them to resist Western domination. Categories of nation and race served this purpose perfectly:

> Colonialism, in order to put into practice the policy of divide and rule, didn't find a better way than making the Islamic tribes and nations to be preoccupied and proud of their tribal, national, and racial differences. It used to be said . . . to the Arabs—who are more vulnerable to prejudices—that you should rely on Arabism (Pan-Arabism) [and in the same manner] to an Iranian that you are Arian, therefore you must have a different account from the Arabs since you are from a high and respected race.[65]

Motahhari, like Ayatollah Sadiq Khalkhali and other clerics, was worried about the nation-state's possible success in convincing the masses that it represented Iranian authenticity, a revival of the true spirit of Iran. What threatened them as clerics of the opposition more than anything else was what Motahhari saw as the attempt to push Shiʿism to the margins of Iranian consciousness. In this attempt, the Pahlavi educational system and secondary agents of memory created a fake similarity between Islam and Arab identity, thus making it easier to denigrate the former in the name of fighting the latter: "We all know that in this last period of time many people under the title of defending Iranian nationalism and tribalism have started a wide campaign against Islam and in the guise of fighting with Arabs and Arabism they make jest of the Islamic sanctities."[66] To the clerics, the type of Iranian nationalism the Pahlavi state tried to promote was just short of modern paganism. It seems worthwhile to quote Motahhari at length here to demonstrate the urgent feeling that he, like other Islamists of his time, was fighting against a cultural crusade:

> The effects of this fighting against Islam in Iran, which we see in books, weekly magazines etc. indicate that it is not by chance and accidental, it is a calculated plan and work that has been designed. Even the propagation of Zoroastrians that got increased and expanded today is a preplanned political activity. All the Iranians of today will never go back to the religion of Zoroaster, the teachings of Zoroastrians will never take

> the place of the Islamic teachings, the personalities of the followers of Mazdak, Manichean, Zoroastrian and all those people that today are introduced under the false title of nationalism and they don't have any specific intention except deviation from Islam—whether formally they carried on their activities in the name of fighting Islam or they took fighting with Arab people to be an excuse they will never take the place of Islamic heroes in the hearts of Iranians.[67]

In his response to this cultural crusade, Motahhari attempted to prove that Islam and Iran are inseparable. He asserted that even though historically Arabs had brought the religion to Iran, because Iranians had joined it of their free will, and—more importantly—had contributed to it so that it grew beyond its original form, the two—Islam and Iran—became one and have thus become part of one religious-cultural entity: if Islam is foreign to an Iranian, then the religion of Christ is also foreign to a European and an American.[68]

According to Motahhari, Iranians have contributed to Islam more than the people of any other nation, which attests to the sincerity and authenticity of their Islam once they received this faith. They have surpassed even the Arabs, who brought this religion to Iran in the first place. Interestingly, this devotion to the faith that came with a foreign invader has become, following Motahhari's logic (and that of others who would follow him), a source of national pride. Other scholars in the Iranian ulema hold the same view, and it can be traced back to the Orientalist view espoused by Corbin, who was a source of inspiration for Shari'ati, as noted earlier.

Whereas, as we have seen, Shari'ati's attitude toward race theories was somewhat ambiguous, Motahhari was unequivocal when it came to racial perceptions. For him, they are nothing but a myth, a superstition: "The race of Semites, Aryans and others were separated and independent of one another only in the past. But now there is so much intermingling, transfer and exchange to the extent that there is no race that has remained independent."[69]

The pretense of knowing one's racial origins is unreal, Motahhari argued, as is the idea that the races still matter or are relevant to people's capabilities or traits: "Many of the Iranian people of today that speak

Persian and call for Iranism are Arabs, Turk or Mogul. Maybe many of the people that are descendants of Cyrus and Darius living in Arab countries exhibit Arab chauvinism, similarly, the descendants of Abu Sufyan may display Iranian chauvinism."[70] History and its tribulations have rendered all racial distinctions irrelevant and absurd.

Motahhari attacked Professor Mohammad Mu'in's theory that the Umayyad caliph Yazid ibn Mu'awiyah (Yazid I, 647–83) was an Iranian by origin. He saw this theory as the fruit of the legacy Mu'in inherited from Ibrahim Purdavud (1886–1968), a linguist who was one of the founders of research on ancient Persian texts and their Indian origins and one of the academic pillars of Iranian nationalism in the twentieth century.[71]

Contrary to Iranian nationalism, which often emphasized biological origins and ancestry, Motahhari disputed the weight often attributed to origins with regard to authenticity. Any national affiliation of Mohammad's prophethood is baseless, according to Motahhari, because "the history of Islam, as well as other religions proves it. . . . Prophets were often ignored in their homeland, only to be adopted wholeheartedly by neighboring societies."[72]

Not blind to Iran's competition in the political field or to its efforts to achieve legitimacy among neighboring countries, Motahhari compared Iran with two of its Arab adversaries in the region: Saudi Arabia and Egypt. Only the former could boast a piety that competed with that of Iran.[73] Piety, then, is the key to national pride, not biological origins or empty claims to authenticity.

According to Motahhari, the nationalist historiography that glorified pre-Islamic Iran did not do justice to the Iranians because at the coming of Islam Iranians were waiting for relief and salvation. That explains why the new faith brought by the Arab conquest circulated among the people at lightning speed.[74] The Arab conquest, according to Motahhari, was essentially different from that of other invasions in Iranian history. The Goliath was not the invaders in this case, but rather the Sassanid Empire: "While the victory of Islam against the Sassanid Empire was in fact a victory of the few against the many, the mercenaries of imperialism, in a most unmanly manner, place the Islamic movement at par with the conquests of Alexander and the Mongols."[75]

The coming of Islam to Iran meshed the two cultures in a way that rendered the modern quest for supremacy of one over the other meaningless. For instance, Iranians' contribution to the development of Arabic studies was far greater than the Arabs' contributions, and the Arab 'Abbasids were more active in promoting the Persian language than Iranians were.[76]

While denouncing the fabrication regarding race that nationalism had spread in Iran, the myth of origin, and the belief in the eternal hostility between Iranians and Arabs, Motahhari did forge one myth of his own: the enduring link between Iranians and the Shi'ite faith. Here one finds Motahhari's ambivalence toward nationalism: although he rejected many of the meanings loaded upon the concept, he actually used it to clarify what he considered to be Iranians' uniqueness among the nations: "Iranians, since the early days of Islam, showed a stronger emotional attachment to the Family of the Prophet compared to other peoples and nations."[77] Indeed, it was the special dynamic of Iranians in Islam that confused Western scholars: some Orientalists tried to color this emotional attachment with ulterior motives, interpreting it rather as a calculated reaction vis-à-vis Islam or at least against Arabs, with a view to reviving old Iranian customs and traditions. According to Motahhari, these persons' views provided a good excuse for the so-called Iranian nationalists, who lauded the Iranians for reviving and preserving ancient Iranian traditions under the flag of Shi'ism. Such, he said, was the erroneous perception of the Shu'ubiyya movement, which was nothing but an Iranian movement to purge Islam of its racist Arab elements.[78]

Both 'Ali Shari'ati and Ayatollah Mortaza Motahhari were facing a powerful state mass-communication effort aimed at inculcating the Pahlavi worldview and repressive measures to prevent competing views from endangering it, even though in hindsight one can surely say that the results of both were mixed. Although these efforts failed in gaining political legitimacy for the regime, the regime's messages sank deep into the Iranian collective memory and shared perceptions in a manner that even the tumultuous events of 1979 did not erode. Despite the repressive measures taken by the notorious SAVAK, the Iranian public sphere was nothing close to dormant or complacent regarding the Pahlavi narrative of Iranian identity and past. One of the figures that best embodied the

Pahlavi worldview regarding the Iranian past and the essence of Iranianness, the mastermind behind some of its most outspoken expressions, was Shojaeddin Shafa'. Turning to him, we see the other side of the struggle for Iranian identity—indeed, for the meaning of being Iranian.

Shojaeddin Shafa': The Historian as a Nationalist Ideologue

Shojaeddin Shafa' (1918–2010) was a central figure in the Pahlavi mass-education machine. He was the manager of the Pahlavi National Library and the ambassador general for cultural affairs during the early 1970s. Shafa' was central in organizing the celebrations of twenty-five hundred years of the Iranian monarchy that took place at Persepolis and Pasargadae in October 1971. According to some sources, the celebrations were in fact his idea.[79] Shafa' tried to explain the reasons for the celebrations that he worked hard to organize: the ceremony around the tomb of Cyrus was meant to convey the message of modern Iran to its ancient predecessor and to renew the contract binding modern Iranians to their ancestors.[80]

Regardless of the role Shafa' played in the initiative, there is no doubt as to his central role in orchestrating the events at the national and international levels. Chairing the steering committee of the celebrations, he coordinated the events that took place in Iran and beyond, including at the Iranian embassies in Canada, Switzerland, Russia, and the United States. According to David Stronach, who headed the British Archeological Institute in Iran at the time, Shafa' was deeply involved in ascertaining that the site of Pasargadae, where the tomb of Cyrus stands and which was the arena of one of the highest points of the celebrations, was emptied of any remains from Islamic periods, which would have been detrimental to the Achaemenid-Iranian message meant to be conveyed in the celebrations. It seems that the Islamic oppositionists' feeling that the Pahlavi state was intentionally downplaying Iran's Islamic past was not unfounded.

To better evaluate his writing and activities, it will help to outline the Pahlavi worldview that Shafa' contributed to shaping. Simply put, the perception of Iranian history promoted by Shafa' viewed modern Iran as a reincarnation of the ancient empire that Iran used to be, starting from Cyrus the Great in the sixth century BCE. In fact, it was the Achaemenid period, named after the dynasty established by Cyrus, that the Pahlavi state sought to commemorate and be inspired by more than any other period in Iranian history. Moreover, this perception of history saw Iran as part of Western civilization, indeed as its predecessor, and attributed to it many of the values that the West appropriated later, such as the recognition of human rights and the tolerance of other faiths and traditions. Although one finds a dominant historical narrative within the Pahlavi establishment, especially in its last decade and a half, it is worth mentioning that the state did support certain religious voices. Seyyed Hossein Nasr (b. 1933), a prolific intellectual and academic, was close to Queen Farah Diba and initiated a circle of sympathetic clerics and intellectuals such as Mortaza Motahhari and Jalal al-Din Ashtiyani (1925–2005).[81]

Shafa' wrote extensively in large part in the wake of the Islamic Revolution, which had forced him, like other officials of the Pahlavi state, to flee Iran. However, unlike most of them, Shafa' did not limit his publicist activity to embellishing his biography or defending his actions as part of the Pahlavi system but rather expanded it to include defending the nationalist pre-Islamic worldview, to which he remained loyal to the end. Shafa' became a torch-bearer of the Pahlavi worldview, continuing to see pre-Islamic Iran as Iran's golden age and maintaining his negative view of Islam's influence on the history of Iranians in the past fourteen centuries. His writings, which did not go unnoticed in the Islamic Republic and among some of the spokesmen of the competing worldview, reflected an Iranian exile's attempt to fight the Islamic historical narrative from outside Iran. His refutation of the Islamic historical narrative, unlike that of other Iranian nationalists, is based on a wide range of sources and shows a great familiarity with the claims of this Islamic worldview and with the speeches and writings of the heads of the Islamic Republic. In fact, his oeuvre stands out owing to the fact that he not only orchestrated some of the most controversial events of the Pahlavi state but also was among the few to wage ideological battle with the Islamic Republic in the aftermath of the Islamic Revolution.

One can take his writing of the book *Iran dar adabiyat-i jahan* (Iran in World Literature) in 1954 as a harbinger of his cultural and political activities. The book was for all intents and purposes a guidebook to French literature for Iranians. Translating some of the French classics where Iranians or Iran are mentioned, Shafa' sought to show the great influence Iranians had on French culture and through that on Western culture in general.

The Last Pahlavi

Shortly after the downfall of the Pahlavi state and the establishment of the Islamic Republic, Shafa' published his monumental work *Tawzih al-masa'il* (Clarification of Questions).[82] This book spells out clearly his view of Iranian history from the pre-Islamic eras to the twentieth century. Shafa' dedicates this book, which could be considered his magnum opus, to "all those who have lost their lives due to cowardly Islamic rulings. The Ferdowsis who were not allowed to be buried among Muslims, the Khayyams and Hafezes whose tombs have been ruined, the Abu-Sinas and Razis who have been declared heretics and were exiled."[83] Shafa' put himself in the shoes of all the great Iranian thinkers who, according to his view, did not receive the honor they deserved. It is no small twist of history that he describes these poets and thinkers as if they were overlooked even though they have been recognized as pillars of Iranian culture for ages. According to him, the great effort of writing this monumental book, which spans more than a thousand pages, was justified as both a "national duty and a cultural one" at a time when Iran was being robbed of its national identity as well as of its Persian and Islamic culture. The indictment of the Islamic Republic screams from every page of this monumental tour de force. Shafa' states that the fundamentalist regime that the revolution brought to power is no better than the worst totalitarian forces of world history: "Hizballah is no better than the SS, viewing their understanding of God as the only legitimate one, just as the former viewed their race as superior to all others."[84]

His reckoning with the Islamic Republic hearkens to earlier periods and their place in Iranian history, the main controversy being the Islamic conquest of the seventh century. It is there that Shafa' locates what he perceives to be the distorted view of history and its repercussions: "Some fourteen centuries ago, with the assault of the newly created religion of Islam on Iran, 1,300 years of monarchy came to an end. . . . Back at that time, Iran was counted among the great empires such as Rome and China, a glory and power it has not recovered ever since."[85] Interestingly, Shafa"s historical narrative is not completely different from that of some of the Islamists we met earlier, such as Motahhari and Shariʿati. The fall of the Sassanid Empire to the Arab invaders was due to the moral crisis Sassanid society suffered in its last days. Shafa' agrees that lack of social cohesion, discrimination in favor of the aristocracy, and the excessive influence of the Zoroastrian clerics over the government administration contributed to Iran's swift downfall in the face of the Islamic invasion.[86] In a rather condescending manner, Shafa' states that whereas for the Arab tribes Islam was an important unifying force, which enabled their progress, it brought nothing of that kind to Iranians, who had achieved these accomplishments long before then. A concept such as "Allah" was equal to the already existing *ahuramazdah* and "Shaytan" to *ahriman*.[87] In other words, Islam did much less in the way of opening the Iranians' eyes to new ideas than Islamists would have it. Shafa' cites James Darmesteter on the continuity that Islamic concepts posed for Iranians, who needed only to translate Zoroastrian terms into the ones that were brought with Islam.[88] Like other Orientalists and Iranian scholars, Shafa' seems to have adopted the idea of the deep roots of Shiʿism in the Iranian soul. Rather than a mere spiritual inclination, the like of which Corbin saw, he sees in the natural inclination of Iranians toward Shiʿism a reaction to the injustice done to them by the Arab ruling elite. It was both a reaction out of deprivation and a deeper longing for a worldview that opposes injustice and inequality.[89] He, too, thus embraces the Orientalist notion that made its way into the writings and perceptions of Shiʿite authorities, clerics and laymen alike.

Analyzing the separate trajectories of Sunni and Shiʿi Islam in *Tawzih al-masa'il*, Shafa' points to the important difference in their relations with the powers-that-be: whereas Sunni Islam was always deeply rooted in government, Shiʿi Islam from the very start was in opposition to it. In addition, there is a discrepancy between the height of the Safavid period with respect to national power and the moral decadence that this period represents. According to Shafa', this discrepancy did not go unnoticed by the ulema, a fact that explains the scholars' suspicion of national heroes. It was rather hypocritical of them, though, because their power went hand in hand with Iran's status. Hence, the clerics' criticism of the Safavid rulers, cruel and morally derelict as they were, was not justified because the clerics themselves had benefitted tremendously from the high tide of Iranian glory during the 230 years of Safavid rule.[90] In a not so different manner, Shafa' argues, the twentieth century has seen the emergence of an alliance of interests between the clerics and the English imperialists: both seem to have benefited from the decadence, xenophobia, and illiteracy of the masses. The clerics appear to be inclined to provide religious backing to political patrons even at the expense of the national interest.

Shi'ism, Shafa' explains, has served the interests of the powers that be through a host of rituals that have channeled elsewhere the need to protest against injustice, such as into the culture of death and mourning, of wailing and sighing, of beating one's breast and lamentation. It is a school that was born out of the vendors of religion. The martyrdom of Husayn became a means of extracting tears from the believers, and Karbala, instead of becoming a symbol of sacrifice, has turned into an evening of festive meals with strangers; instead of serving as a tool for opposing injustice, it has the silly instigation to martyrdom, whose goal is to send the believer as quickly as possible to palaces of great heavenly pleasure and to the girls who await him there.[91] Shafa' claims that the wailing over the imams has become a deep element of the religious culture of Shi'ites and has influenced other spheres of the believers' lives.

Crucifying Shi'ism

Shafa''s indictment of Shi'ism extends to the field of arts, to which, according to him, Shi'ism is an enemy. Music is the victim of Shi'ism's condemnation more than the other arts, which has stifled any artistic drive. Shafa' often merges and blends his criticism of the Shi'ite faith with his criticism of the Islamic Republic. Ironically, he seems to affirm the Islamic Republic's claims to represent the religious principles it stands for. Its hypocrisy and double standards are evident when its leaders, first and foremost Ayatollah Khomeini, tried to narrow the gap between Shi'a and Sunna in what has become known as the *taqrib* movement. This scholarly trend, which started in Egypt, was welcomed warmly by some members of the ulema in

Iran, among them Khomeini. Shafa' attacks this tendency, which he sees as hypocritical, exposing the double standard of the Shi'ite clergy. Even as they play down the differences between the two currents of Islam in their speeches and writings, the Islamic Republic represses its Sunni minorities, such as the Kurds and the Baluchis. The ostensible rapprochement between the two currents of Islam, Shafa' argues, is nothing compared to the harvests of hatred and mutual slander they have been sowing for hundreds of years.[92]

Shafa''s concern with the gap between the rhetoric used by the Shi'ite clergy and the actions they take in reality extends to other fields as well. For instance, Shi'ism glorifies the term *sayyid*, which it understands to mean special privileges bestowed on its owner. But it overlooks the fact that so many crimes and evils have been done by people who bear this title with great pride. Shi'ism is not true to its own belief because many a SAVAK agent and other officials of the Pahlavi state who were executed in the revolution were also sayyids.[93]

To bolster his argument for Iranian continuity, Shafa' refers in *Tawzih al-masa'il* to the story of the marriage between Shahrbanu, the daughter of the last Sassanid shah, and Husayn, the son of 'Ali. This legend, dating back to the ninth century, played a significant role in the revival of Iranian pride under the rule of Islam.[94] Regardless of the story's veracity, it has a few national elements besides the obvious one of the continuity of the Iranian dynasty from the monarchial period to the Islamic period. First, it means that following the coming of Islam, Shahrbanu retained her dynastic title and monarchial name, indicating that they were not something to be ashamed of. Second, according to the same tradition, she converted to Islam after her marriage to Husayn, which means they got married when she was still a Zoroastrian (*majus*). This tradition was abused to lend credibility to Islam, which—even if the tradition is taken for authentic—should not have been done. For Shafa', Iranian Muslims are merely descendants of the unfortunate Zoroastrian Iranians who recited the *shahada* under the threat of the sword, without even comprehending its meaning.[95]

Shi'ism's lack of authenticity to Iranians is evident in the field of art as well. In contrast to the consciousness that the Islamic Republic is trying to raise, Iranian artists speak of Iranian arts and literature but make no mention of Karbala. Even the names of their publications, such as *Aresh*, refer to pre-Islamic myths of the same name: "It is a national story, but it surprised me that this name had such resonance in their soul, to the degree that they dedicated poems to it. But at the same time, Husayn, around whom such great events and human and divine values crystallized, does not receive that attention."[96]

Shafa' argues that ridding Iran of the theocracy is necessary not only for Iranian culture but also for the Islamic one. Removing this layer of rulers who rule in the name of religion, who cultivate and lead "forged Shi'ism" (*tashayyu' taqallubi*), will clear the way for real religion to be observed by the people. The clerics have created a religious discourse that serves their interests perfectly, deceiving the naive believers, who are incessantly exposed to their sermons and messages. Shafa' cultivates the conception that official Shi'ism is essentially different from folk Shi'ism and that the latter is manipulated by the former. The great conspiracy, then, is the stealing of religion by a gang of clerics who have made it a tool for their own promotion: "For eleven hundred years this shameful school has ruled Iran and has caused it the greatest calamities. If only the ones who govern it were to be removed, the true, authentic face of Islamic Iran would come to light. Both the nation and religion will come out as victors in that case."[97] The alliance of state and religion, in his view, is nothing but a precondition for stifling both and using the people along the way.

Shafa', then, reiterates the Iranian sense of superiority that is presumably based on the great gap between the conquerors and the conquered during the Umayyad period. To lend more power to his argument, he bases it on the writings of the famous and oft-cited historian Ibn Khaldun (1332–1406), who is expected to lend it great credence, of course: "The historical truth is that . . . during the first centuries of Muslim rule Iranian culture took nothing from the Arab and Muslim worlds but only gave them its own foundations and methods of thought."[98] The 'Abbasid rise to power in the middle of the eighth century was nothing but Iranian ascendancy in the guise of a changing of the guard within the Islamic struggle for power.

Shafa' wishes to set straight what he sees as credit mistakenly appropriated by Arab scholars in the Middle Ages. In the process of translation and transmission of texts in Arabic written by Iranian scholars in the Middle Ages, these scholars were wrongly identified as Arabs but were Iranians through and through. Iranian arts such as miniatures, carpet weaving, and embroidery were mistakenly labeled as "Islamic art," even though some of them were distinctively Iranian. Miniatures, for example, could not have flourished under Islam because of the religious ban on images and icons. They thus deserve to be labeled Iranian and nothing else.[99]

Shafa' criticizes harshly the claims that monarchy is an outdated form of government and not democratic in nature, asking, "Is Assad's republican regime of Syria more democratic than the Swedish monarchy? The point is not that one kind of political order is superior to another, but rather that each society should have the one that has developed over its historical, geographical, social, and cultural foundations."[100] In *Tavallud-i digar* (Another Birth), he argues that "this millennium that has just ended is the millennium of Iranian historical bankruptcy in that it began with Ferdowsi's *Shahnameh* and ended in Khomeini's *Tawzih al-masa'il*."

> The great divide of the Islamic conquest is, indeed, evident if we consider the fact that in the fourteen centuries that preceded the coming of Islam, with a short interval of some seventy years, Iran was a world power in the ancient world. And in the fourteen centuries that have elapsed since then, not only has it not maintained this position, but also for about half of this period it did not even retain its sovereignty but was subjugated to some other empire, be it Arab, Moghul, Seljuk, Turk, or Tatar.[101]

In a manner that reminds one of the idealization of pre-Islamic times, Shafa' tends to present a dichotomy between the periods preceding the Islamic conquest and those following it. The first periods are imagined as ones where legitimacy emanated from the people, whereas during the latter periods it was the sword that made the people obedient to the ruling dynasty. It has been argued, states Shafa', that the Arab conquest removed the Sassanid caste system, which had existed in Iran and was detrimental to the social fabric. The opposite is true, though. Not only did the Arabs not remove the prejudices that had existed in Sassanid Iran, but they added their own racial discrimination and deprived Iranians of the freedom and the pride they had before then.[102]

Shafa' wishes to distance Iranian history and culture from Khomeini's idea of *vilayat-i faqih* (rule of the jurisprudent), which is a pillar of the Islamic Republic and its constitution. For Shafa', the association of Iran with the idea that there is a person who embodies the will of God (i.e., *vilayat-i faqih*) is an embarrassment because it is the only country on earth where this idea is practiced in the twentieth century. However, according to him, this idea is in fact alien not only to Shi'ism but also to Islam in general. It emanated from Judaism, biblical research has shown.[103]

In a somewhat condescending manner, Shafa' states that a great portion of the people in the Muslim world these days practice Islam more as a matter of retaining their identity than out of religious conviction. Without this identity, they actually have none at all. Without clinging to their Islamic identity, countries such as Pakistan and Bangladesh would be nothing but part of greater India, to which they were attached throughout history. Without their Islamic essence, the sheikdoms of the Persian Gulf lack history, culture, and identity. After all, one should bear in mind that 80 percent of Muslims do not speak the language of the Qur'an and the prayers.[104]

Conclusion

The thought and influence of these three intellectuals—'Ali Shari'ati, Mortaza Motahhari, and Shojaeddin Shafa'—reveal another aspect of the continuity before and after the Islamic Revolution. They show that continuity does not mean agreement or consensus. The revolution brought to the fore yet another phase in the ongoing struggle between different ideas of the right balance between the various components of Iranian identity. This is a struggle among these three figures (as representatives of prominent voices in this debate) as well as more subtly within each and every one of them individually. By following Shari'ati, Motahhari, and Shafa', we can trace the tensions inherent in Iranian identity and especially its religious and ethnic-national divide through the thought of three remarkable characters. Though not exhausting the discussion of the dilemmas of Iranian affiliations, these three thinkers and influential figures articulated the tension between Iranians and their religious affiliations but left the matter unresolved for future generations. In fact, two out of the three, Shafa' and Motahhari, witnessed the Islamic Revolution. Motahhari still enjoyed a following in the wake of the revolution, but Shafa' had to flee Iran and seek asylum abroad.

It is noteworthy, then, that not only did all three enjoy admiration, whether as a representative of the government (Shafa') or as bitter critics of that government (Shari'ati and Motahhari), but it was their privilege to influence the more practical aspects of national mythmaking. Shafa' was the first in this regard, particularly in his role as a pillar of the Pahlavi state's cultural administration. Writing history was in fact his later occupation; shaping and, more importantly, orchestrating ceremonies and state celebrations were his prior occupations. It is interesting therefore to examine the figure identified with the nationalist worldview more than any other: Cyrus the Great.

3

A Lost King Rediscovered

> Thus saith the LORD to his anointed, to Cyrus, whose right hand I have holden, to subdue nations before him; and I will loose the loins of kings, to open before him the two-leaved gates; and the gates shall not be shut;
>
> I will go before thee, and make the crooked places straight: I will break in pieces the gates of brass, and cut in sunder the bars of iron;
>
> and I will give thee the treasures of darkness, and hidden riches of secret places, that thou mayest know that I, the LORD, which call thee by thy name, am the God of Israel
>
> —Isaiah 45:1–3

> "Your book is all too true," Pari said, "but why write it down? It's of no importance. You should have written about the ancient kings, the glories of the past."
>
> —Anne Sinclair Mehdevi,
> *Persia Revisited*

The Return of an Idealized King

In October 1971, SAVAK, the Iranian secret police, fired Jahangir Taffazuli from his job as director of the national radio authority of Iran. When Ibrahim Bastani Parizi (b. 1925), an Iranian historian who worked as a cultural adviser for the Ministry of Information, inquired into the matter, he discovered that SAVAK's order had to do with a revised edition of the translation of a book on Cyrus the Great that Taffazuli was in charge of distributing. At the heart of the book was a controversial theory by Abul Kalam Azad (1888–1958).[1] Azad—an Indian national activist, politician, and India's first minister of education, wrote a commentary on Surat al-Kahf, "The Cave," the eighteenth sura of the Qur'an. According to Bastani Parizi's inquiry, SAVAK "had received information that the radio is about to publish a book on Cyrus the Great and that the translator is going to claim in the introduction that Cyrus was the son of a Jewish mother and that his mother tongue was Hebrew."[2] This seemingly false piece of information made SAVAK suspicious of Taffazuli's intentions concerning this publication and afraid that the Pahlavi state would be embarrassed at a sensitive period of national aggrandizement of Iran's historical glory.

What can we learn from this story, told years later by Ibrahim Bastani Parizi? First, it shows how a mere historical "fact," such as Cyrus's origins, could become a sensitive issue for Iran's secret police. This sensitivity should be understood in light of the Islamic opposition's criticism of the shah and the state's worship of the pre-Islamic past. This criticism often made good use of Iran's warm relations with the Jewish state.[3] These relations were not given publicity and were handled with a high degree of delicacy, so the publication of a book that claimed that Cyrus, whose memory and image the state promoted in every way possible, was Jewish, could provide the Islamic opposition with plenty of rhetorical ammunition in its fight against the regime.

What caused the memory of Cyrus to become so highly politicized? What legacy and image did the Pahlavi state try to inculcate regarding the founder of the Achaemenid Empire, and how were the state's messages received by Iranians of different backgrounds? Finally, how did the Islamic opposition deal with the Pahlavi perceptions of Cyrus, and what alternative view of Cyrus has the Islamic Republic encouraged in the past two decades? The question of change and continuity regarding the image and legacy of Cyrus the Great are of concern here.

Cyrus the Great was the founder of the Achaemenid Empire (558–330 BCE). No Persian sources regarding his life have survived, and modern historians have had to rely on Greek sources to learn about his period of rule. However, the Cyrus cylinder—a broken clay cylinder discovered during a British archaeological excavation carried out in the ruins of Babylon in 1879—was written in Akkadian and cuneiform script. The question of the historical sources on Cyrus is central in my attempt to assess the "marketing" of Cyrus to Iranians of various backgrounds in the period dealt with here as I seek to understand the logic behind the symbols chosen by the agents of memory in their efforts at nation building. According to this approach, the choices they make cannot be dismissed as mere tools and taken for granted as such. It is, therefore, illuminating to understand the historical and pedagogic manipulation of a figure used as a national symbol. The gap between what we know about a historical figure and the knowledge created and marketed about this figure is significant because this filtering and adding lie at the heart of the mythmaking process.

For example, the lack of certainty about Cyrus's religious affiliation left room for historians and court intellectuals to manipulate it according to their ideological needs, such as claiming that it included Western values or established Iran's tolerance toward religious minorities. Another, somewhat thornier issue is Cyrus's absence from Persian sources altogether. This fact is most significant; he is missing even from the most famous and popular national epic, the *Shahnameh*. Written by Abul-Qasim Ferdowsi, the *Shahnameh* (Book of Kings) relates the adventures of legendary and historical Iranian kings from the Creation to the fall of the Sassanid Empire in the seventh century CE. The book is known as an important agent of Iranian national identity far beyond a narrow circle of literati.[4]

Until well into the nineteenth century, when the Cyrus cylinder—which attests to the declaration attributed to Cyrus after the conquest of Babylon—was found, no written source outside the Bible and Greek historians concerning the life or even existence of Cyrus was known. The interest in and then glorification of Cyrus that followed the cylinder's discovery was from the beginning connected to Western scholarship and historiography (broad and inclusive as this term is), a fact that was to have significant consequences for the memory of Cyrus in modern Iran. In her study on Xenophon's *Cyropedia* (c. 370 BCE), a fictional biography of Cyrus, Deborah Levine Gera deals with the question of the absence of Cyrus from Zoroastrian sources and states that until not long ago it was thought that Cyrus was a contemporary of Zoroaster, and therefore it was assumed that he did not believe in Zoroastrianism, which had not yet passed through its formative period.[5] Today, however, historians and archaeologists tend to push Zoroaster farther back in time, making it possible for Cyrus to have been a believer in that religion. It remains to be revealed whether there are Persian sources on Cyrus. The Danish historian Arthur Christensen deduces the existence of such sources from the biblical story of the Book of Chronicles being recited to Ahasuerus at his command.[6] The historical accuracy of that book, though, remains disputed, if not refuted altogether, which renders Christensen's deduction quite problematic, to say the least. In any event, there is no solid proof for the existence of Persian accounts of Cyrus, only the possibility of oral histories that found their way into Greek historiography and from there into the Greek sources we have today. The historiographical controversy concerning the reliability of the Persian sources on which the Greek ones were based is significant here because the question of reliability seems to have been one of the obstacles to the popularization of Cyrus on the part of the literati in the twentieth century, who felt alienated from the cultural activities of the Pahlavi state.[7] Unlike the figures of poets and national heroes of the early Islamic period whom the Pahlavi state tried to set up as role models worthy of admiration in the first half of the twentieth century (such as Hafez, Sa'adi, Khayyam, and, of course, Ferdowsi), Cyrus the Great had to be introduced to Iranians because he was unknown to many of them. Poets such as Ferdowsi and Hafez were known not only to the educated classes but also to the wider public, but the image of Cyrus had to be built from scratch.[8]

This process limited the degree of popularity that Cyrus could gain among the masses because he was absent from oral folklore and the forms in which it was disseminated, such as poetry. This limitation should be seen in the wider context of the symbolism that the Pahlavi state tried to attach to Cyrus. Cyrus the Great was a figure imagined and venerated by Pahlavi state propaganda and marketed to Iranians by historians and publicists as the founder of the first Iranian state and as a source of inspiration for the modern state under Mohammad Reza Shah.

Pahlavi historians were keen to bridge the gap between their time and ancient Iran, often manipulating the historical timeline to jump over long periods of Iran's subservience to an Islamic entity that did not fit into their desired ethos. Analysis of these manipulations can help us demarcate "eventful" periods in contrast to empty historical "lulls," to use Eviatar Zerubavel's terminology.[9]

The struggle over the memory and legacy of Cyrus the Great in Iran over the past four decades encapsulates conflicting views of Iranian identity. In the decade and a half preceding the Islamic Revolution, Cyrus's historical importance was buttressed by a regime vying for historical linkage and the appearance of continuity. Beyond that, the fact that he was a character well appreciated in Western history and in the scriptures of two of the three monotheistic religions gratified the regime's desire for global recognition of Iran's past greatness.

However, these same facts also made the aggrandizement of Cyrus controversial; it seemed to be entirely devoid of authentic Iranian sources, a fact that bewildered and concerned both advocates and opponents of the Cyrus myth. In addition, the pagan origins of ancient Iran made it difficult to convince both the more traditional nationalists and the clerics to identify with Cyrus and his dynasty.

Indian scholars' hermeneutic innovation (in replacing the Macedonian emperor with the Persian king)—warmly embraced by the Iranian Pahlavi state and its scholars, who had a strong incentive to cultivate that innovation—brought Cyrus closer to the Iranian pantheon of national heroes than could be accepted by wider circles, including some commentators on the Qur'an. It was these commentators, in particular those not "officially" of religious rank, who brought Cyrus to the general public, which recognized him as one of the precursors of Islam, and who assumed his monotheistic belief along the way. It is interesting to note that the continuous effort to accept Cyrus into the pantheon of national heroes persisted despite political shifts, surviving even the Islamic Revolution. Though the Cyrus myth seemed to disappear for about a decade after the revolution, it was ready to reemerge as the Islamic Republic began to come to terms with its Persian ethnic legacy and history.

The different and conflicting ways in which the image of Cyrus has been understood, interpreted, and contested during the past four decades provide a window onto the nuanced balance between religious and ethnic components of Iranian identity in this period. The heated polemics over the historical figure of Cyrus and his legacy reveal undercurrents of Iranian identity dilemmas and conflicting ways of resolving them among intellectuals, lay historians, and religious scholars. Beyond mere historical or religious discourse, the debate over the "correct" memory of Cyrus presents an interesting case of shifting emphasis on identity and sources of political inspiration in Iranian society from the late 1960s to the present. Moreover, putting the debate over the ancient king in perspective, there emerges a wider picture of the religious adaptation of what once seemed pagan or secular. The Pahlavi legacy, rather than being abandoned, is manipulated into an inclusive framework of Iranian identity infused with and appropriated by religion. Another question I examine here is the social and political image of the figure of Cyrus in the effort to make it not only admired but also politically helpful to the Pahlavi political elite. Because very little is known about Cyrus, especially in terms of his beliefs or political convictions, his identity was flexible and easily imbued with the values held by the agents of memory who propagated his image.

Cyrus as a National Hero

From the mid-1950s on, in the wake of the Mosaddeq crisis the monarchy tended to be placed at the center of Iranian identity as the embodiment of the nation.[10] Earlier Iranian monarchs may well have seen themselves as pivotal to the identification and uniqueness of their country, but the identification of citizenship and the nation in its modern sense with the king was a modern phenomenon. This tendency began with Reza Shah but gained much more strength with the colorful personality cult of his son, in which birthdays of members of the royal family were celebrated as national holidays, monuments depicting the king were erected throughout the country, and the tabloids gushed over the world fame of Mohammad Reza Shah and the benevolence of various *bunyad*s (foundations) under the auspices of Empress Farah Diba and Princess Ashraf.

The context of the personality cult in Iran after 1953 is connected to the need to generate legitimacy for a regime that had recently revealed a high degree of fragility and dependence on foreign aid for its very survival. The fact that it was the deep and violent involvement of foreign intelligence agencies that brought the shah back from his short-lived flight to Rome that year catalyzed the need to reconstruct his image with historical foundations. Moreover, this political-cultural endeavor to substantiate

Iran's pre-Islamic roots and especially the need to imbue it with westernized themes of freedom should be seen in light of the political necessities of Iran's foreign policy, which required legitimizing.

One of the leading figures behind the state effort in instructing Iranians in the "important" history they should know was Shojaeddin Shafa', the shah's court historian and the initiator of many of the steps taken by the state apparatus during the 1970s, including the controversial celebrations of twenty-five hundred years of Iranian monarchy at Persepolis in October 1971. It would not be an exaggeration to say that Shojaeddin Shafa' was the animating spirit behind the Pahlavi mythmaking project of the 1970s.[11]

The need to find a historical narrative that would go beyond personal adoration of the shah became pressing, and the historical narrative developed by Shafa' from the early 1960s on and distributed by means of the media under the control of the Pahlavi state—radio, television, newspapers, scientific journals, and (following the White Revolution) the Literacy Corps—was supposed to serve this end.[12] According to the Pahlavi historical narrative, Iran's cooperation with the West resonated well with its golden age as an empire, when it was a source of admiration for and imitation by the West (represented by ancient Greece). This narrative served the purposes of the Pahlavi regime in more ways than one: in addition to placing the king at the center of Iranian identity and ipso facto legitimizing his decisions as desirable for the nation, the historical narrative was meant to make the fact that Iran was politically part of the West seem natural, a continuation of its long-established cultural heritage and political legacy.

Against the formation of the "nonaligned" bloc, spearheaded by Gamal 'Abdel Nasser of Egypt (a staunch rival of the Pahlavi regime), Iran aligned with the West in the Cold War. As part of its ideological rivalry with Egypt and other countries, it had to present a competing narrative that would defuse its rivals' claim to political authenticity. The historical claim to authenticity, then, had to assert deep and long-standing roots. The theme that Iran was actually the source of Greek values served this perception and was supposed to make it easier to swallow Iran's alignment with what at the time seemed to be the enemies of some of its neighbors in the region. It was thus seen as not unnatural for Iran to be detached from its neighbors (the Arab countries) and from the Third World as such because it did not belong with them essentially—that is, historically.[13]

The ways the figure of Cyrus the Great was imagined, described, and utilized in Iran during the two decades preceding the Islamic Revolution are of great significance when seen in the wider context of the struggle among competing social and political forces over the right to claim authentic Iranian identity.[14] My inquiry into the forms of representation of this ancient king, often described as the founder of the first Iranian state, has two aims: first, to see the representations of a figure from Iran's ancient past in their historical context, thus exposing the political and social forces and the social agents who served these representations; and, second, to attempt to extricate the main moral and political themes that Iranian historians, publicists, and public figures derived from the Achaemenid period and its founder as well as the lessons from ancient history that they thought would be useful to modern Iranians.

However, the story of the making of Cyrus's image cannot be confined to state initiatives or to the participation of individuals in programs run by the state ministries and organizations. It is to a large degree a story of the contest between the state and its opposition over what it means and what it should mean to be Iranian. These questions obviously had dire political implications as the confrontation between the Pahlavi state and its political opposition seemed inevitable. This story is one of protest to and rejection of the state's political message disguised as a figure from Iran's ancient history.

Because the focus on Cyrus in publications from Iran rose in the modern period, the question of sources on his life is of understandable importance. Little wonder, then, that the desire to find religious grounds for the adoration of Cyrus gained momentum in the twentieth century—especially in the Islamic Republic, where emphasizing a figure's religious identity could usher him back into the national pantheon.

As the coronation of Mohammad Reza Shah and Empress Farah Diba in 1967 approached, with the shah feeling that his throne was solid enough to celebrate the coronation, a book on the life of Cyrus was published by Frederick Talberg, a graphic designer with Pahlavi University in Shiraz.[15] The book's title, *Az Korush ta Pahlavi* (From Cyrus to Pahlavi), proclaims its view of Iranian history as a continuum in which Cyrus is the precursor of Mohammad Reza Shah. The work seems to address the younger generation more than adults and covers history from the Achaemenid Empire through the early Islamic period and the Qajar period to the time of Mohammad Reza Shah. The timeline all but excludes intervening periods that do not serve the Pahlavi historical narrative.

On the first page of the book, which was presented to the shah by Asadollah 'Alam, chairman of the Pahlavi University board of trustees, there is a translation of one of the inscriptions from Persepolis. Interestingly enough, the original cuneiform inscription appears in the background of an illustration of the ruins of Persepolis, with a translation of the inscription into modern Persian below it.[16] The effect this opening could have on the modern reader is dual and contradictory: on the one hand, there is the virtual proximity to the site, which appears accessible on the sheet of paper in front of the reader; on the other, the inscription is, of course, unreadable by the modern Iranian, and its translation obviates the fact that were it not for that translation, there would be no way to understand the text. Although modern Iranian readers need this mediation to understand their ancestors, it nonetheless brings them closer to the writers of the inscription.

The timing of the book's publication is explained as fitting "these glorious days, when the Iranian nation is commemorating the coronation of H. M. Mohammad Reza Pahlavi . . . and Empress Farah Pahlavi. . . . The history of Iran is a manifestation of the life of its people and the service of its kings."[17]

Iranian history, according to *Az Korush ta Pahlavi*, started with the Aryan tribes and their migration to the Iranian plateau.[18] The book divides Iranian history into two parts: periods when the country was ruled by foreigners and periods in which it was independent. This division reflects an approach to Iranian history quite similar to that of Mohammad Reza Shah, as he expresses it in his book *Mission for My Country*.[19]

The choice of Cyrus as a historical icon used formally in Iranian political life was made public by Prime Minister Amir Abbas Hoveyda, who declared in his budget speech to the Parliament in February 1971 that this year would be the year of Cyrus the Great in honor of Mohammad Reza

Shah: "Since the beginning of its glorious history, our country has been famous for peace, friendship, and humanity, and this can be clearly proved by studying the methods and measures of the great kings such as Cyrus the Great, whose efforts made possible our celebration next year of the 2,500th anniversary of the Iranian monarchy."[20] A final element in the process of Cyrus's cultivation as an Iranian icon in preparation for the celebrations of twenty-five hundred years of Iranian monarchy was politicizing his character to fit with the way the shah was intended to be perceived by his people.

History writing was another means of disseminating the Pahlavi national discourse and was supposed to complement the other media used for this purpose. Books concerning the Achaemenid period and especially its founder appeared ever more often.[21] These books mediated between professional archaeologists and the public on developments in archaeology because most archaeological sites were not accessible to the Iranian public. Pictures and illustrations in books, journals, and newspapers were often the only means to bring firsthand information on excavations and archaeological findings to Iranian readers.

Shapur Shahbazi (1942–2006), a London-trained archaeologist and an Iranian authority on Achaemenid history and archaeology, participated in the government's cultivation of the importance of this period in history and gave it the academic dimension necessary to imbue it with a scientific aura. His book *Korush-e Bozorg* (Cyrus the Great) combines history with the manifesto of the Pahlavi establishment in terms of its perception of Iran's ancient history and that history's relevance to the era of the book's publication.[22]

According to Shahbazi, throughout history Iranians "had many laws that were a memorial to Cyrus and Darius. They enacted many constitutions and rules specifically to oversee these laws."[23] The theme of continuity prevails in Shahbazi's book and finds expression in two ways: the way in which Iranians adopted Cyrus's legacy in their role as pioneers of the message of political freedom in the ancient world and the way in which Iran survived despite various tribulations it endured. Shahbazi suggests a dichotomy in Iranian history: periods of independence and national pride versus periods of national humiliation and foreign rule.[24] This dichotomy developed as an alternative to the classic Islamic division of history into the pre-Islamic (i.e., Jahiliyya) period and the period following the bringing of Mohammad's message to Iran. As for an archenemy, which is necessary for a national hagiography of this kind, it can be found in the figure of Alexander the Great, the Macedonian king who destroyed Persepolis:

> The Achaemenid dynasty reigned supreme for two centuries after Cyrus's death until it was taken over by Alexander of Macedonia in the year 330 BCE. It is noteworthy that whereas the Achaemenid monarchy emerged with the declaration of human rights and freedom of prisoners by Cyrus the Great, the empire of Alexander rose out of the destruction of Persepolis, setting fire to its remains.[25]

During Cyrus's rise to primacy, as witnessed by the numerous publications bearing his name and dealing with his life during these years, the attitude to Alexander also underwent significant change. This change occurred in more than one way; however, it is important to note here that the national cult of Cyrus meant ipso facto the demonization of the person who brought his empire to an end—Alexander the Great.

Shahbazi represents a genre of authors who wrote about the Achaemenid period and built a narrative with common lines. They were not necessarily Iranian—consider Albert Champdor and Harold Lamb[26]—but the fact that their works were translated into Persian at a time when the political establishment wanted more Iranians to have access to such works is telling. Other Iranian authors, such as Mohammad Qa'imi,[27] used European research extensively, but one can assume that their contribution was especially valued in that the public saw such works as coming from the pens of local intellectuals rather than of foreign scholars. This was especially important in light of the claim to authenticity so central to the Pahlavi historical narrative.

The steps taken by the Pahlavi government to promote awareness of Cyrus's greatness included, among others, the initiative to present the Cyrus cylinder at the United Nations headquarters in New York and the restoration of archaeological sites throughout the country, with an emphasis on Achaemenid sites. A private government document emphasized the hope that "the entire population of Iran will recognize the importance of the archaeological sites in their country . . . and will regard the awareness of them as a national duty."[28]

Shojaeddin Shafa''s publication on Cyrus contains a series of reports he gave to the Iranian committee in charge of preparing the celebrations, which by then had already been in the works for a year, in an effort to promote the Iranian historical narrative favored by the regime. The central committee for the coordination of the celebrations was established at the shah's order and was supervised by Empress Farah. It was staffed by the Pahlavi political and bureaucratic elite and included figures such as court minister Husayn 'Ala', most of the cabinet members, and heads of the military as well as the head of the broadcast authority.[29] This committee and satellite committees in several countries, including most European countries, Canada, and the United States, were formed to promote the image of Iran as a modern country in the developed world. The satellite committees comprised local scholars on Iran, usually with an Iranian representative from the embassy in the country. Beyond being a mere exercise in public relations, the promulgation of the image of a modern Iran abroad had a central role in confirming Iran's self-perception as a society marching forward toward progress.

The writings of Shapur Shahbazi[30] and of other Iranian historians and researchers, such as Sa'id Nafisi, Ibrahim Purdavoud, and Ibrahim Bastani Parizi,[31] to name a few of the prominent spokesmen of this trend, bring us to a distinction that should be made between the state apparatus and more popular forms of culture in Iran during the 1960s. The former brought to the forefront the cosmopolitan elements in Iranian national mythmaking, whereas the latter emphasized the xenophobic elements in it. This tension can be described as being between "cosmopolitan-universal nationalism" and "chauvinistic nationalism." Of course, there is no clear-cut definition by which one can classify every publication, activity, or national rite as belonging to either type of nationalism. However, it is hard to avoid relating these two poles as not only expressing two intellectual trends, voiced by the same speaker sometimes side by side, but also—more than that—expressing two conflicting social forces divided by the mid-1970s according to intellectuals' attitudes toward the Pahlavi regime and its cultural creation. This division of different aspects of Cyrus is thematic and does not necessarily divide the historical works on him by different authors. Xenophobic expressions were more popular in extragovernmental publications, but they were not entirely absent from state ones. It is noteworthy that the attitude toward the non-Iranian, as part of the self-definition of what is good about being an Iranian, became the battleground between the state and opposition cultural avant-gardes from the mid-1970s on. Some of the latent revolutionary agitation in the new middle class found expression in the cultural struggle over Iranian identity.

A children's book, *Korush-i Kabir* (Cyrus the Great), focused on the personality and character of Cyrus, the founder of the Achaemenid Empire. Its author, Mahmud Ashrafi, who taught art history and interior design at various institutes, dedicated it to "the heir of twenty-five centuries of Iranian monarchy, His Majesty Mohammad Reza Shah Pahlavi Aryamehr, who adores art and is an admirer of culture."[32] The book was directed at children, and its purpose was to recount the greatness of Iran, which, it aimed to demonstrate, is manifest in the greatness of its kings throughout the ages. Ashrafi tells his young readers of a legend in which Cyrus

> was playing the kings' game [*shahbazi*] one day with his peers, all sons of Median nobility. Cyrus, who was the son of a shepherd, seemed older than the rest. The children chose him as their king. He started right away with dividing realms of authority to the children: he gave some weapons, some were made guards . . . and if someone showed disobedience, he would let them know they would be punished.[33]

Two recurring themes in this historical narrative of ancient Iran come to the fore. One is the ruling class's sense of entitlement—Cyrus is recognized as the king by his peers, which readers are expected to understand because he "seemed older than the rest." The second is Cyrus's identification with the shah by his deeds and by the authority that he, as a member of the ruling class, feels entitled to—although he is only a boy in the story. That is, he has the right to punish the rest for disobedience. According to Barbara Johnstone, "discourse arises out of the world or worlds that are presumed to exist outside of discourse."[34] This is one of the ways in which a text can be analyzed to extract the meaning that lies within it. In Ashrafi's children's book, even as the text shapes the world (of Cyrus as a child), it is being shaped by the world (of Iran under the rule of Mohammad Reza Shah). It is a world where everyone has a role that should not be confused with anyone else's. The game the children play in the story is actually a microcosm of Iran in its ideal form, its reality under the Pahlavi state, according to the author.

In relation to the question of the origins of the Iranian nation, an issue that is well positioned for embellishment and glorification, Ashrafi defines Iranian history as beginning with the immigration of Aryan tribes from India to Iran around the year 3000 BCE. The way that Ashrafi describes the appearance of Zarathustra (Zoroaster) cannot but remind one of the descriptions in Muslim tradition of the appearance of Mohammad and his mission as a prophet against the background of polytheism and ignorance. Ashrafi seems to be trying to paint Zarathustra as an Iranian version of the prophet of Islam. Zarathustra started to preach when the Aryans were steeped in "idolatry, worshipping the sun, the moon and stars, praying to the water, fire, wind, and earth."[35] In the account of Cyrus's life being saved many times by God, Ashrafi may even be alluding to the many unsuccessful assassination attempts on the shah from the beginning of his reign.[36] The shah interpreted the failures of these attempts on his life as proof of Providence, a sign that he was chosen and especially protected by the Almighty.[37] The history of Cyrus lent the attempts on the shah's life a historical dimension, reflecting a reenactment of the history of royalty in Iran.[38] This was another element, sometimes referred to as "the Cyrus Complex," that worked in the service of the Pahlavi narrative.[39] The historical awareness of the shah's apparatus definitely encouraged parallelism between the shah and Cyrus the Great, to the point that the former was ostensibly considered to be a reincarnation of the latter. Although it is highly doubtful that the similarity was valid in the eyes of Iranians at the time, various state officials expressed it repeatedly. An Iranian diplomat in India put it succinctly when speaking to an audience who came to pay their respects to the Pahlavi commemoration of twenty-five hundred years of Iranian monarchy: "It is manifest . . . that the present Shahenshah Aryamehr has continued the glorious tradition of Cyrus the Great and has devoted his mind and energies to the heroic task of achieving the maximum prosperity for the people of Iran. . . . Iran has progressed by leaps and bounds and has taken its place as a great progressive country in the Family of Nations."[40] The theme of tolerance and freedom was reiterated in Pahlavi parlance even at the same time that oppression of opposition groups—real and imagined alike—was being carried out. This gap between terminology and the reality of ever-growing oppression by the security agencies was a catalyst in building the opposition's animosity toward the Pahlavi state.

The historiography of ancient Iran thus expressed by implication two contradictory approaches to Iran's place among nations in the modern period: one emphasized the common heritage and diffusion of values, the other stressed an isolationist view of Iran as superior. The two approaches, though contradictory at first glance, actually went hand in hand. For example, Gholam'ali Homayun, a lecturer in art history at Tehran University, published in 1971 a booklet called *Korush-i Kabir dar asar-i hunariy-i Urupa'iyan* (Cyrus the Great in European Art).[41] This publication illustrates the intellectual atmosphere accompanying the preparations for the celebrations of twenty-five hundred years of Iranian monarchy. In the introduction, Homayun—who had published a few books on the perception of Iranians in Europe and their influence on Western culture[42]—laments the fact that the greatness of ancient Iran has been forgotten and that many Iranians are ignorant of Iran's central role in the development and evolution of Greece and Rome and in turn of Western culture in its entirety.

Homayun opens his argument by stating that Greek historians tended to be loyal to their ancestors to the degree that they twisted and changed historical "facts" to glorify their nation. An example is the myth they created of Greece being the motherland of freedom: "Greek writers used to brag about their country being the cradle of freedom and that they are the first nation to have a parliament while other countries were ruled by dictatorship alone." This view, he states, is incorrect and misleading. These Greek writers "tended to overlook the fact that in the Achaemenid era Iran also had a parliament, a jury close to the king, which used to include seven wise men who served as a parliament. This council would advise the king on matters of importance and would prevent him from taking dangerous or harmful steps." He further explains that the Persian parliament was even more representative of the population than the one in Athens—where only representatives of the elite debated. Therefore, Greece was not unique in establishing a parliament, as one might think in view of the self-pride Greek writers cultivated: "No Greek historian has pointed out that the first great liberal in the world came from Iran—that was Cyrus, who published the first declaration of freedom in the world. In consequence, he set free millions of people."[43]

The message of freedom endorsed so proudly in Iran by a mouthpiece of the state collided with the reality of rising suppression of the opposition by SAVAK—Iran's secret police and intelligence organization—and the police. The security apparatus's firm hand was felt ever more strongly with the imminent celebrations in October 1971. This might explain why government-sponsored publications emphasized two competing and contesting themes of a just and progressive society: freedom alongside order and control. In *Korush-i Kabir-i*, Homayun tries to balance the call for freedom with the social need for order and state control: "Freedom should coincide with order. Cyrus cultivated order side by side with freedom and did not let freedom turn into chaos [*harj u marj*]."[44] According to Homayun, tight control over the empire was a necessary condition for its survival because of its immense size. Unlike the Greek islands, the Achaemenid Empire had to rule a vast territory, a fact that served as a bond that tied different provinces together. Although the Greeks regarded the Achaemenid regime as tyrannical and oppressive, Homayun claims that it was in fact the only regime that succeeded in restoring order and peace to such a variety of peoples. The allusion to modern Iran is quite clear, despite the difference in size and conditions; modern Iran, where about half of the population belongs to either an ethnic or a religious minority, is also anything but homogenous. In the introduction to the exhibition showcasing the manner in which Cyrus was portrayed by European artists, Homayun laments the fact that no inscription has been found that describes the real features of Cyrus or any of the other Achaemenid kings. This longing for the true face of one's ancestors is only natural, especially in light of the festival of icons surrounding the shah and the royal family during those years. Depictions of the shah and other members of the royal family filled Iranian newspapers and journals and appeared in public venues as statues in the squares and as postage stamps. The profiles of Mohammad Reza Shah and Empress Farah as well as of other members of the royal family seemed omnipresent. From the time of the coronation in 1967, they were presented on plates, trays, and even dolls.[45]

In contrast, Cyrus's physical features were unknown, which made it harder to "market" him to the Iranian people. As Delicia Harvey and Lance Strate have asserted about the promulgation of an image, "Having a human being pose for a drawing, painting, or sculpture artists could obtain better results than . . . working from imagination or memory."[46] The comparison of Mohammad Reza Shah with Cyrus the Great and the shah's presentation as a modern Cyrus could be counted as an exercise in mutual complementary imagination: Cyrus was meant to lend the shah a historical greatness and depth he lacked, and the shah was meant to be the visible, tangible expression of a king whose image was unknown. It might have seemed possible that the image of Cyrus would also provide the shah with a sense of legitimacy and authenticity, but later developments proved otherwise.

Cyrus as a Universal Hero

The image of Cyrus as a national hero developed by Iranian historians seemed to be part of a great paradox in the Pahlavi self-perception of Iran. On the one hand, the focus was on the country's great power, on its people drawing inspiration from its rediscovered history, and, in fact, on the re-creation of its contemporary history to reflect the legacy of this ancient glory. On the other hand, this symbolism suffered from an authenticity complex because even the symbols used to cultivate ancient Iranian glory were to a great degree influenced by Western research, ideals, and attitudes toward ancient Iran. A token of this issue was the question of the sources on Cyrus, which were either Greek or biblical. This want of original Persian sources called into question the state's choices of cultural-historical icons as symbols deserving of modern Iranians' admiration.

This cultural cognitive dissonance spread to another dimension in a different though related field: Iran's foreign policy. The choice to align with the West in the Cold War had to be justified, especially in light of Iran's bitter memories of Western occupation and economic exploitation over the previous two centuries. It was necessary to find a precedent for Iran's connection with the West in its historical narrative. However, other aspects of Iran's foreign policy had to be contained within a more comprehensive line of thought, fitting history with the present to conform to one seemingly continuous line from the Achaemenid Empire to the present.

An example of such universal nationalism is Hadi Hedayati's work on Cyrus, which was published in 1956 and was one of the pioneering works on the founder of the empire written after World War II but a decade before the popularization of Cyrus by the state. In his characterization of Cyrus, Hedayati emphasizes the ancient monarch's benevolence, depicting him as the total opposite of his contemporaries with regard to the treatment of conquered peoples:

> The first step Cyrus took [after conquering Babylon] was to attract the admiration of the Babylonians by declaring himself the friend and liberator of its oppressed minorities, and he allowed them to return to the shrines from which they had been expelled by Nabonidus [the king of Babylon at the time of the defeat by Cyrus]. Cyrus blamed Nabonidus for sacrilege and disrespect of holy sites.[47]

Beyond the personal motivation behind the Pahlavi historical discourse, often described as the shah's megalomania, the paradox of that discourse was exemplified in the gap between Iran's self-image and foreign policy: on the one hand, Mohammad Reza Shah fortified his military, spending billions of dollars to modernize it; on the other, the military was meant to keep the borders safe and not antagonize its enemies.[48] Iran was engaged only in occasional skirmishes with Iraq and the deployment of Iranian forces in Oman. Despite its chauvinistic rhetoric and the notion of superiority over its neighbors, Pahlavi Iran succeeded in simply maintaining its borders and not giving military expression to its nationalist aspirations to become a regional power. The Pahlavi narrative went hand in hand with this contradictory combination of self-perception of greatness and a policy that was peaceful rather than belligerent, the unprecedented fortification of the armed forces while keeping the army out of politics, and the espousing of a nationalistic rhetoric while cooperating with what the regime's opposition (and Third World rhetoric) termed American imperialism.

The themes dwelled upon in the universal narrative of Cyrus aimed to answer this need to bridge such contradictions and can be delineated as follows: Iran's power does not need to be overt but rather should be concealed, and its best expression is self-control and containment. In relation to the minorities in Iran, its power is expressed in tolerance, just as the Achaemenid Empire was the paragon of tolerance in the ancient world. The religious minorities in Iran, especially the Zoroastrians and the Jews, bear witness to this long-established Iranian tradition of tolerance because they have enjoyed it ever since Cyrus the Great. Each of these two minorities has its special place in this narrative. The Zoroastrians bear witness to the religion of Cyrus and his dynasty, and, hence, their costumes and rites are a relic from that period and should be cherished accordingly. The Jews of Iran, descendants of the Jews who were held captive in Babylon and released once Cyrus took over, are living witnesses to Cyrus's liberal and tolerant policy. Therefore, their role is no less important; they are reminiscent of those who enjoyed the fruits of this policy and expressed their thankfulness in their scriptures. The fact that the Bible is holy to Christianity (i.e., the Western world at large) guarantees that the Jewish appreciation of Cyrus would not go unnoticed.

The treatment of the religious minorities within the Achaemenid Empire served a dual purpose for Hedayati and others: it was proof of the empire founder's enlightenment and, hence, his relevance to the modern nation of Iran, and it demonstrated the founder's power and self-confidence. A third aspect of this historical fact is that it served as implicit justification for the policy toward minorities in Pahlavi Iran, in particular the Jews.[49] It was the attitude toward the Jews, connected to the memory of Cyrus, that became the hallmark of Sadeq Khalkhali's wrath against the Pahlavi state in his antisemitic treatise *Korush-i dorughin* (False Cyrus).[50] This policy was consistently under attack by the Islamic opposition as revealing just another aspect of Iran's submission to foreign influence in that it was compelled to restrain the Islamic worldview in the public sphere. The policy was yet another aspect of the struggle over the sources of authenticity between the Pahlavi state and its opponents. In the state's discourse, the minorities were remnants of the Achaemenid past, so treating them equally showed loyalty to that past, whether directly (Zoroastrians) or indirectly (Jews). In the opposition's discourse, however, these minorities (especially the Jews) were yet another aspect of foreign intervention in Iran, and their being treated as equals was yet another sign of Iran's subservience to foreign pressures and interests.

These two minorities played an important role in the aggrandizement of the shah and in the Pahlavi regime's claim that it was loyal to the ancient traditions of Iran. This issue was demonstrated at a conference in honor of Cyrus the Great in Bombay in 1971. Both Iranian officials and researchers from Indian and Western academic circles presented papers on Cyrus and his legacy. The Iranian embassy and the Parsi community of Bombay (as the Zoroastrians of India are known) collaborated to host the conference. In the foreword to the book of proceedings published following the conference, it is stressed that Cyrus's rule over India was not perceived as a national humiliation. India was the home of many Iranians who fled their land of origin due to religious persecution. The connection between Iranians and Indians is "not of recent origin but go[es] far back in time and originate[s] from the common source and stock of the great Aryan race." That connection was dormant but came back to life in the time of Reza Shah when the two peoples came closer together, "realizing their shared heritage, especially in the fields of culture and fine-arts."[51] The author of the foreword attempts to go along with the enlightened self-image painted by the Pahlavi discourse in order to distinguish the Indians from other Asian peoples, who were obviously less refined:

> Iran was helped by the king of India to achieve success over the cruel rulers of western Asia. By this success the bright Aryan civilization of western Asia was founded, based on freedom and human dignity. . . . When Alexander of Macedonia, intoxicated by his victories, overran the entire land of Iran, the sympathies of India were with the Iranians, and because Iran was subjected to the attacks before India, a group of countless Iranians came to India and brought with them the culture and traditions of Iran, which powerfully influenced the Indian thought.[52]

According to Gholam'ali Homayun, it is not Iran that owes ancient Greece its rich cultural merits, but the other way around. In *Korush-i Kabir*, Homayun gives some examples of Greek historians who recognized and appreciated the great cultural traits of the Iranians they knew or learned about.[53] Western culture is therefore deeply influenced by the culture of ancient Iran. Because of Iran's pro-Western foreign policy in the Cold War years and the tensions that policy raised, as was evident in the Mosaddeq crisis, it seems that this view, encouraged by the Pahlavi state, was meant to mitigate the feeling of humiliation at being "sold to the West," a sentiment expressed by the Iranian opposition.

The universal aspect of Pahlavi history writing in its various forms therefore went deeper than merely serving the shah's political needs or giving him the legitimacy he sought. It served the regime's and the intellectual elite's political agenda in more than one way. First, it built Iran's self-image as a society much more progressive than those of surrounding countries, a benevolent kingdom where the minorities sing a song of praise and bear witness to its justice and wisdom. Second, it revealed Western values (human rights, religious tolerance) to be part of the national legacy, as one of the speakers at a Zoroastrian conference dedicated to Cyrus in India put it:

> The greatest contribution of Cyrus to posterity is his charter of rights. Today freedom of speech, freedom of expression, freedom of worship and individual liberty are greatly priced and cherished, but 2,500 years ago Cyrus the Great had the insight to recognize these principles and guaranteed them. . . . History has known many tyrants who ransacked, oppressed, exploited, and killed the people they had subjugated. But there are rare instances of kings like Cyrus the Great who after their conquests have treated the subjugated in exemplary fashion, respected their rights, and worked wholeheartedly for their happiness and improvement of their lives.[54]

The intolerance displayed by Nabonidus, the last king of Babylon before its fall to the Achaemenids and the representative of Babylonian culture, is juxtaposed against the tolerance shown by Cyrus. For Hedayati,

Babylon represents barbarism and cruelty, but Cyrus, representing Iran, is the embodiment of civilized culture. His book includes a description of the atrocities committed by Ashurbanipal, the Babylonian king who ravaged the cities he conquered and executed their inhabitants but was finally defeated by Cyrus in the year 539 BCE. Cyrus's civility is presented here in contrast to the barbarity of his enemies and other kings in his time. Thus, it is the background of his time that lends Cyrus his greatness or allows everyone (i.e., Iranian subjects, to whom Hedayati's booklet is directed) to assess that greatness. As the best evidence of Cyrus's greatness, Hedayati brings up the fact that even the Greeks, the archenemies of ancient Iran, glorified Cyrus and praised him in the biographies they wrote about him.[55]

Of interest is the importance Hadi Hedayati attaches to archaeology as proof of Cyrus's benevolence: "What a great lesson it is for someone who expects the ambiance of a hero to be felt in the battlefield amid dead bodies and those fallen in the war!" As an example of Cyrus's greatness, Hedayati states that Cyrus did not present himself as the conqueror of Babylon but rather as its savior and the beneficiary of Marduk, its god: "He released the soldiers of the city with no harm. Not only did he not enforce his own deities upon the Babylonians, but he did not try to promote them in any way. That is the reason why the entire populace of Sumer and Akkad went to kiss his feet."[56]

Hedayati claims that the Jews of Babylon expected Cyrus to wreak vengeance on the land of their captivity and were disappointed that he refused to do so. This way of narrating the story might stem from Hedayati's intention to downplay the harmony between the Jews of Babylon and Cyrus. After all, the justification for political ties between Pahlavi Iran and Israel that could stem from the Pahlavi historiography concerning Cyrus the Great was a highly sensitive issue in Iran at the time.[57] Interestingly, Hedayati attempts to explain Cyrus's policy toward the Jews in utilitarian terms as a prudent political move. According to him, a possible explanation for this act was that the Persians needed Palestine as a gateway to Egypt. In order not to waste energy and troops on this passage, Cyrus needed a population that would have at least a neutral stand in the war, if not a positive relationship with the Achaemenid Empire.

Shojaeddin Shafa' also treats with care the emphasis on the Bible as a reliable source for Cyrus's greatness. He reminds his readers that Cyrus's greatness is reported in the Bible:

> These words of praise appear in the Bible, a book of praise, considered to be of celestial origin by all three religions—Islam, Christianity and Judaism . . . which lends great honor to Cyrus. . . . In order to exemplify the special status Cyrus has in the eyes of the Torah, it is enough to mention that the fundamental book of the Torah, the Book of Chronicles, finishes with the name of Cyrus and that the book of Ezra starts with the name of Cyrus.[58]

The universal narrative assisted in providing historical proof of Iran's superiority in both might and virtue. Thus, Cyrus's merits as a ruler were juxtaposed with the cruelty of the kings he defeated in order to emphasize his moral superiority. The negative view of Babylon was more than a hint at Iran's superiority over its neighbors, especially Iraq. The symbolism played both ways here in that the Iraqi Ba'ath Party was also developing national symbols pertaining to ancient Mesopotamia, Assyria, and Babylon.[59] The rivalry between Iran and Iraq, considered from this perspective, was a modern version of old contentions, each claiming to be the heir of the mightiest and—in the case of Iran—the more just and human side of that ancient conflict.

Shafa' uses various Babylonian inscriptions to prove the barbarity of Ashurbanipal and Sennacherib, the Assyrian kings (taken to be Babylonian either out of confusion or, as suggested earlier, because of their identification with modern Iraq). This interpretation makes the conquest of Babylon into the salvation of humanity as a whole, not merely an Iranian cause for celebration, according to Shafa'. Moreover, for Shafa', Cyrus's defeat of Babylon marked the end of an era in world history, that of the old kingdoms. Pahlavi historiography described the Arab states as the heirs of those morally inferior old kingdoms. This alliance between the mighty and the just also served the Pahlavi narrative well by presenting the king's righteousness and the order that he bestows on his country as proof of his greatness.[60]

The Word of God

Until well into the nineteenth century, when the Cyrus cylinder was found, no written source concerning the life of Cyrus was known outside the Bible and the Greek historians.[61] The interest in and then glorification of Cyrus that followed the cylinder's discovery was connected right away to Western scholarship and historiography—a fact that would not go unnoticed by either the critics of the Pahlavi worldview or its supporters, who developed an apologetic discourse in order to come to terms with this annoying fact.[62] The thirst for indigenous, "authentic" sources on Cyrus was an important contributor to the promotion of the idea that Cyrus is mentioned in a source familiar to most Iranians and needing no further introduction—the Qur'an.

This sensitive field of discourse in the debate over the "right" image of Cyrus rose to such prominence that the Islamic Republic has been inclined to adopt it, at least according to some voices. Several scholars throughout the twentieth century tried to locate the admired king in the Qur'an, thus adding religious support to national pride.

The eighteenth sura of the Qur'an, "The Cave," refers to the story of a person, apparently a king or a military leader, code-named Dhul-Qarnayn—literally, "The One with Two Horns":

> They will ask you about "Dhul-Qarnayn." Say: "I shall render an account of him for you. . . . We established things on earth for him, and gave him access to everything; so he followed a [certain] course until when he reached the place where the sun sets, he found it setting in a mucky spring alongside which he (also) found some people. We said: 'Double Horn, either you will punish [them] or else act kindly toward them.'"[63]

Like a few other characters mentioned in the Qur'an, Dhul-Qarnayn is mentioned only by his code name, which leaves room for speculation as to the figure behind the name. Both Islamic commentators and modern researchers of the Qur'an most commonly identify Dhul-Qarnayn as Alexander the Great (356–23 BCE).[64] In fact, the story recited in the Qur'an praises Dhul-Qarnayn in a manner that many Islamic scholars have understood as implying belief in one god, placing him potentially in high esteem.[65]

Interestingly, the first to suggest that the Dhul-Qarnayn mentioned in the verses of "The Cave" could be the founder of the Achaemenid Empire was not an Iranian but rather an Indian intellectual and politician. Sir Sayyed Ahmad Khan (1817–98) was a political leader and historian of modern India who had close connections with English intellectuals of his time—among them Sir Henry Rawlinson, famous for his decoding of the cuneiform inscriptions. Khan expressed his closeness to Rawlinson and deep appreciation of Orientalist scholarship in his commentary on the Qur'an regarding the question of Dhul-Qarnayn. Rawlinson did not hide his admiration for Sir Sayyed and eulogized him as "the finest and most representative Mohammedan in the annals of British India,"[66] which attests to the close relationship between the two.

Sir Sayyed believed that Islam was in dire need of a new interpretation in order to shake off conservative dogmas that were the main cause of its weakness at the time he was writing. Like other Islamic modernists, he believed in the compatibility of Islam and rational principles. The need to make Islam compatible with the scientific revelations of his time is evident in his enthusiasm regarding a statue revealed in Persepolis that fits the description of Dhul-Qarnayn.[67] The motivation to find Cyrus in the Qur'an was multifaceted and involved the view that Islam was compatible with local pre-Islamic traditions. Another Indian scholar to adopt this view was S. M. Taher Rezwi. In his book on the Parsis (i.e., the Zoroastrians in India) published in 1928, Rezwi maintained that Dhul-Qarnayn was Darius, Cyrus's heir.[68]

Rezwi assumed both Dhul-Qarnayn and Darius to be, beyond doubt, adherents of Zoroastrianism. It was in their time, according to him, that "Zoroastrianism attained its golden age for the last time."[69] More importantly, this assumption was part of his wider theory that attributed monotheism to Zoroastrianism. The main purpose of Rezwi's study was to prove that Zoroastrianism was in fact monotheistic, thus rendering it compatible with Islam. This proof would be of great value to Pahlavi scholars because it could bridge an inconvenient gap between the Zoroastrianism of the Sassanid period of the third to seventh centuries and the coming of Islam to Iran in the seventh century. As in the question of the identity of Dhul-Qarnayn in the Qur'an, there was uncertainty regarding Cyrus's religious convictions, which left plenty of room for speculation by those with nationalist motivations.[70]

Interestingly, the scholar who would mediate this new interpretation regarding the identity of Dhul-Qarnayn to the Pahlavis was Abul Kalam Muhiyuddin Ahmed (1888–1958), better known by his pen name, Abul Kalam Azad.[71] Azad—an Indian national activist and politician and India's first minister of education—was also a prominent scholar who was well aware of the importance of archaeology in building a national identity. In a speech he gave to the Indian Advisory Board of Archaeology in 1949, he complained of the seemingly underdeveloped state of the field in India compared to its state in other countries, especially in the Middle East. Among the reasons for the lack of interest in archaeology in India as compared to Egypt and Iraq, he mentioned European interest in the Bible, which directed European archaeologists mainly to the other two countries.[72]

Azad recognized the deep historical roots shared by India and Iran. In his welcome speech to Mohammad Reza Shah and Empress Farah, he announced that the Indian Council for Cultural Relations was establishing a special section to "deepen and strengthen Indo-Iranian relations."[73] The same body sponsored the work of a professor of Indology at Tehran University and facilitated the study of Sanskrit there. Influenced by theories suggesting the Aryan roots of Iran, Azad declared: "The relations between India and Iran go back to thousands of years. In the early dawn of history we already perceive that men of the same stock were settling in India and Iran. . . . The religious beliefs and practices of these early peoples are so akin that one cannot have any doubts about their common origin."[74]

Azad's commentary on the Qur'an was part of his call for the liberation of Islam from false traditions, which, he believed, had accumulated over centuries of influence by Greek philosophy.[75] Like other reformers of Islam, he testified, "I was not content with the religion inherited by birth from my ancestors."[76] His travels to Iraq, among other countries, might have also exposed him to the original commentary on Dhul-Qarnayn. The identification of Cyrus as the Qur'anic Dhul-Qarnayn fit well with Azad's

3. The winged figure found at Pasargadae, from ca. sixth century BCE. Photograph from Ernst Wallis et al., *Illustrerad Verldhistoria* (Chicago: Svenska Amerikanaren, ca. 1875–79). Wikimedia Commons.

intention to refute the notion of the evolution and development of faith by his claim that monotheism had existed thousands of years ago.[77] More importantly, he asserted, because Iran and India share a historical legacy that goes back thousands of years, finding the founder of ancient Iran in the Qur'an linked India, if only indirectly, to the Holy Book and bestowed it with a special connection to Islam.

True to his intent to establish Islamic scholarship on scientific pillars, Azad adapted archaeological findings to support his theory. His focus on "finding" Cyrus is tangible in his view that the winged figure in the relief in the monumental gate structure found at Pasargadae represents Cyrus.[78] Azad did not hide his admiration of Cyrus. Ibrahim Bastani Parizi went further, saying that Cyrus's appearance on the scene "ought to be considered one of the wonders of history, particularly to the descendants of the Aryan race."[79]

Qur'anic Exegesis in the Service of the Pahlavi State

Azad's identification of Dhul-Qarnayn as Cyrus the Great attracted little attention at the time of its publication and received few echoes in commentary on the Qur'an. However, as the October 1971 celebrations commemorating twenty-five hundred years of Iranian monarchy approached, the Pahlavi state used every shred of evidence pointing to the greatness of Iran, and it was in this context that Azad's theory was resuscitated.

Azad's commentary on the eighteenth sura, translated into Arabic, was distributed at the shah's order to all guests from Muslim countries who attended the celebrations held near the ruins of Persepolis, the Achaemenid capital in the centuries following Cyrus's death. Pahlavi state ideologues were keen to make use of this interpretation in the service of the Iranian national message. Among the directions to the committee for the celebrations of twenty-five centuries of Iranian monarchy, one finds the urgent need to cultivate the notion that Cyrus the Great is indeed mentioned in the Qur'an: "Each head of state that hosts a committee for the celebrations should receive an issue of the journal *Iran Bastan* that presents the theory of Abul Kalam Azad, former Indian Minister of Education, which refers to Cyrus the Great and the attribution of Dhul-Qarnayn from the

'Sura of the Cave,' to him."[80] The cultivation of Cyrus was at the center of the Pahlavi state's efforts at this point, so much so that publications on Cyrus were monitored by SAVAK, Pahlavi Iran's notorious secret police. As mentioned at the beginning of this chapter, Ibrahim Bastani Parizi was involved in issuing a revised edition of the translation of Azad's commentary identifying Cyrus with Dhul-Qarnayn. According to his story, "SAVAK had received information that the Ministry of Information's radio station press was about to publish a book on Cyrus the Great and that the translator [of the book into Persian] was going to claim in the introduction that Cyrus was the son of a Jewish mother and that his mother tongue was Hebrew."[81] Bastani Parizi promised that he had no such intention, and so the publication process continued unimpeded. This incident testifies to the high degree of politicization of the historical figure of Cyrus and the way his image became deeply entangled in the political ferment in the years prior to the Islamic Revolution.

In the introduction to that Persian translation of Azad's commentary, Bastani Parizi reminds his readers that it was Cyrus's wisdom that enabled him "to become central and powerful in the land of Iran and rule over the territory of the Aryans and to subjugate their enemies."[82] However, the glory of the past is relevant above all for its echoes in the present:

> It is thanks to him [Cyrus] that to this day, 2,500 years later, the land of the Aryans is safe in a world where the[re is] collision according to the rules of eat or be eaten, torn apart between the worldview of the North, the turmoil of the East, the dashing from the South, and the revolutions of the West and in general [is stable compared to the] Indians, Turks, Kurds, and Arabs. It is thanks to him that we can celebrate his kingdom after 2,500 years.[83]

Bastani Parizi was skeptical, however, regarding Azad's "scientific" proof of Sir Sayyed's theory:

> It is true that it is not possible to verify Azad's investigation into the matter completely, and indeed many doubt the conclusions he reached, but even if we admit that the question of the identity of Dhul-Qarnayn in the Qur'an is a matter that has not been solved . . . none of the other

> personalities identified with Dhul-Qarnayn is any closer, in terms of the spiritual and political characteristics, than Cyrus the Great. Therefore, we can appreciate the value of Abul Kalam [Azad's] inquiry—particularly from the Iranian national point of view.[84]

In the historical context of late Pahlavi Iran, proselytizing the identity of Dhul-Qarnayn as Cyrus the Great served as a way to tie the Pahlavi state to the greatness of ancient Iran without discarding most Iranians' religious affiliation. Such a promotion of the Cyrus myth could be seen as yet another attempt to merge Iranian ethnic identity with the sacredness of the Qur'an—an attempt that as a consequence contributed to the popularity of the founder of the Achaemenid Empire. After all, the shah depicted himself as Cyrus's true heir. Sa'id Nafisi, an intellectual and writer who was also one of the propagators of the Pahlavi historical worldview, confessed:

> This riddle of more than a thousand years was eventually solved recently by a scholar named Abul Kalam Azad . . . who did a great service to Islamic studies. The great admiration of Iranians is increased due to the fact that he proved beyond doubt that Dhul-Qarnayn of the Qur'an is Cyrus the Great, the Achaemenid king. It adds to our great pride in the glories of Iran that the holy Qur'an sings a song of praise to a great Iranian king. . . . The scientific and literary community of Iran would like [to] thank this great scholar who did a great service to Iran and its people.[85]

An Ambivalent Heritage

Once Azad's claim was published in Persian, the possibility that the founder of the Achaemenid Empire is mentioned and even praised in the Qur'an enchanted Iranian commentators on the Qur'an. Once the interpretation that Dhul-Qarnayn was Cyrus the Great became an option, the temptation to disperse and promote it affected many Iranian scholars, clerics, and laymen alike.

Possibly the highest authority to grapple with the theory was 'Allamah Mohammad Husayn Tabataba'i (1903–81), one of the most prominent Shi'i clerics of the twentieth century and author of the magisterial work *Tafsir al-mizan* (The Balance in Interpretation, published in two versions—one in 1981 and the second in 1985).[86] In his commentary on the eighteenth sura, "The Cave" (al-Kahf), Tabataba'i shows awareness of the claim that Dhul-Qarnayn was the Persian Achaemenid king Cyrus, who founded the Iranian Empire and believed in one god.[87] Tabataba'i surmises that if Cyrus was so admired by the Jews (as revealed in their holy scriptures), there is good reason to believe that he did not worship idols; otherwise, they would not have held him in such great esteem as "Messiah, adherent, and companion of God."[88]

Tabataba'i was deeply impressed with the archaeological find of an inscription of a king with two horns coming out of his head, which fits well with the description of Cyrus from the book of Daniel (8:1–9). According to Tabataba'i, the inscriptions regarding Darius, composed only eight years after Cyrus's death, also attest to his monotheistic inclinations, which therefore are very likely the legacy of his predecessor.[89] As noted earlier, there are two versions of *Tafsir al-mizan*, the first published in the early 1980s following the Islamic Revolution and the second in the mid-1980s. The difference between the versions is telling: in the first version, Tabataba'i accepts Azad's theory, if only for lack of any other convincing explanation for the identity of Dhul-Qarnayn, but he tends to reject it in the second, which was published after his death. It seems that the rise of the Islamic Republic with its strong (temporary) rejection of Pahlavi discourse on the Achaemenid Empire left its mark on Tabataba'i. Nevertheless, even when rejecting this identification in the second version, he admits that it is not altogether groundless and compares Cyrus with Alexander the Great. Tabataba'i, who first wrote his commentary under the rule of Mohammad Reza Shah, felt the need to accept the theory of Cyrus the Great in the Qur'an despite his lack of conviction regarding the evidence Azad offered in support of this theory. He walked a fine line in this matter so as not to be unpatriotic while remaining loyal to the traditional interpretation of the identity of Dhul-Qarnayn.[90]

In the second version of *Tafsir al-mizan* published after the Islamic Revolution, Tabataba'i gives an interesting account of the memory of Cyrus and the reason it was tarnished by the opposition to Pahlavi rule during the 1960s and 1970s. He theorizes that Cyrus was presented not only as the first Iranian king but also as the one who established the

Iranian monarchy. Thus, the ulema viewed every reference with suspicion ever since the Pahlavi state tried to gain legitimacy from it, out of fear that it would be just another attempt to abuse the memory of Cyrus for political gain.[91] According to Tabataba'i, Cyrus did not establish the Iranian monarchy but continued the legacy of the dynasties that preceded him, the Medeans and Elamites. Tabataba'i uses the figure of Cyrus as inspiration for the republican message he wishes to deliver in his commentary on the Qur'an. According to him, Cyrus was actually antimonarchical—part of the innovative message he brought to the ancient world because monarchy was contradictory to the original Iranian values. Paradoxically, then, Cyrus's republican inclinations are what make him special among Iranian kings. Neither the Medeans before him nor his heir, Darius, shared his cosmopolitan outlook; they tried to base their rule solely on Iranian elements. Cyrus was the only ruler who valued tolerance and coexistence among the different peoples who constituted the Achaemenid Empire. Thus, Tabataba'i aligns his reading of the Qur'an with the politically correct message dictated by the political vicissitudes of Iran in the early 1980s.[92]

The suspicion with which the ulema viewed the monarchy as an institution in Iran, a view tacitly criticized by Tabataba'i, was new in the 1970s and formed part of the struggle between the Pahlavi state and the ulema during this period.[93] The animosity that had once been directed narrowly toward the Pahlavi monarch and his establishment widened to include the monarchy as a political institution. Cyrus then became a symbol of the long-lasting malaise of Iranian despotism, and desecrating his memory became tantamount to rooting out that malaise. The importance of Tabataba'i's commentary lies mainly in his role as a leader in the revival of the madrasas in Qom in the 1950s, which situated him on the fine line between the religious and the social importance of the ulema in Iran at that time.[94] The most vociferous of the ulema in his rejection of the monarchy was Ayatollah Ruhollah Khomeini, who developed a republican doctrine out of the collision between the Pahlavi establishment and the ulema:

> Tradition relates that the title *Shahanshah* (King of Kings), which is borne by the monarchs of Iran, is the most hated of all titles in the sight of God. Islam is fundamentally opposed to the whole notion of

> monarchy. Anyone who studies the manner in which the Prophet established the government of Islam will realize that Islam came in order to destroy these palaces of tyranny. Monarchy is one of the most shameful and disgraceful reactionary manifestations.[95]

The most vehement attack, though, came from one of Khomeini's aides, Ayatollah Sadeq Khalkhali (1926–2003), a Qom graduate and a disciple of Khomeini as well as of other scholars such as Ayatollah Husayn Boroujerdi (1875–1961) and 'Allamah Tabataba'i. Khalkhali spent several years in prison and exile successively and was a prominent activist in the extreme Islamist group Fida'yan-i Islam (Those Sacrificing Themselves for Islam).[96]

During the months leading up to the celebrations in October 1971, which, as we have seen, served as an arena for the contestation of Cyrus's legacy, Khalkhali composed a treatise titled *Korush-i dorughin* (False Cyrus). In the forty-odd pages of this booklet, Khalkhali tries to counter and refute the various sources used by Pahlavi propagandists to establish the historical greatness of the founder of the Achaemenid Empire. He attacks the Greek sources that praise Cyrus and tries either to empty them of any historical validity or to show that they were misused and misinterpreted by the Pahlavi public educational apparatus.

Khalkhali loathes the idea that Cyrus—who, according to him, was nothing better than a bloodthirsty and immoral monarch—is mentioned in the Qur'an in a positive light. He claims that Azad's theory is baseless, after which he moves on to demonstrate that Azad, perhaps unknowingly, was delivering historical propaganda in support of the Pahlavi regime and the Zionists. According to Khalkhali, both the Cyrus cylinder and the Jewish Bible, which Azad used to prove his case regarding Dhul-Qarnayn's identity, are unreliable. The cylinder was created by Cyrus himself, making it an undependable witness to the king's deeds and character. As for the Bible, Muslims should not trust it because of its various misinterpretations and corruptions.[97]

In Khalkhali's view, Cyrus was in fact "a cruel king, who was most fond of taking revenge on his enemies and succumbing to his carnal desires."[98] His benevolence toward the Jews was nothing more than a direct outcome of his desire for Esther, the Jewish queen he married.[99] The Jews, Khalkhali states, were thankful to Cyrus "for declaring their rights and letting them go to Palestine."[100] As a token of appreciation, they depicted him positively in their scriptures. It was, therefore, a foreign conspiracy that lent Cyrus such a positive image and resonance in the eyes of Iranians.

Ironically, though, Khalkhali adopts the parallelism and continuity between the Achaemenid Empire and twentieth-century Iran presented by Pahlavi propaganda. However, he turns the moral meaning of this continuity upside down, from being positive to having the most despicable nature. In his narrative, conspiracy is the thread that links the past with the present. It is no wonder, then, that he finds many similarities between the hypocrisy of Cyrus's regime and the hypocrisy of the Pahlavi state, which had imprisoned Khalkhali and adored the image of Cyrus. Just as Cyrus cloaked his opportunism as clemency and benevolence, so the United States tries to paint its imperialistic ambitions as the exporting of peace and freedom to various nations around the globe. Khalkhali's appropriation of the Pahlavi paradigm does not stop here.

Third Worldist thought is prevalent in this discourse on Cyrus, who is depicted as yet another conqueror of Iran; hence, boasting of being of his lineage amounts to the same thing as a woman bragging of being raped. The hypocrisy of representing Cyrus as someone who established peace in the Ancient East is as ridiculous to Khalkhali as the claim that the United States is keeping the peace in the Third World during the Cold War. Hence, Khalkhali argues, one should not be surprised at the Western historical narrative describing Cyrus as a benevolent king.[101]

Mainstreaming Innovation: The Religious Appropriation of Cyrus in the Islamic Republic

The first decade following the Islamic Revolution marked a receding of the historical narrative dealing with ancient Iran, despite the need to incorporate ethnic Iranian elements into war propaganda that revived some pre-Islamic symbols along the way.[102] However, regarding the Achaemenid Empire, it seems that the interval of uninterest in it was temporary, and it was rediscovered in the early and especially mid-1990s.[103]

The rapprochement with nationalist tendencies seems to have started during Akbar Hashemi Rafsanjani's presidency (1989–97). In November 1996 a conference was organized in Shiraz under the title "Fars: Mahd-i tamaddun-i Irani Eslami" (Fars: Cradle of Islamic-Iranian Civilization).[104] During the two-day conference, the guests heard several speakers illuminate various topics in the history of Fars Province, Shiraz in particular. And, in fact, half the conference was dedicated to the debate over the identification of Dhul-Qarnayn as Cyrus the Great.

The interest in Cyrus has continued to gain momentum, as a cursory search for this name in the Iranian National Library database proves. The number of publications on the Achaemenid Empire has fluctuated, peaking at more than seventy in 2005. Interestingly, the most popular topic that books about the Achaemenid Empire deal with in the Islamic Republic is its founder, Cyrus the Great.[105] Numerous publications now identify Dhul-Qarnayn as Cyrus, and it seems that many Iranian publications on Cyrus the Great see the idea as a theory that needs no debate, if not one altogether well proven.[106]

The historical connection between contemporary Iran and its ancient past is evident in these publications as well. President Mohammad Khatami (1997–2005) expressed a new political discourse regarding the cultural heritage of Iran, foregrounding its pre-Islamic legacy and seeking to mitigate the tensions inherent in the official ambivalence toward this legacy and its relation to the religious affiliation of the Islamic Republic.[107] His visit to Persepolis was yet another symbolic step in this direction. One book on Cyrus published during Khatami's presidency reads: "Khatami is the follower of Cyrus, leading Iran in times of great crisis and despair, in light of the American efforts to take control of the region. By electing Khatami, the youth have expressed their desire to return to past glories."[108] Yet another publication expresses Khatami's dialogue of civilizations in a manner suitable for the masses. The author tries to mitigate the tensions between pre-Islamic Persian history and the Islamic periods following it: "There were those who tried to present the memory of Cyrus and recognition of his greatness as an alternative to Islamic values. This was done out of animosity to the Islamic Republic in the wake of the revolution that brought it into existence. . . . It is a great mistake to try to describe the national heritage as opposed to religion and its values."[109]

A resuscitation of pre-Islamic symbols in general and of the founder of the Achaemenid Empire in particular could satisfy the Islamic Republic's need to reinvigorate revolutionary zeal. Thus, a monograph on Cyrus published in 1997 states in its introduction, "We should strive to inculcate the legacy of Cyrus in the generation of the revolution, which seems desperate and hopeless. We need to draw inspiration from ancient Iran in the time of the great war with Iraq."[110]

The chauvinistic tone adopted by those who argue that Cyrus appears in the Qur'an is also present in the work of those who reject this theory—namely, by pointing to the anomaly that the classic understanding of Alexander the Great as the destroyer of Persepolis seems to pose. It thus comes as no surprise that a recent publication on Cyrus, which takes for a fact that Dhul-Qarnayn is Cyrus, states that the story in the Qur'an regarding Dhul-Qarnayn cannot refer to Alexander the Great because Alexander was not monotheistic, whereas the Persians were. Alexander lost any traces of humanity after he conquered Iran, according to the same publication.[111]

Conclusion

The Cyrus cylinder received a warm and official welcoming ceremony when brought from the British Museum to Iran for exhibition in September 2010.[112] The arrival of the cylinder, which was preceded by a long debate and tension between the British Museum and Iranian authorities, was followed by a formal and well-orchestrated ceremony that included a speech by President Mahmud Ahmadinejad (2005–13) in which he referred to Cyrus as the godfather of all *basiji*s (young recruits to the auxiliary militia of the Revolutionary Guards) in Iranian history.[113] The president, considered to be the political quintessence of the Islamic Revolution of 1979, also referred to "twenty-five hundred years of Iranian history" in his visit to the National Museum in Tehran.[114] Conservative members of the Majles were also alarmed to learn that the president was planning a festive reception and Nowruz (the Iranian new year in the week of March 20) ceremony at Persepolis, the Achaemenid capital that lies to the south of Shiraz in Fars Province. This would have been the first state-sponsored ceremony at the site since the fall of the Pahlavi state and the establishment of the Islamic Republic.[115] It was definitely the memories to which Persepolis, one of the most famous archaeological sites in the Middle East, was connected that made President Ahmadinejad wish for a Nowruz ceremony there, but it was the site's connection to the Pahlavi state that undermined this aspiration.

4

Persepolis Revisited

Oh Cyrus, great king, king of kings, Achaemenid king, king of Iran: I, king of kings of Iran, salute you, on behalf of myself and my nation. Rest in peace, as we are watchful and shall remain forever so.

—Mohammad Reza Pahlavi at Cyrus's tomb in Pasargadae, October 1971

Islamic civilization acted like scissors and has cut us off completely from our pre-Islamic past. The pundits, such as archaeologists and historians of antiquity, may know much about the Sassanids, the Achaemenids, and even older civilizations. But our people know nothing about such things. They do not find their roots in these civilizations. They are left unmoved by the heroes, myths, and monuments of these ancient empires. They remember nothing from this distant past and do not care to learn about these pre-Islamic civilizations.

—'Ali Shari'ati, *Bazgosht be khish* (Return to Self)[1]

National Holidays, History, and Memory

The process by which a historical artifact, whether a site, figure, or event becomes a national symbol has attracted the attention of many historians, social scientists, and political scientists.[2] Some of the issues involved in the discourse on the making of symbols touch upon the choice of the symbol, its appropriation and marketing to the masses as such, and the (sometimes conflicting) way in which the symbol is perceived by different sectors in the society involved. An inquiry of these issues with respect especially to Persepolis, the site that became the arena for the Pahlavi state's most famous and controversial performance of power, will enable us to see the ways in which a historical symbol becomes a political battlefield.

It seems that no other site in Iran symbolizes the reign of Mohammad Reza Shah more than Persepolis, capital of the Achaemenid kingdom from Darius's time until it was burned down by Alexander the Great (fourth to sixth centuries BCE). Iranian nationalists recognized Persepolis as an archaeological site of national importance from the 1920s on. Iranian interest in Persepolis developed out of a growing recognition of the site's importance to Iran's pre-Islamic historical heritage. This interest constituted a break from the previous situation in which archaeological digs, conducted at several sites in Iran during the nineteenth century and the beginning of the twentieth, stemmed from Western researchers' interest in sites related to the Bible. Iranian interest in the site seventy kilometers northeast of Shiraz developed alongside the transfer of responsibility for archaeology in Iran from Western to Iranian hands. The Pahlavi monarchy used several archaeological sites for the production of national-historical events aimed at generating legitimacy for the shah's rule. Persepolis was foremost in importance and the site of the festivities celebrating twenty-five hundred years of Iranian monarchy.

In the second half of the twentieth century, archaeology in Iran developed considerably and underwent thorough professionalization. The entrance of Iranians to research in the field could be regarded as dramatic, preventing the perception of archaeology as a field of foreign influence even though it was not until the 1960s that Iranians filled positions of power in the Iranian Antiquities Authority. Nevertheless, the deeper question of the object of archaeological research has continued to be the glory of ancient Iran. This aim also affected the question of the periods under research in favor of the Achaemenids and Sassanids rather than the Elamite (ca. 3200 to 1500 BCE) and other periods. Even the Achaemenid period was not studied in a scientific way but rather with the aim of exhibiting the glory of that period and little else. At the same time, developments in archaeological methodology in the West began to focus on the study of everyday life in ancient periods. As Roman Ghirshman confessed to a reporter in 1968:

> The problems with both Iranian and foreign teams currently working in this country . . . lay in the fact that on the whole they were neglecting six major historical periods. These periods are very important. . . . For a start very little work has been done on the Elamite Empire. . . . Then there is the Median Empire. . . . The Achaemenian period is even more neglected; all we seem to hear about from this time is Persepolis.[3]

It seems that despite the changing of the guard in the upper levels of the Iranian Antiquities Authority, there was a great degree of continuity in the goals that the people who held these positions sought—namely, to reveal the greatness of ancient Iran at the national level through the dynasties and the kings who led them.[4] Some of the problems observed in the late 1960s were the lack of local experts to conduct archaeological research in Iran and the neglect of urban sites, such as old bazaars in the centers of cities (Isfahan, for instance).[5]

Kamal Niknami, an Iranian archaeologist, has observed that "archaeology in Iran from its very beginning has always been observed as an ideological link with national patriotic aspirations." In his opinion, that was the reason for the lack of connection to the field of anthropology as it developed in the West from the 1960s on. The objects of research, archaeological sites, and the way they were studied were also meant to serve the nationalist cause: "archaeology very quickly entered into the service of the glorification of the past, and a very definite patriotic content was included." According to Niknami, the change in the nationality of archaeologists in Iran (from British and French to Iranian) did not entail a change in the methodology used in the research conducted there, where "anti-theoretical traditions continued to be dominant."[6] Archaeology was perceived as a background for nationalism, supplying it with scientific "raw material" to prove its historical narrative.

Pierre Nora argues that what he terms "the acceleration of history," a typical by-product of modernity, confronts us with the brutal realization of the difference between real memory—social and unviolated, exemplified in but also retained as the secret of so-called primitive or archaic societies—and history, which is how our hopelessly forgetful modern societies, propelled by change, organize the past. In other words, Nora sees the modern forms of remembering as compensation for the traditional, authentic ones, which became extinct in the wake of the Industrial Revolution and the urbanization of Western societies. The outcome of this historical development is that "we must deliberately create archives, maintain anniversaries, organize celebrations, pronounce eulogies, and notarize bills because such activities no longer occur naturally." The state's need to mediate memory for the public emanates from a void that modernity left behind in the field of genuine feeling of connection to the past. Nora sees a tight connection between "the irrevocable break marked by the disappearance of peasant culture" and "the apogee of industrial growth."[7]

Therefore, state celebrations like the one held in Persepolis do not necessarily demonstrate the power of the state, nor do they guarantee it a higher degree of legitimacy in society, but rather they express the need to compensate for modern societies' lack of natural, traditional means of remembering. States of various types, democratic as well as authoritarian, invest great efforts in the generation of national festivities such as the one under discussion here. From Elizabethan England through imperial Germany and Japan of the early twentieth century to Java and Morocco, states have tried to promote their right to rule in the eyes of the people they govern by holding celebrations and ceremonies that are supposed to enhance this right.[8] The research literature provides three main explanations for the role of such events—parades, festivities, and commemorations of national days—initiated by the nation-state in the modern era. First, the state needs to achieve legitimacy. According to Clifford Geertz, "at the political center of any complexly organized society . . . there is both a governing elite and a set of symbolic forms expressing the fact that it is in truth governing."[9] Second, the state wishes to shape the national identity and make its presence felt in the public sphere. In this context, Antony Smith argues that "in many ways national symbols, customs and ceremonies are the most potent and durable aspects of nationalism. They embody its basic concepts, making them visible and distinct for every member, commemorating the tenets of an abstract ideology in palpable, concrete terms that evoke instant emotional responses from all strata of the community."[10]

Third, the elite need to justify their rule in their own eyes—that is, as members of the elite. In contrast to the first two reasons, which see the general public as the target of the festivities, the third reason points to the ruling elite as having a double role in the event: the elite create the event, shape it, and are its main consumer. Rodney Barker describes the process of creating legitimacy as follows: "It involves . . . a self-referential or self-justifying activity characteristic of rulers pursued with great intensity at the centre of government and with those engaged in the business of government as its principal consumers."[11]

The selection of an archaeological site for the ceremony as well a series of symbols that attempt to reawaken the past with which the site is identified are not to be taken for granted. Eric Hobsbawm and Terence Ranger coined the oxymoron *invented traditions*, which they define as "a group of actions which are usually controlled by clear rules, in an open or hidden manner, of a symbolic nature and whose purpose is to instill norms of behavior and certain values by repetition, which automatically suggests continuity with the past."[12] Even though the celebrations at Persepolis under discussion in this chapter were not repetitive but rather singular, they did encourage a view of an ostensible continuity of Iranian history. This phenomenon characterizes societies undergoing modernization processes and trying (consciously or not) to "establish a basis for continuity with the desired historical past." Another important characteristic, although inherently a subjective one, that Hobsbawm and Ranger find in these traditions is that they are created and forced "from above": "Where there is reference to a historical past, what is unique in 'invented' traditions is the fact that their continuity is essentially forced. In short, they are reactions to new situations, shaped as old situations or creating their own past by forced repetition."[13] The artificial and coercive nature of modern inventions has the effect of awakening opposition from competing political currents over the right to shape historical consciousness and to disseminate it in the public sphere. Other scholars, however, have challenged the dichotomy between tradition and modernity espoused by Hobsbawm and Ranger. Richard Handler and Jocelyn Linnekin attack what they see as "a false dichotomy between tradition and modernity as fixed and mutually exclusive states."[14] Nevertheless, accepting the somewhat porous boundaries between tradition and modernity does not invalidate the notion of the evolution of "invented traditions."

Underlying the impulse to create new traditions we find the distress created by the feeling that modern life is disconnected from the past, which makes society uneasy, as if it is rootless. As Hobsbawm puts it, the motivating factor behind the creation of these traditions is the "collision between frequent changes and the novelty of the modern world and the need to establish at least some parts of the social life as stable and unchanging."[15] From October 12 to October 16, 1971, festivities commemorating "two thousand five hundred years of Iranian monarchy" were held on the plains of the Persepolis site. In these festivities, attended by presidents, heads of state, and monarchs, the Pahlavi regime presented, on the one hand, the continuity of the Iranian monarchy and especially its own affiliation to the Achaemenid dynasty established by Cyrus the Great and, on the other hand, the progress and development that the regime had established in Iran to lead the country to a brilliant future.

My analysis of the Persepolis events points to the connection to the distant past and the dissonance experienced by the shapers of Iranian memory at the time discussed as well as by a large part of the population and justifies considering the Persepolis events as an invented commemoration, borrowing from Hobsbawm and Ranger's analysis of ostensible modern traditions that are in reality new creations.

Pierre Nora describes a process where transition from a traditional society to a modern one entails the vanishing of spontaneous memory and its submission to history—that is, the official version of memory orchestrated from above, the state. "Societies based on memory are no more: the institutions that once transmitted values from generation to generation—churches, schools, families, governments—have ceased to function as they once did."[16]

Critics of Nora have pointed to the dichotomy he presents between premodern and modern society in the field of memory.[17] Nora's attitude in this matter, it seems to them, reveals a somewhat romantic view of premodern society, as in the following description by Nora: "The 'acceleration of history' thus brings us face to face with the enormous distance that separates real memory . . . from history, which is how modern societies organize a past they are condemned to forget because they are driven by change."[18]

Whereas Nora has emphasized the role of the state, which has the advantage of its enormous resources in commemoration of what it sees as the right memory to be endorsed, other researchers, such as Jay Winter and Emmanuel Sivan, John Bodnar, and Kirk Savage,[19] have sought to delineate a more balanced equilibrium between the state and civil society (i.e., private initiatives) in national commemoration.[20] In other words, against the tendency to see the state as a central or even sole designer of memory in the public sphere, some researchers have tended to limit the role attributed to the state in this field and to allow room for other players.

Therefore, an important place in shaping memory must be reserved for unofficial agents who do not act on behalf of the state but rather mediate and argue with the memory that the state attempts to instill, affect it, and are affected by it at the same time.[21] Israel Gershoni has distinguished between primary and secondary agents of propagation of knowledge in relation to national awareness and emphasized the latter's importance, especially in their ability to reach a wider public than the former.[22] By concentrating on one test case at one site and on an event that was extensively planned and produced by the state without negotiating with secondary agents of memory, I wish to point out the price that the state sometimes pays for its demand for exclusivity in instilling the "correct" national heritage. The lack of secondary agents, a result of the state's efforts at monopolizing the national memory, can prove counterproductive to the state's goal. In the absence of the diffusion of memory making through varying and competing agencies (except clandestinely), the official apparatus may backfire strongly, as indeed happened in Iran in the two decades preceding the Islamic Revolution.

Nora draws our attention to the modern forms of the search for legitimacy on the part of modern states. The need for such formal, institutionalized forms of memory, according to this interpretation, rises in an industrial society. This occurs hand in hand with the diminishing power of traditional society, in which the mimetic model of memory, one based on the transmission of traditions from one generation to the next, was more common and "natural." The need for formal ceremonies to commemorate events in the national past has a greater weight in a society that is going through a process of modernization, and one may even surmise that the less the state feels certain of its right to exist, the greater the efforts it might invest in events to assert its power and celebrate it.

In this manner, I argue that the elaborate festivities conducted on the vast plains near the Achaemenid capital of Persepolis in October 1971 were actually a sign of the degeneration of the Pahlavi cultural project that had begun during Reza Shah's rule. Beyond the question of their success in creating legitimacy for the shah's regime, the Persepolis events were a perfect presentation of the process of the institutionalization of memory and its reversion to history in the sense that Nora uses these terms. Therefore, the festivities symbolize not the high point of the regime's ability to create legitimacy for itself but rather a milestone in the Pahlavi regime's loss of legitimacy in Iran.

Widespread activity concerning the fostering of heritage was stimulated by two developments, the first being the Mosaddeq crisis (1951–53), in which the popular prime minister Mohammad Mosaddeq challenged the shah while expressing economic patriotism—that is, nationalization of the oil industry—at the shah's expense. The other development was the declaration of the White Revolution in 1963. This "revolution," which included several measures regarding land ownership, education, and infrastructure, was the starting point for the training of a cadre of youths in order to send them to distant districts to teach the locals to read and write and to provide them with basic notions of loyalty to the state and connection to its history, in addition to the spreading of the "correct" national and historical consciousness among modern Iranians. These educational activities must be seen as bestowing far more than knowledge upon the rural population because they were concerned with the political socialization of areas that the modern Iranian state had not yet managed to penetrate. Fostering the national symbols, first and foremost the shah himself, was an attempt to utilize that affiliation for the purpose of legitimizing the regime and creating an ideological alternative to the opposition (Marxism on the one hand and religious affiliation on the other). The show of strength at Persepolis must be seen in the wider context in which the regime had to deal with ideological challenges from within while trying to leverage the internal confrontation outward toward a regional claim for power. However, because the celebrations were supposed to enhance the regime in the eyes of its own supporters and members, they should not be viewed merely as a propaganda effort but rather as expressing the Pahlavi state's deep belief in its unique role in the history of Iran.

The Pahlavi regime used Persepolis to glorify the pre-Islamic heritage in a number of ways—beginning with intensive digging and restoration efforts from the 1920s on, inviting official visits by dignitaries, and culminating in using it as the stage for the ostentatious celebrations in October 1971. Persepolis was the capital of the Achaemenid Empire during the reign of Darius (fifth–sixth centuries BCE), and as far as we know, it was not built in the time of Cyrus.[23] This is a significant point because that means the site did not in fact fit well into the worldview of the shapers of national heritage in Pahlavi Iran, who desired above all to create the facade of an uninterrupted, harmonious historic continuity.[24] For this purpose, the Pahlavi state and its agents of socialization marketed Persepolis as the capital of the empire and attempted to connect it with the figure of Cyrus, despite the chronological leap this connection entailed.

In ancient Islamic chronicles, the site is identified as Takht-i Jamshid, the Throne of Jamshid, named after a mythical Persian king. The authors of the Muslim chronicles identified Jamshid with King Solomon, which gave the site an additional name: Solomon's Mosque. After Alexander the Great burned Persepolis in 330 BCE, it fell from greatness, although it still served as a regional center of authority. In the Sassanid period, it was located near the capital city of Istakhr, and inscriptions there show that the Sassanid kings also attempted to sing the ruins' praises in order to portray themselves as the successors of the Achaemenids.[25] European travelers and adventurers, especially in the nineteenth century, drew, sketched, and described the ruins of Persepolis as a remnant of Iran's glorious past.[26]

In the state's effort to link Persepolis with Cyrus and a national celebration, one publication in a historical journal presented Persepolis as the place where the Achaemenid kings celebrated Nowruz, the Iranian New Year. In this way, a sort of national "trinity," made up of a historical figure, a site, and a specific (and familiar) time, was constructed as part of the national heritage.[27] Thus, for example, 'Ali Sami (1910–1989), one of the first Iranians to excavate Persepolis and the founder and director of the Archaeological Institute of Persepolis, presented the history of Iranian folk festivals (Nowruz, Mehrgan, etc.) in a lecture held at the Iran Bastan Museum in 1971 under the title "Celebration of Nowruz in Takht-i Jamshid."[28] Despite the promising title, he did not actually claim that the site was used for the celebration of Nowruz. He did, however, mention the site as the place where inscriptions from the time of Darius, which list twelve festivals that the ancient Persians used to celebrate every year, were found. The juxtaposition of the site with a national festival is telling in that it shows modern Iranians' great need to bridge the gap and connect a particular point in time (Nowruz) with a particular locus, site, in order to enhance the feeling of continuity and harmony between the people of Iran and the land's history.

The name Persepolis was coined by Greek historians and apparently originated in its identification with the center of power of Fars Province, the district in which the site is located.[29] Besides being the site of historical antiquities, Fars Province was the center of power of Karim Khan Zand (r. 1749–79), the Qajars' archenemy. As Firoozeh Kashani-Sabet, who studied the production of maps of Iran in the nineteenth century, has remarked, "The province of Fars (Pars) maintained an exalted position as 'the seat of empire of the kings of Iran' in texts as well as on maps."[30]

Iranian court officials showed interest in the Persepolis site as early as 1850, when Nasir al-Din Shah ordered Jules Richard, a French professor who was teaching at Dar al-Funun, to photograph the ruins and inscriptions of the Achaemenid remains there. Owing to financial difficulties, the assignment was not completed until seven years later by Luigi Pesce, an Italian officer.[31] Despite sporadic attempts at discovering the greatness of the archaeological site in the late Qajar period, these efforts depended on either the shah's or the foreign mission's personal initiative. However, neither the last shahs of the Qajar dynasty nor the foreign archaeological missions tied the site to a well-articulated political cause. This connection had to wait until well into the 1930s to be made.[32]

The turning point in the status of the Persepolis site can be traced to 1930, when Ernst Herzfeld, a German archaeologist, was granted the right to excavate the site as part of a wider deal struck between the French

Archaeological Mission, the Iranian government, and the Oriental Institute of the University of Chicago, whose activity in Iran was led by Herzfeld, a German immigrant to the United States. Herzfeld's request of court minister Abulhusayn Taymurtash for a permit to excavate the site was an expression of the "need to safeguard Persepolis," an issue that had been bothering him for twenty years by that time. His expectations from Taymurtash in this matter went further than funding the excavations. Herzfeld wished to lead and prioritize the excavations and in this way to leave his mark on the meaning attached to them by Iranian officials and, he hoped, by the wider public as well.[33]

Numerous findings from the Achaemenid and Elamite eras were made at the site, foremost among them Darius's reception hall, known as Apadana.[34] The finding that attracted the most attention was undoubtedly the tablet showing various state ministers arriving from the far reaches of the empire, presenting tribute to Darius, bowing to him, and greeting him (apparently because it was a holiday).[35] The presence of Iranian archaeologists at the site increased toward the end of the 1960s, together with the preparations for the festivities of 1971, when 'Ali Akbar Tajwidi (1927–2017) received funding to continue research there. The regime was not interested in archaeology for its own sake, so it included funding for digs at the site in the budget for the festivities, but Tajwidi discovered immediately following the festivities that his funding was cut off.[36]

Before the twentieth century, visits of Iranian officials to archaeological sites in general and to those of Fars Province in particular were quite rare and sporadic. It was, however, a journey to these sites that caused the intellectual Mohammad Nasir Fursat al-Dawla (1854–1920) to compose *Asar-i 'ajam* (Heritage of the Persians), a detailed description, with illustrations, of some of the sites in the province.[37] At a conference held at the Ministry of Culture in Tehran in 1927, Prime Minister Mohammad 'Ali Foroughi expressed his deep disappointment at the condition of the ruins of Persepolis and the hope that Iranians would do their duty in this matter.[38] One of the first official visits to the site was made by 'Isa Sadiq, an educated young man and a future minister of education and lecturer at Columbia University. His familiarity with Iranian history was heightened upon his visit to the United States, where he met a series of researchers of the ancient Near East. Sadiq later described the excitement that gripped him while visiting Persepolis with Western researchers in 1932 as part of an Iranian mission: "It was the first time I saw Persepolis and Naqsh-i Rostam,[39] and I was awestruck by the size and magnificence of the palace and the pieces of art and a great sense of national pride awoke in me."[40]

From the 1950s on, Persepolis became the official site for foreign diplomats to visit. The regime's growing fascination with this site can be identified by two events initiated by the cultural architects of the Pahlavi regime: the first was an annual event, the Jashn-i Honar-i Shiraz (Shiraz Arts Festival), which included stage performances in Shiraz and its environs, including the ruins of Persepolis, and the second was a one-time event, the commemoration of the passing of twenty-five hundred years since Cyrus's reign. Together, the two events came to symbolize the Pahlavi regime's and its supporters' arrogance and detachment from most of the nation, especially the masses.[41]

The celebrations in Persepolis were preceded by an annual event that took place in Shiraz and the vicinity—the Shiraz Arts Festival, including the archaeological site. The festival included visual arts of various kinds and presented various avant-garde and provocative shows that aroused the anger of both the middle class and students from the right and left.[42] In this way, the site identified with Iran's glorious past also came to be identified with the Pahlavi regime, which a growing part of the populace hated. This identification also explains the Islamic Republic's tendency to neglect the site in the years after its rise to power.[43]

Some viewed the Shiraz Festival as the meeting point of East and West, but others saw it as the collision of the two. Its patron was Empress Farah Diba, and it was directed by Sharazad Ghotbi, the wife of Reza Ghotbi, head of National Iranian Radio and Television, which sponsored the event.[44] A young Iranian student, asked about her impression of the meeting of East and West in the festival and its effects on Iranian culture, answered: "I think we should keep our traditional music the same as it was."[45] This emphasis on traditional music contrasts sharply with the exotic impression created by Iannis Xenakis, a Greek musician who performed in the festival in August 1971, just two months before the celebrations of the twenty-five hundred years of the Iranian monarchy. Xenakis later reported how he was awestruck by the contrast between the ancient ruins and the modern music that emanated from them, assisted by microphones hidden at various points in the ruins, which sounded spectacular to him.[46]

Before this point, though, Shojaeddin Shafa''s idea of a national celebration that would claim continuity between the Achaemenid Empire and Pahlavi Iran had rattled around the corridors of power for many years, while the committee appointed to manage the festivities—a complicated, multifaceted undertaking—suffered from continual personnel changes for no less than two decades. An examination of the committee appointed to manage the festivities in its various forms, from the early 1960s on, reveals the extent to which the highest echelons of the Pahlavi regime and its various extensions were involved in this endeavor. Shafa' himself figures prominently, as do Court Minister Asadollah 'Alam, almost all the cabinet ministers, and a number of army generals.[47] The preparations for the festivities were accompanied by a comprehensive domestic propaganda campaign and a wide-reaching public-relations effort in many countries, especially in the West.[48]

At home, the campaign included a variety of publications such as a special issue of each daily newspaper covering the steps the government had taken to promote Iran's image in the West, a host of articles covering the important periods in the history of Iran, and a survey of the leaders who had changed the history of Iran from the Achaemenid period on. The leaders chosen as representatives of the periods of greatness in Iran were Cyrus the Great, Darius, the Safavid emperor Shah 'Abbas (r. 1588–1629), and, of course, Reza Shah.[49]

As the celebrations were held in Iran, exhibits of the arts and artifacts of ancient Iran were put on display in leading museums around the world, among them the Louvre, the British Museum, the Hermitage in Leningrad, and the Metropolitan Museum in New York. The purpose of these exhibits was twofold: to present "a culture of 2,500 years of Iranian monarchy" and "to put Iran of Aryamehr [i.e., the present-day Iran of Mohammad Reza Shah] side by side with ancient Iran, the Iran of Cyrus, and [the Iran] preceding his appearance in the time of the Aryan tribes."[50] The aim of such exhibitions was to connect the visitors to the past and make them relate to the present because, it was emphasized, the ruins are a link to the modern heirs of this ancient civilization.[51]

Another aspect of the preparations had to do with the ruins at the site. Because these ruins included archaeological artifacts from Islamic periods, it was necessary to remove such artifacts because they could "obscure" the Achaemenid period. When Professor David Stronach, director of the British Institute of Persian Studies in Tehran, went to Pasargadae to attend the ceremonies held there in late 1971, he was surprised. It was evident that all the various small-scale stone remains that had long stood beside the tomb of Cyrus the Great had been removed. Turning to Shojaeddin Shafa', who had orchestrated many of the events held in honor of Cyrus in that year, Stronach inquired about the missing remains. Shafa''s reply was telling in that he admitted that he had "taken care" of the different worked stones that had been placed in the vicinity of the tomb in medieval times, which he felt stood in the way of the Achaemenid ruins and thus blunted the site's message.[52]

Another symbol of the celebrations was the Shahyad (Shah's Monument), built on the route from Aryamehr Airport to Tehran the same year. Rising forty-five meters high, the monument was meant to incarnate twenty-five hundred years of Persian history.[53] Besides the monument's obvious grandiosity, its design was intended to be a modern interpretation of the old architecture of past periods, especially the pre-Islamic periods. The idea behind the edifice was "a need to express in the best way possible the greatness of 2,500 years of Iranian power, side by side with sites of antiquity such as Takht-i Jamshid [Persepolis], Bisotun, Susa, and Pasargadae."[54] Combining Sassanian, Roman, Parthian, and Safavid elements with modern ones, the monument proclaimed the theme of continuity the Pahlavi state wanted to convey to the public.[55] The Shahyad was meant to combine pre-Islamic and post-Islamic architecture by borrowing elements from both.[56] As exemplified in the monument, the tangible connection between the two monarchs, Cyrus and Mohammad Reza Shah, separated by two millennia, was supposed to be yet another expression of the main visual message of the celebrations at Persepolis: the new and the old intertwined, the old empire bringing into full expression the new empire's potential and inspiration.

Writings by Western scholars who admired and praised the Achaemenid Empire, such as Arnold Toynbee and Andre Aymard,[57] were translated into Persian and served a dual purpose: to bring knowledge of historical research to the Iranian reader who had no access to foreign scientific journals or history books and to show Iranians that the greatness of ancient Iran had drawn Westerners' attention. Western attention was yet another element of retrieved glory because it was tantamount to a modern repetition of Greek authors' praise of the ancient Persians. The descendants of the Greeks (at least culturally, as Westerners were perceived by Iranians) were again acknowledging the greatness of ancient Iran, a fact that made it almost compulsory for Iranians to do the same.

The Iranian academy complemented efforts of this kind, rallying around the flag for the events and producing publications ranging from history books to maps and atlases to scientific editions and translations of ancient inscriptions from Iran's archaeological sites.[58] Their overarching theme was that the Achaemenid period represented the highest achievements of Iranian civilization both politically and culturally. The underlying message was the bridging of the Achaemenid period with contemporary Iran, the only period in the country's history in which the achievements of the past could return. All of these publications were in the service of the Pahlavi historical narrative, in which modern Iran represented the values and spirit of ancient Iran, acknowledging its debt to that glorious past and hence paying tribute to it.

The preparations for the celebrations of the foundation of the Iranian monarchy can be divided into two parts: domestically, the festivities were accompanied by indoctrination through every possible venue available to the regime, from schools and youth movements to workers' committees and sports clubs. The Iranian media were flooded with reports about the preparations, their benefits to Iranian society, and the respect the country would achieve with their success.[59]

Ali Ansari has emphasized the strong militaristic aura that surrounded the celebrations at Persepolis: "One may argue that this was the beginning of the relegation of 'militarism' within the umbrella of 'Pahlavism.'"[60] Indeed, the soldiers' parade at the plaza of Persepolis was one of the highlights of the ceremony, but not necessarily the central theme there. The soldiers' parade and the military presence in general seemed to stress the site's place in the history of Iran. This historicization, however, came at the expense of the military as a national icon in the present. Thus, while soldiers marched in the parade, they did it against the background of the ruins of Persepolis and made way later on for the show's climax—the audiovisual performance at the site. We should add to this the fact that during the White Revolution, military terminology was used for essentially civilian purposes. The best example of this practice is the Literacy Corps, in which soldiers taught literacy and principles of hygiene and housekeeping in rural areas to bridge the gap between rural and urban Iran. The recruitment of soldiers for this project was conducted through the military system, and the language used was military, yet the purpose of their service was civilian through and through. Despite their affiliation with the military, the conscripts were, according to Farian Sabahi, "housed and trained apart from regular army personnel."[61] There is no doubt that the Iranian army played a symbolic role in the celebrations in October 1971; however, the military presence was a somewhat archaic one and was overshadowed by other, civilian elements that were considered more useful in "marketing" the ceremonies to Westerners.

The preparations inside the country were accompanied by a diplomatic campaign outside the country that included a fair amount of pressure to secure a list of as honorable and high-ranking guests as possible. Subcommittees took care of advertising and creating public relations for the important event by organizing conventions and exhibitions about Iranian culture in countries as varied as Soviet Russia and Switzerland.[62] The message was adapted to the host country, so that, for example, even though the ceremony at Persepolis had a military character that included soldiers marching in procession, the Iranian embassy's activities in Canada included the combination of scientific and cultural validation of Iran's exotic and glorious past.

Mohammad Goodarzi, Iran's ambassador to Canada, declared during the event that "the history of Iran is more a history of civilization and culture than a history of military conquest and political domination. The Persian Empire . . . was based on humanitarian values of equality and freedom. This idea first appeared in Cyrus' declaration of human rights.

4. Period-costumed soldiers parade at festivities celebrating the twenty-five-hundred-year anniversary of the Persian Empire, Persepolis Tent City, October 1971. Nik Wheeler/Alamy Stock Photo.

Since then, the maxim of freedom for all, regardless of race, skin color or religion permeates Iranian life."[63] To demonstrate this multicultural message, the Iranian government granted four scholarships in Canada to "four children, one from each race—black, yellow, white and red." This variety was explained by the need to "symbolize the values of equality and freedom declared by Cyrus the Great, founder of the Persian dynasty." The symbolism, however, did not stop there—each child had to be exactly twenty-five hundred days old upon receipt of the scholarship on October 14, 1971, at the time of the festivities in Persepolis.[64]

The universal element of the celebrations contradicted the particular nationalist element somewhat, a fact that did not go unnoticed by the Pahlavi educational machine. The regime had to tackle the monarchial element of its own rhetoric, which seemed outdated, and adapt it to modern terms. It did so simply by creating an apologetic discourse, which explained that "the shah is no emperor, and his monarchy [*shahanshahi*] is different from an empire."[65] The state's apologetic discourse expressed the dual message of the celebrations, a message to Iranians coupled with a message to Western guests.

Darius ex Machina

The festivities held on the wide plains of Persepolis lasted for four days, October 12–16, 1971, and consisted mainly of three events: a speech by the shah at Pasargadae in front of Cyrus's tomb, a parade of Iran's armies, and the aforementioned audio-visual performance at night.

Held on the first day of the celebrations, the shah's speech at Pasargadae, whose main point appears as the epigraph to this chapter, included an address directed at Cyrus the Great, who is presumably buried at the site. In this manner, Mohammad Reza Shah declared himself the successor of Cyrus the Great, demonstrating the idea fostered by the Pahlavi historical narrative that under the rule of a strong leader Iran was awakening from its long slumber, in contrast to previous periods in which the state of the monarchy as well of the nation itself was dreadful. This "decline thesis" was a recurring theme in Pahlavi historiography and served as the foundation for the concept of Iranian history in the last two decades of the Pahlavi state.[66] At a convention held two months later in honor of the event, the Canadian historian Roger Savory, who was among the guests at the celebrations—a group that included heads of states, monarchs, and many other diplomats—voiced his deep impression of the shah's speech: "We are celebrating this anniversary because the present Shahanshah of Iran sees himself as being, in a very real sense, the heir of Cyrus the Great and the inheritor of his empire. No one, I think, who was present at the dignified and moving ceremony at the tomb of Cyrus, could doubt this for one moment."[67]

The audio-visual performance that accompanied the royal dinner at the tent site next to Persepolis is perhaps the best example of the essence of this display: a combination of modern technology at an "authentic" archaeological site, the old making way for the new, the power of the present radiating from the site of a glorious past. The sound and light show was received with mixed emotions on the part of some of the archaeologists working at the site because it appeared not "to render due respect to the perspective of that solemn place."[68] The voice of Darius spoke (in French!) from the ruins of Persepolis, while the most sophisticated and powerful light projectors revealed to the guests a site that had come alive. In this presentation, the guests were privileged to hear Iran's past kings talking, inviting them to visit the site, expressing their joy at Iran's glorious present and the even more magnificent future awaiting it. In this way, the shah and his reign were connected to the past in the most tangible manner. Thus, too, the Pahlavi project was tied to technology over the ruins of the empire it presumed to represent. Technology was one of the hallmarks not only of the events in Persepolis but also of the atmosphere surrounding them, exemplified in the effort to light the site at night, a significant task for the production team.[69] Another such effort at juxtaposing the old and the new was a car race, which was planned to pass by the site in the same week as the celebrations. This event was a tour de force of the Pahlavi state's cultural campaign and self-exoticism—combining a modern sport (car racing) with archaeological sightseeing and shopping for traditional Iranian handcrafts.[70]

Diane Barthel has argued that the tension and anxiety caused by the entrance of technology into everyday life are a central factor behind the preservation of historical sites. When the familiar is faced with the risk of being erased by modernity, the need to preserve authenticity is raised. As a reaction, there is a movement toward the preservation and conservation of historical sites. Referring to this reaction, Barthel concludes that "it was in large part a response to industrialization: its social dislocations and discontents."[71] Yet, despite the tension between technology and a yearning for the past that fuels preservation, the Pahlavi project in fact expressed a strong desire to combine the two, to bridge the gap and turn it into a source of strength. The modern was to show its splendor by projecting its light on the past and bringing it to life. Iran was, after all, supposed to be "a show window of the blend of ancient and modern. . . . Side by side with these ruins (of Persepolis), and with other fascinating reminders of our antiquity, are seen countless instances of modern progress," as the shah had put it in his memoirs ten years earlier.[72]

The celebrations themselves, as one can surmise from the national propaganda that preceded them as well as from the reports concerning them in the Iranian media, were a sort of ceremonial rite testifying to Iran's return to glory under the rule of a strong shah.[73] This is clear in how the propaganda and reports relive the historic visit described in the famous tablet at Persepolis, in which the state ministers of the Achaemenid Empire pay tribute to Darius. The historical context of the pilgrimage made by the world's dignitaries to honor the shah at the celebrations was emphasized over and over again, as if to proclaim, "We will renew the days of old." In a feedback loop, the pictures from the event were used in government propaganda to describe the regime's power and to provide evidence that the entire world recognized that power. Thus, the event turned into the reliving of a climactic moment commemorated at the archaeological site and at the same time served as proof of the regime's worldwide legitimacy.

Regarding the audio-visual performance at the celebrations, Talinn Grigor argues that its purpose was "to prove that Iran could and had transcended its 'Orientalist traditions' while remaining true to its heritage. Ultimately, Iran could be, if it wanted, as modern as the West and as ancient as the Orient."[74] However, this part of the festivities had an additional dimension in that it was a self-conscious piece of fiction at an impressive archaeological site, which possibly granted this fiction a completely different depth and capacity. This combination of modern audio-visual effects with antiques from Iran's glorious past as background was the message of the festivities.

The military parade held two days after the famous speech and next to the archaeological site (about ten kilometers from the tomb) was another featured component of the Pahlavi presentation. The soldiers embodied the nation's physical power.[75] The dynasties chosen to represent Iranian history in the parade were the Achaemenids (fourth–sixth centuries BCE), the Parthians (third century BCE–third century CE), the Sassanids (third–seventh centuries CE), the Safavids (sixteenth–eighteenth centuries CE), the Afsharids and Karim Khan Zand (together about fifty years in the eighteenth century), the Qajars (end of the eighteenth century until the rise of Reza Shah in 1921), and, of course, the Pahlavi state.

Hundreds of Iranian soldiers, dressed as soldiers of the dynasties held to be prominent in Iranian history, participated in the parade. The parade clearly represented the continuity being emphasized, showcasing the symbol of national power and strength, the army—the new replacing the old.

This presentation was a visual expression of the "commemorative density" characteristic of the construction of national memory. Dynasties that had ruled Iran for centuries but were seen as non-Iranian—such as the Arab dynasties following the conquest of Iran, the Mongols, and the Timurids (who ruled for about three hundred years)—were omitted because their origins did not fit the modern national presentation. But some very short periods of rule, such as those of Karim Khan Zand and Nadir Shah, who together ruled about half of the eighteenth century, received a place of honor in Iran's history. Thus, the viewers were spared the representations of non-Iranian dynasties as well as of those dynasties that were not able to preserve large parts of the motherland.[76] In addition, the voice of Orson Welles, who read out the text of the whole production, juxtaposed each and every period presented by the soldiers with simultaneous developments in the West.

I believe that the three parts of the festivities symbolized the rationale underlying them: glorification of the monarchy, historic continuity in the form of the armies of various dynasties, and Iran as a body returning to life, a sort of "vision of the dry bones," as mentioned in the Book of Ezekiel

(37:1–14), in the shape of an audio-visual performance. In this way, the past and the present became one, foretelling a great future for Iran.

Research on legitimacy has apparently taken it as a matter of course that state ceremonies are designed to contribute to the positive image of a ruler in his or her subjects' eyes.[77] However, the Persepolis ceremonies in 1971 lend themselves to an alternative analysis. Rodney Barker's view is of particular interest here because it offers a different angle on the phenomenon of state ceremonies, one that does not entail a desperate need to search for their ostensible contribution to the legitimacy of the groups in power or for their intentions to do so.[78]

Barker's theory rests on the premise that politics and government are "self-generating activities, occupations with their own rewards, and their own justifications and legitimations." Therefore, it is wrong to be tied to the need to find a justification for the ruler's activities because, according to Barker, ruling is "a distinctive activity with its own aims, justifications, and culture" and not "solely or principally . . . an instrumental activity." The gist of Barker's argument is that "rulers legitimate themselves in the sight of their subjects. But though they do so in part to impress their subjects, they do so also in order to impress themselves. The self-legitimation of government, and of governing identity, is an activity which appears to have little regard to the views or approval of the larger part of the population."[79] If we adopt this approach, we might be able to eliminate the discrepancies that otherwise emerge when applying the research on nationalism and the role of state celebrations to the celebrations of twenty-five hundred years of the monarchy in Iran. According to Barker's analysis, the audience at which the celebrations were directed and whose hearts they were supposed to win were neither the Iranian people nor the foreign dignitaries who were invited, but rather the Pahlavi elite who planned and attended the events. Lack of access to state ceremonies existed in the Qajar period as well, when official ceremonies were held far from the eyes of the regime's subjects. The great difference between the two periods lies mainly in the sphere of the expectations regarding such accessibility. In the Qajar period, the dynasty's subjects had very few expectations of first-hand contact with state ceremonies because these ceremonies were held within the precincts of the court or palace, and there were obviously no means of transmitting their content in real time to the world outside these precincts.[80] By the time of the celebrations in October 1971, however, such expectations had developed because the event was promoted in public for a long time, including the demand for the presence of workers and schoolchildren in well-orchestrated ceremonies all over the country. Above all, the fact that the celebrations were broadcast on the official television channel, which brought them to many homes in Iran, made ordinary Iranians' lack of access all the more present.

National Glory ex Cathedra

The connection between Western scholars and the shapers of national historiography in Pahlavi Iran began before Reza Shah's rise to power and was prominent in expatriate publications between the two world wars. Articles by Western scholars of the ancient Near East, such as Oskar Niedermayer, Wilhelm Geiger, and Arthur Christensen, adorned nationalist publications in the interwar years.[81] *Kaveh* was a platform for a considerable number of such translations of research on various topics of Iranian history. The scientific platform blurred the line between historical research on Iranian history and the glorification of Iran, a process that had begun in the 1920s and had not stopped since then. This connection between Western academia and the agents of memory in Iran extended beyond the site of Persepolis in 1971. In parallel with the grand ceremony at the site, numerous conventions were held for researchers of Iran in major cities, with Iranian officials, usually the Iranian ambassador, being involved in their organization.[82]

The main conference for the celebrations was held in Shiraz, October 13–16, 1971, where historians, linguists, archaeologists, and researchers of literature from many academic institutions, mostly Western ones, gave lectures. The convention was held under the slogan "the continuity of Iranian history,"[83] and the motif of the "timeless Iranian spirit" was invoked in most of the lectures given. An example of this was the lecture given by Arnold Toynbee, one of the prominent historians of the twentieth century. One of Toynbee's main themes in his analysis of the ancient Near East was the contribution of each empire to world civilization.[84] Toynbee was popular in mass-education media in the West not only for being a great historian but also for the fact that his theoretical views lent themselves to useful adaptation to the historical self-perception of past glory revived in the modern period.[85] It was the deterministic aspect of Toynbee's perception of history that made him perfectly suited to the Pahlavi establishment's needs.

According to Toynbee, empires and the rulers that led them had a historical essence that cut across time and that could be revived and come back to life at any point, despite long periods of slumber. Toynbee was introduced to Iranian readers as "a pillar of civilization" "who has attributed to history a much deeper meaning than a mere collection of events."[86] The most significant part of his historical work concerned "civilization" as a central unit of historical analysis. From the Iranian national point of view, as presented to the Iranian audience, the most important element of Toynbee's thought was that he "had developed the philosophical view which follows the continuity of the creation of civilizations. He has pointed out the essence of the content of those civilizations. In this way, the future of these civilizations can also be determined. Toynbee believes in the essential connection between civilizations and their reincarnation in other civilizations."[87]

It was not the past for its own sake that mattered, but rather the ability to learn from it or even foretell the future according to it because of the recurrence of historical destiny. In a lecture Toynbee gave in honor of the celebrations of Iran's twenty-five hundred years, he claimed:

> The Achaemenian Empire was the first Persian Empire in a series. . . . The second Iranian empire, which the Sassanids maintained for four centuries, was overthrown by foreign conquerors as suddenly as the first Iranian empire had been. Yet the Abbasid caliphate, which was almost conterminous with the Achaemenian Empire, was a resuscitated Iranian empire under an Arab veneer; and the third Iranian empire, which was founded by the Safavis, is the Iran of today.

He then concluded his lecture in the spirit of the day: "It is worth repeating that the first Iranian empire also has relevance for mankind's future.

The tolerant spirit of the founder, Cyrus II, and his successors is the spirit that our present-day world needs in the statesmen whose task it will be to unify mankind on a literally world-wide scale."[88]

Georgi Tsereteli, a Georgian researcher (representing Soviet academia) who lectured at the same convention, emphasized Cyrus's leadership with the following words: "Cyrus' policies and actions were an expression of the social needs of his time and therefore there are grounds to regard him as an outstanding leader of the ancient world." According to Tsereteli, the Achaemenid Empire's greatness stemmed mainly from its ability to control a large area and many peoples while maintaining law and order and justice as well as respecting the various local traditions and customs. Clearly, Tsereteli was attempting to maintain the most harmonious picture possible, as even with regard to Persian and Greek relations he tried to emphasize the mutual cultural influences and not the many wars the two empires waged with each other. In the spirit of Soviet historiography, Tsereteli summed up: "The Achaemenid period was an important period in the historical and cultural development of the peoples of the Soviet Union."[89]

This scientific stamp of approval was an important component of the Pahlavi discourse, and certain researchers were chosen to support the desired theses. Conferences like the main one in Shiraz in October 1971 were held in various academic institutions in Europe and the United States and involved the participation of the local Iranian embassy and experts on the history of Iran.[90] For example, the Iranian ambassador to Canada initiated a conference in Montreal in December 1971. In his opening words, Roland Michener, the governor general of Canada, expressed his views on the relevance of Iranian history to Canada's citizens: "Because our Canadian culture has its main roots in Indo-European civilizations, these studies are relevant and interesting."[91] Professor Roger Savory expounded his view concerning the continuity of Iranian history, reiterating the thesis that Iran had been resurrected:

> We are not celebrating 2500 years of unbroken empire, still less 2500 years of monarchy, with king following king in unbroken dynastic succession. . . . After the Arab conquest, for nearly nine hundred years, Iran

> had no independent existence and was little more than a geographical abstraction, either forming part of a larger unit as the caliphate, or broken up into a number of smaller units. During this period of nearly nine centuries, Iran was subject to the rule of a number of foreign rulers—Arabs, Turks, Mongols and Tatars.[92]

According to these words, it seems Savory was willing to "sacrifice" the thesis of the continuous, uninterrupted history of Iran. He apparently could not bridge the gap in the Pahlavi historical narrative, which demanded recognition of historical continuity yet emphasized the revival of modern Iran under the Pahlavis and thus implying a break in history between the remote past and the present. Even though Savory's account of Iranian history sacrifices one element of the Iranian historical narrative encouraged by the state, it does so in a way that emphasizes another element of this narrative: Iran's reawakening from a centuries-long slumber.

It seems that the academic element of the celebrations was much more than a veneer for the Pahlavi legitimacy efforts. It touched on a deep ethos of scientific objectivity that had been at the heart of the Iranian project of modernity and creation of national awareness from the early twentieth century. Together with the presence of dignitaries from all across the world at conferences and events celebrating twenty-five hundred years of the Iranian monarchy, the theme of Iran at the center of the universe and the recognition of it as the beacon of progress served the Pahlavi elite's self-perception well. This drive for academic recognition and support for Iran's claim to greatness led by the modernists of the early twentieth century and then by the Pahlavi educational apparatus was imbued with a modernistic message that replaced the religious source of (limited) state legitimacy with a secular source.

From Hasan Taqizadeh's translations of the work of leading scholars of the ancient Near East in his journal *Kaveh* to the connection 'Isa Sadiq made with researchers of ancient Iran during his visit to the United States as a student, the Pahlavi establishment came to be deeply influenced by Western historians, archaeologists, and art collectors, who instilled a feeling of superiority in Iranians and a perception of their continuity throughout the ages. The scientific gospel was part and parcel of Pahlavi self-esteem as a guarantor and a tool for the acquisition of legitimacy by the social and political elite.

A Fighting Opposition

To understand the rage that the festivities awakened in many circles of the opposition to the Pahlavis, mainly leftist groups and Islamists, one must view it within the wider context of the alienation of increasingly large parts of Iranian society from the regime, its institutions, and its symbols. This alienation was of concern to many intellectuals, and it caused many of them to seek a more authentic framework for their identity. Among the answers they found were those given in the tapes recorded by Ayatollah Ruhollah Khomeini.[93]

The shah's apparent intimacy with his people, a connection he believed to be so close that he could feel the people in a supernatural way, as he claimed to have done occasionally, turned out to be completely without foundation. According to Anthony Parsons, "the propaganda went to Orwellian lengths to sustain the myth of the Shah's mystical union with his people and to disguise the reality of his remoteness. Television was an invaluable aid to this deception."[94] As in some of the criticism aimed at the festivities by the opposition, which used the comparison of the current regime to more ancient monarchies, so also Parsons, in a somewhat Orientalist manner, saw the shah's separation from his people and his artificial connection with them as the continuation of an ancient Persian tradition.[95]

The facts that most of the guests at the celebrations were foreigners and not Iranians and that the site had been isolated and secured many days beforehand contributed to the masses' alienation from the events. Problematic activities such as the removal of a neighboring village's cemetery added to the negative feelings toward the festivities.[96] The reports generated by SAVAK, Iran's secret police, expose its relentless surveillance of the opposition as well its impressive surveillance of the general public. Its archives are replete with reports of growing discontent on the part of many citizens, mostly of the lower classes, with the extravagance of the celebrations.[97]

The opposition's criticism can be divided into two main areas: one objection common among wide swathes of society concerned the exaggerated expenses incurred by the celebrations while many Iranians lived in poverty, and intellectuals of various political leanings criticized the celebrations mainly as a representation of Western influence and the shah's personality cult.[98] It seems that the further the preparations came along, the greater the alienation to them deepened among both intellectuals and the common people. In this respect, one may see in the growing disaffection a factor uniting educated people with secular and religious people as well as uniting both of these social forces with the masses, who were not foremost among those benefiting from the social-economic arrangements established in Iran at this time. Alienation went hand in hand with the state's growing effort to take over and control the cultural scene by "co-opting intellectuals, closing down newspapers and magazines and establishing cultural councils and inaugurating cultural festivals."[99] These venues and events were meant not only to "revive" Iranian arts, crafts, and culture in general, as they were marketed to the public and guests from abroad, but also to dictate what was performed and by whom.[100] For instance, the Shiraz Arts Festival (started in 1967), born out of an initiative by Empress Farah Diba and reflecting the tastes of the Pahlavi court, mixed Western avant-garde with Iranian folklore. It is beyond the scope of this study to analyze this festival and the performances staged there, but it suffices for my argument to mention that of the six annual festivals in the 1960s and 1970s, at least the one in Shiraz definitely added to the alienation of the middle class, when the clerics moved the public to protest against what they considered to be promiscuous performances there.[101] This sense of alienation should not be limited to a specific incident but rather should be seen in the wider context of rising resentment toward the Pahlavi cultural initiatives during the 1970s. Besides the middle class's lack of connection to the Shiraz Festival, this cultivation of ancient Iran was perceived as Sharqzadeqi, "Eastoxication," no more than a superficial mimicry.[102]

Examples of popular local criticism may be seen in Firuzabad, where SAVAK noticed unrest among the merchants at the bazaar, who complained about the high taxes they had to pay so that a sports hall could be built for the festivities. Low-ranking clerics from Shiraz testified that nomads from the tribes in the area turned to them because of their deteriorating economic situation while the expensive and flamboyant celebrations were being held in front of their eyes.[103]

One official noted that "these celebrations are the most ridiculous exhibition seen in Iran in the twentieth century . . . at a cost of millions of dollars."[104] A truck driver reported hearing a conversation between two villagers about the possibility of a general revolt breaking out as a result of the celebrations. Both estimated that the events would raise the animosity to new heights.[105] Another argument recurring in the criticism was the celebrations' lack of authenticity. The same government official, serving in France at the time, testified: "[Those of us] who live in France [have to] read what they write there in ridicule about these celebrations in various ways: caricatures, satire, pointing out Iran's poverty, the irony in preventing the nation from participating in these celebrations. . . . They express the deep confusion of this country, whose gardens, as the poet wrote, 'are laden with flowers,' yet it imports them from Holland."[106] Such reports are abundant in the SAVAK records.

The point repeated in the words of those opposed to the celebrations was that not only were the masses not invited to the celebrations, but they were also denied access when several kilometers around the area of the festivities were turned into a sterile zone two weeks before the events for security reasons. The paradox in such criticism is evident in the desire to be present at the celebrations and to enjoy the power they project.

Clerics of various ranks also frequently gathered to discuss the spiritual challenge that the celebrations posed with regard to the sympathy they would supposedly create for the regime. However, neither side was assured of winning over the hearts of the people. Therefore, the events served as a catalyst for the opposition groups to the degree that they may be defined as the formative event for the opposition, religious as well as liberal and socialist, to the shah's regime during its last decade. Members of the opposition wrote and dispersed several popular treatises in response to the celebrations or following them. Among them we may count *'Are barodar, inchunin bud* (Indeed, Brother, so It Was) by 'Ali Shari'ati as well as *vilayat-i faqih* (Rule of the Jurisprudent) by Ayatollah Ruhollah

Khomeini.[107] The latter collection of lectures delivered by the future leader of the Islamic Revolution was distributed a short while after the celebrations, the preparations for which accelerated the acceptance of his message. Some eight months before the events, in light of the preparations for them, Khomeini exhorted Iranian pilgrims to Mecca on February 6, 1971: "Let the world know that these festivals and celebrations have nothing to do with the noble Muslim people of Iran, and that all those who organize and participate in these festivals are traitors to Islam and the people of Iran."[108]

The question of authenticity (or the lack thereof) lay at the center of the struggle to win over the hearts of members of the middle class, a struggle conducted between the regime on the one hand and the religious clergy and intellectuals on the other. It seems that the more the regime tried to emphasize its authenticity by external symbols (such as uniforms, setting, and presentations), the more its image was degraded in the eyes of a growing number of social groups, led by the shapers of these groups' consciousness, the religious scholars and the intellectuals.

The celebrations were apparently the last straw in shaping Khomeini's antimonarchic view, a new and unprecedented political aspiration among the ulema. Moreover, they had a great part in shaping both Khomeini's perception of the state and its central role in the indoctrination of society and his negation of the central role the monarchy claimed to have in modern Iranian identity. In a series of harsh sermons against the Pahlavi projects surrounding the celebrations of 1971, Khomeini asked his audience: "What benefit have our people ever derived from such rulers that we should now celebrate and light up our cities? Are we to commemorate Agha Mohammad Qajar, that bloodthirsty savage? Or the monarch who massacred people in the mosque of Gauhar Shad in such numbers that the walls were stained with blood and the gates of the mosque had to be closed so that none might see the spectacle?" In this vein, Khomeini turned to a more general conclusion concerning the Iranian monarchy:

> It is the kings of Iran that have constantly ordered massacres of their own people and had pyramids built with their skulls. Even those that were reputed to be good were vile and cruel. It is related that one such "good" monarch, for whose soul prayers are said, once on the way to

> Shah 'Abd al-Azim ordered a group of soldiers that had assembled about his coach to ask for bread to be strangled with a rope. . . . This was one of the "good" monarchs; the deeds of the evil monarchs one can scarcely comprehend.[109]

Considering the ulema's traditional support of the Crown during the Constitutional Revolution (1905–11) and the rise of Reza Shah, their opposition to the Pahlavi state could be considered one of the most dramatic manifestations of the general opposition. One might argue in this regard that the Pahlavi state efforts were counterproductive and detrimental to its survival and were at the same time a necessary component in the opposition's formation of a new, unprecedented, and radical approach to Iranian history and the Crown's place in it.

But in order to widen the discussion and avoid narrowing it down to the question of the shah's legitimacy, I would like to analyze some of the most vociferous expressions of resentment toward the celebrations. They are important mainly for two reasons: the popularity of these expressions among wide audiences, especially the urban, young, and educated, and what we can learn about the elements contested between the Pahlavi narrative and that of the opposition as well as the elements that were absorbed or infiltrated into the discourse of the national historical narrative, if only unconsciously.

The publications of the Islamic opposition, such as Ayatollah Khalkhali's book *Korush-i doroghin* (False Cyrus), reflect an atmosphere in which radical clerics, especially those of the second rank who were afraid of losing their standing with their flock owing to the Pahlavi propaganda machine, were engaged in a struggle for the hearts of the people:

> It is deeply regrettable that the authorities in Iran know these things and decide to ignore them. They hold the masses mentally backward by brainwashing them. They use every media at their hands, such as radio, newspapers, and television, in order to prevent this nation from waking up and realizing in what a condition they are. [Khalkhali uses the word *bidar*, used by Mohammad Reza Shah and his ministers to describe the "awakening" of the Iranian nation under their rule.] The worst of the

> historical periods of Iran is being "served" to the stricken and deprived masses who own nothing, while they are preparing the celebrations of twenty-five hundred years. Should we celebrate crime, bloodthirstiness, murder, and carelessness? Are those things to be proud of? Is it not tantamount to going backward to the Middle Ages? . . . Those who run this circus, when will they control the minds of the masses?[110]

The foreign involvement in the celebrations, which indeed existed from the planning phase but was made manifest mainly in the presence of foreign guests in this presentation of power, played a key role in the propaganda against the regime. Here one can see a mirror image of what the regime tried to gain from the presence of various world-renowned dignitaries at the Persepolis events. Whereas for the shah the dignitaries' presence was incontrovertible proof of the renewal of Iran's glorious past, this same presence accelerated the alienation of the masses from the celebrations. To this must be added the almost mythical role of foreign intervention in Iranian politics, especially since the shah's return to rule with the assistance of the Western powers in 1953.[111] The involvement of foreign companies and guests in the events was used as the ultimate proof that the celebrations were alien to the true spirit of the Iranian people and that the masses were upset by them.

Beyond refuting the historical narrative describing the Achaemenid period as the pinnacle of Iranian history and the monarchy as its center, Khalkhali's treatise also contains a plea arising from the clergy's real distress. They, the representatives of Shi'i Islam, felt endangered by the rapaciousness of the Pahlavi state, which was leading a national project in which Islam played a marginal role. Khalkhali apparently tried to turn words into deeds in his approach to archaeological remains from the Achaemenid period. According to Ayatollah Majd ad-Din Mahallati, a clergyman and member of a family of clerics, Khalkhali even planned to destroy Persepolis at the height of the Islamic Revolution until he gave up that plan when local residents, led by Mahallati, opposed such a move. Answering a journalist's question on this matter, Mahallati said: "[Persepolis] is the greatest symbol we have."[112] As we shall see, this approach would become more salient among religious circles of the next generation in the 1990s.

Another prominent spokesman against the Persepolis celebrations was ʿAli Shariʿati, the social scientist and thinker, who became a lecturer popular for his ability to combine socialist and progressive views with religious revival. This ability and his captivating character made him into a speaker for a generation of young, educated Iranians who were becoming ever more alienated from the state and the ideology it represented.[113]

In a booklet Shariʿati wrote on the eve of the celebrations, we see another aspect of the criticism aimed at them. The feeling of alienation is clearly expressed here as Shariʿati adopts the cultural weapon used by the regime, pre-Islamic history, for his own protest. *Indeed, Brother, so It Was* is the story of Shariʿati's visit (real or imaginary is not important for our purposes) to the pyramids at Giza in Egypt. Shariʿati uses the pyramids, a symbol of Egypt's magnificent past, to attack the Pahlavi regime's cult of the Achaemenid past and to tell of a dramatic change in his own social views. As part of a group, he listened to the guide recounting the wonders of the pharaohs and the monumental structures that they left behind them. Arriving at the site, Shariʿati was an enthusiastic tourist of the pyramids, as expected of whoever visited the famous site:

> I was deep in this wonder and magic when my eyes fell upon a pile of rocks, slightly touching each other:
>
> "What are these?" I asked the guide.
>
> "Just a pile of stones," the guide answered.
>
> "Just a pile of stones?! I am curious to know what they are," I demanded.

The guide, forced to satisfy Shariʿati's curiosity, explained that the pile of rocks is the tomb of the slaves who built the pyramids: "Thirty thousand slaves carried these rocks from afar for thirty years; many of them died from the weight of these stones."[114]

Shariʿati pleaded and begged to see the skeletons of these slaves, but the guide saw no point in this. Shariʿati lost his temper and declared:

> "I don't need your guidance anymore; I'll carry on from here by myself."
> I left the group and started toward the pile of rocks, where I sat down.

> At that moment I felt a deep connection to the souls buried there; I felt we were of the same kind. And then I felt alienated from all the majesty surrounding the great pyramids. To be precise, I deeply hated and despised the cultures [*tamaddunha'*] that built their empires with the flesh and blood of my forefathers. . . . I returned to the lodgings that day and wrote a letter to one of my many brothers and explained to him what happened to us in the past five thousand years. Five thousand years in which he wasn't present but in which slaves and slavery existed in various forms.[115]

This text demonstrates the process through which a popular lecturer, one of the leading voices of protest to the Pahlavi state, turned his back on official propaganda in general and on the historical narrative it cultivated in particular.[116] The term *tamaddun* (civilization or culture), which was central to the Pahlavi historiographical discourse, receives here the opposite meaning: abusive and exploitative regime. The term *alienated* appears here, too, and expresses many Iranians' feeling toward the celebrations. The fascinating thing about the text is that the author uses a powerful cognitive mechanism of identification with the past until it is felt in the present against the regime and the extensive use that the regime made of this very same mechanism. The author identifies with the slaves buried underneath the rocks, and this feeling bridges the five thousand years separating him from them. Interestingly enough, though, Shari'ati had already proved himself a master at carving out social and political themes, using well-known Islamic symbols such as Zaynab, 'Ali, and Hasan and Husayn. He definitely was a "banker" who recognized the great value that could be earned from using the "spiritual currency" of symbolism, to use Kenneth Burke's terminology.[117]

Shari'ati's criticism fits into the discourse of other Iranian intellectuals who viewed the Pahlavi effort to cling to historical sites as a case of "gathering mummies from the past," as Dariush Ashuri put it.[118] It was a shallow and rootless grasp of history and was therefore tantamount to forgetting that history altogether. Museums, cultural festivals, and art and archaeological exhibits—all were perceived by Iranian intellectuals during the 1970s as westernized forms of analyzing Iranian culture in a way that rendered it irrelevant and detached from the lives of ordinary Iranians. Al-e Ahmad expressed this feeling succinctly in his oft-cited treatise *Gharbzadegi* (Westoxication): "We are all equally acceptable to Westerners, the makers of our machines, as contented museum pieces. We are to be objects of research in the museum or the laboratory, nothing more. Watch that you don't alter this raw material!"[119]

Conclusion

The feeling of alienation 'Ali Shari'ati expressed was closely connected with the main issue with which Iranian intellectuals grappled at the time—the question of authenticity.[120] Negin Nabavi came to the conclusion that "whereas in the 1950s history had by and large been dismissed as irrelevant for the 'progressive' and 'forward-looking' intellectual, now it was considered increasingly important, since it was a time when there was a general vacuum in society. So the past, in the form of cultural and religious values, provided a framework for the understanding of the present."[121]

There was a competition over authenticity between the rival historical themes by which it was felt Iranian history should be represented. The theme of authenticity had several expressions in the publications surrounding the celebration of twenty-five hundred years of Iranian monarchy. I argue that this discourse was not only conducted by both sides, the regime and the opposition (whether religious or not), but also expressed a deep conflict of identity on the part of both sides, especially the Pahlavi establishment. Unlike the political situation, which was resolved by struggle, upheaval, and political power, this conflict of identity was not resolved with the Islamic Revolution and the establishment of the Islamic Republic on the ruins of the Pahlavi state. Rather, it haunted the Islamic Republic, even if it was temporarily subdued during the republic's first decade. But then it resurfaced with the war effort against Iraq in the 1980s and with greater ferocity in the course of the 1990s as the Islamic Republic came of age.

5

Celebrating Iranianness in the Islamic Republic

The Islamic Republic came to the world with a promise and commitment to cross the barrier of nationality, carrying the message of a universalist ideology: Islamic unity. To understand the ideological evolution of the Islamic Republic, one has to turn back to the formative period of the Islamic opposition to the Pahlavi state—the decade and a half preceding the Islamic Revolution. Despite the Sunni–Shi'i divide, Iranian clerics and activists were deeply influenced by the unfolding of relations between the nation-state and Islam in the Arab world. Unlike the inclusion of Islamic undertones in the call for Arab unity, which Arab leaders, first and foremost Egypt's president Gamal 'Abder Nasser, tried to recruit for political benefit and which bore echoes of Arab nationalism, Islamists in Iran could not connect in any way to a message of Arab unity, if only because of the simple fact that they were not Arab. Besides the mere ethnic difference, nationalism in Iran during the Pahlavi years became very closely identified with what was perceived as the anti-Islamic policies of the nation-state and even with the allusion to pagan pre-Islamic cultures performed in some of the state's public events.

To gain a wider perspective on the relations between Shi'i identity and Iranian nationalism in modern Iran, I distinguish between four distinct phases: the late Pahlavi period, especially from the early 1970s to the revolution at the end of that decade; the revolution (1979) and the Iran-Iraq War (1980–88); the 1990s and early 2000s (President Mohammad Khatami's term); and the present. This division is based on the stages of evolution from a supranational tendency, which began during the years of opposition to Mohammad Reza Shah's monarchial project, continues through the years of coming to terms with Iranian nationalism and Persian ethnic identity, and finishes with the embracing of Persian ethnicity and some of its elements. Its culmination is religious appropriation of Persian pre-Islamic symbols in the Islamic Republic, a process that is still in its infancy. This phenomenon is interesting because, as I suggest, it places the Islamic Republic in a wider context with other religious movements in the Middle East that have become more nationalistic in their aims as well as in the symbols and rites they have adopted.

To understand better the trajectory of nationalism in the Islamic Republic, we should consider the late Pahlavi period as the formative period of the Islamist opposition in Iran. Opposition movements, whether acting openly in democratic conditions or mainly underground owing to repression by the state, are deeply influenced by the establishment they wish to replace. The Iranian Islamic opposition during the Pahlavi era is no exception. While speaking in the name of fourteen hundred years of Islamic legacy, the main Islamic opposition ideologues were deeply influenced by the Pahlavi state and by other opposition movements from the left.[1]

Ayatollah Khomeini, 'Ali Shari'ati, and Mortaza Motahhari, three leading ideologues of the Islamic criticism of the Pahlavi state, learned two important lessons from their adversary, distinct yet not disconnected from each other. The first was the importance of the state—or, rather, the nation-state. While these ideologues were preaching Islamic unity, the relevance of the state became ever more evident as the struggle with the Pahlavi regime continued and demonstrated to them the massive power the regime held in indoctrination as well as in coercion and repression. The second lesson came with time and was in fact a ramification of the first: the acceptance of nationalism, with some modifications and adaptations that would suit a state whose role is to realize Islamic ideas. Whereas the first lesson, realizing the state's power and necessity, was learned swiftly (and took place hand in hand with the unfolding of the revolution), the second lesson, the shift in the state's raison d'être, was slow and took shape only in the aftermath of the Islamic Revolution. It developed over time and knew many twists and turns.

During the last decade and a half of the Pahlavi state, the Islamist opposition promoted Shi'i Islam as the overriding ideology and means of achieving the ideal government that would lead to a just society. Khomeini, like other prominent voices of opposition to the Pahlavi state and its worldview, such as 'Ali Shari'ati and Jalal Al-e Ahmad, was also searching for the authentic Iranian experience and its political expression. Indeed, his political answer was a combination of Third Worldist, populist, anti-Western rhetoric, with a religious core of national cohesion. Shi'i Islam belonged first and foremost to Iranians, expressing their authentic spirit, their genuine self. One of Khomeini's right-hand men and Iran's supreme leader after his death, 'Ali Khamenei, distinguished between what he termed "positive" nationalism and "negative" nationalism. The first represents one's natural affinity and loyalty to one's homeland, one's willingness to sacrifice even one's life for it. The second is nationalism as created and used by the Western powers, whose purpose is to divide Muslims and prevent them from uniting.[2]

The evolution of nationalism espoused by the Islamic Republic was originally directed against foreign influence and interests, first and foremost the United States and whoever was identified as its ally (Iraq and Saudi Arabia, to name two nations). It later included certain elements of popular sovereignty. Indeed, the latter was also encouraged by Khomeini's rhetoric, but it was swept aside during the violent process of the institutionalization of the revolution in the early 1980s and reemerged only in the period of rehabilitation following the end of the war with Iraq. While both elements existed in the thoughts and rhetoric of the Islamic Republic even before its establishment, nationalism as a content of political life is still struggling to assert its presence and relevance in the republic's social and political sphere.

The war with Iraq, known in Iran as the Holy Defense, had an important role in the flexibility that the Islamic Republic learned to acquire regarding the ways in which the state can infuse enthusiasm into and demand loyalty from its citizens. In addition to the obvious need to galvanize the masses to the war effort, Iran suffered a great disappointment from its failed attempts at instigating rebellions among Shi'ites in the Persian Gulf, which would have raised the option of pressing Iraq (through its Arab neighbors) to halt its onslaught on Iran. Iran's lack of success in destabilizing the Gulf states by inciting their Shi'ite minorities caused it to divert its war propaganda from religious justifications to national ones. Akbar Hashemi Rafsanjani, Speaker of the Majles, claimed in 1984 that Iran's superiority over its enemies stemmed from national reasons, not religious ones: "We are the greatest nation in the Persian Gulf, greater than all our enemies. Our coastline along the Gulf is longer than theirs, and our resources are greater."[3]

When the moment of a final cease-fire came and with it the peace agreement, which some perceived as a national defeat, Ayatollah 'Ali Khamenei came to the republic's defense by using national arguments: "This is the nation that has stood up and resisted for eight years, fighting with no support but that provided by Allah, against an enemy well assisted. A nation that has stood in the way of a pernicious enemy and defended its homeland, its people, and its revolution. No nation is greater. What you, great nation, have done in the course of the past eight years is a source of great national pride."[4]

"If we look at historical records," Khamenei argued, "and if Saddam were to examine them, he would find out that Iraq is actually part of Iran. Ctesiphon [the Sassanid capital, thirty-five kilometers southeast of Baghdad] belongs to Iran. There are proofs of that. Cyrus's great palace stands in what is today Baghdad."[5] The image of Saddam Hussein in Iranian propaganda is an extreme example of demonization of the enemy as a collective of barbarians. Thus, for example, Saddam was described in one publication simply as an animal. In a poem distributed among the troops, he was called "a wild animal of the jungle."[6] These descriptions are reminiscent of the Iranian historiography of ancient Babylon during the Pahlavi years.[7] There, as we saw, the Babylonian kings were depicted as wild and cruel in comparison to the civilized and benevolent Persian kings.

Although the Islamic Republic and its constitution placed strong emphasis on the Islamic identity of Iran, with the Iran-Iraq War, which broke out almost simultaneously with the collapse of the Pahlavi state, this paramount emphasis on Islamic identity was replaced by a more nationalistic approach. Shahram Chubin and Charles Tripp claim that Iraq on one side and Iran on the other tried to "universalize" the war.[8] Yet another side to the war propaganda becomes clear with hindsight: both Iraq and Iran tried at the same time to nationalize the war and turn it into a cause célèbre for their societies. Neither side spared any symbol, religious or national, around which to rally its population.[9] The war propaganda was a great step toward the nationalization of religious symbols, and all symbols in the war iconography were obviously used for national ends—to obtain control over the Persian Gulf and defeat the demonized enemy of the nation.

Ali Ansari argues that by the end of the war between Iran and Iraq, "the tensions implicit in religious nationalism were being resolved in favor of nationalism." Ansari further argues that this nationalist bent mirrored Iraqi war propaganda against Iran as an "extension of historic Persian/Arab antipathies."[10] Shireen Hunter contends that "in order to rally support for the war effort, the [Islamic Republic's] government had to appeal not only to Islam, but also to Iranian nationalism."[11] Whether this process began as a war propaganda tool and developed into a substantial return to an emphasis on pre-Islamic identity or was a well-planned move is beyond the scope of this discussion and can hardly be proven anyway.

Whatever the explanation, soon after the overthrow of the Pahlavi state, the leadership of the Islamic Republic realized that there was no point in trying to cover layers of Iranian collective memory and identity under an Islamic cloak. This decision might have been the result of, among other things, the local population's reaction to attempts to erase pre-Islamic symbols. Thus, for instance, when Ayatollah Sadiq Khalkhali proposed to raze the ruins of Persepolis to the ground, he was stopped by local tribesmen, who made him realize this would not happen without a fight.[12] Even without having the intellectual depth of research into cuneiform inscriptions, the locals most likely felt respect for the place and had no intention of letting Khomeini's zealot right-hand man destroy the site situated near their villages.

Scholars tend to interpret the nationalist elements in the Islamic Republic's policy making mainly in two ways. One view is that the Islamic Republic, not unlike other revolutionary regimes, diverged from its revolutionary zeal once it obtained power. Mohsen Milani argues that "Shiism became a unifying ideology for uniting all groups in opposition to the late Shah, [and] nationalism may play a similar role against the Islamic Republic."[13] Farideh Farhi adds that what characterized Iranians in the twentieth century is the fact that they "afforded, or . . . produced, more opportunities to recreate themselves in a bombastic and dualistic fashion, energetically vacillating between extremes of contentious Islamism and secularism, pre-Islamic and Islamic imagination."[14] These "extremes," however, were due to meet farther down the road, and that became the state's main ideological challenge.

One should remember the origins of this tension within the Islamic Republic's political elite. Following the overthrow of the shah and then the dispersal of the emergency government, Khomeini appointed Mehdi Bazargan (1907–95) as prime minister. However, barely a month passed before Bazargan realized that the plans Khomeini had for the Islamic Republic differed significantly from his, and so he resigned in March 1979. Hamid Ahmadi proposes that following the withdrawal of National Front leaders from the Bazargan government, "the term 'national' was considered to be non-Islamic and its use was interpreted as an overt act of opposition to Islam and the Islamic regime." He defines the Islamic Republic's foreign policy as one shifting between "contradictory trends regarding the issue of national interest."[15] According to him, the structural dualism embedded in all aspects of the Islamic Republic of Iran is the main reason behind the dilemma of national interest in its foreign policy.

Some scholars suggest that the Islamic Republic's change in attitude toward its national identity demonstrates adaptation and flexibility on its part, proof that it is not blind to public sentiments. David Menashri tries to grapple with this seeming anomaly thus:

> On the whole the Islamic Republic's pursuit of its goals has been based on the ideology of the revolution . . . and considerations of both national interests and those of the ruling regime. Although national interests were alien to Khomeini's general principles and theory of foreign relations . . . his regime nonetheless chose to conduct its regional policy from a perception of Iran's state interests."[16]

Another scholar calls this discrepancy between supranational aspirations and national interests "a dual policy," wherein the logic of state interests and the logic of the revolution coexist uneasily.[17]

Other scholars tend to see the policy changes as an answer to challenges faced by the Islamic Republic, such as the war with Iraq and the tensions with the West.[18] All views, however, take the dichotomy between nationalism and religion as a given. The characterization of a divisive path, however, is due for reevaluation in light of four decades of policy making and cultural activity by the Islamic Republic.

What has been given mythic proportions as a Manichean struggle between contentious or conflicting identities needs to be addressed instead from an Iranian internal context that goes beyond the tumultuous events of the Islamic Revolution, dramatic as they were.[19] The main reason why scholarship explains away the tilt toward a more nationalist policy has much to do with the lens through which scholars analyze and judge the Islamic Republic—namely, that of foreign affairs. However, in order to see "the other side" of the transformation in the way the Islamic Republic has shaped its national interests, one has to turn to its domestic policies. An understanding of these policies, I believe, will shed new light on the way the Islamic Republic perceives itself inwardly as well as on its view toward the region and beyond.

Although the more nationalist policy is often seen as an ideological price the leadership of the Islamic Republic paid for the cooperation and legitimation it needed from the population, I argue that this policy grew from a deep change in the worldview of at least some of these leaders. Rather than conceal the revolution's aims and beliefs, the nationalization of the Islamic Republic expressed the national message of the overthrow of the Pahlavi state. Instead of seeing this nationalization as a change from a state-based ideology to an Islamic-based one, we should see it as a shift in the emphasis on the role of religion in the Iranian national agenda—in other words, as a shift from one form of nationalism to another. Shabnam Holliday has demonstrated this shift as the tension between Iraniyyat and Islamiyyat: the former represents Iranian national exclusivity, the latter its Islamic identity.[20] This political discourse, according to Holliday, expresses the tensions of Iranian identity over a longer period of time, on the one hand, and has ramifications regarding other aspects of public life in the Islamic Republic, on the other.

During its first years, the Islamic Republic tried to erase any remains of the old order, both on the personal level (i.e., the removal and often the mass execution of former officials of various ministries and government agencies) as well as on a public level by removing symbolic traces of the Pahlavi regime, which included changing school textbooks, destroying monuments of the royal family, and renaming streets and squares.[21] However, despite all its efforts at refashioning Iran in an Islamic style, a decade after the outbreak of the revolution it became evident that much about the Islamic Republic was, in fact, national. The shift from a religious focus to a national focus was gradual and yet, in hindsight, decisive. Pre-Islamic elements of Iranian identity were not discarded, as some of the founding fathers of the Islamic Revolution had hoped, but rather were incorporated into Islamic practices and the public sphere.

The Pahlavi state left a deep imprint on the ways Iranian symbols have been perceived and interpreted over the past four decades in the Islamic Republic. Symbols such as Persepolis and Cyrus the Great (and even Nowruz for the more extreme clerics) were identified with Pahlavi self-aggrandizement and the negative memories it had left among many Iranians from various walks of life. This approach, developed in the course of the 1970s in the face of the Pahlavi national-cultural project, was also the impetus for the development of the anti-Pahlavi historical narrative. As noted earlier, this narrative was emphasized in Ayatollah Sadeq Khalkhali's attack on the figure of Cyrus the Great. Although the counternarrative Khalkhali constructed regarding the founder of the Achaemenid Empire ran along pretty much the same lines as the Pahlavi narrative, he reached different conclusions. The conspiratorial element of Khalkhali's analysis regarding the sources on Cyrus (especially the Bible) queried the positive image the ancient king has in these sources as well as any attempt to make him a role model for modern Iranians.[22] However, despite the fact that Khalkhali was prominent among the young revolutionaries who destroyed the old establishment, supervising the execution of the highest echelons of the Pahlavi leadership, his point of view on Iran's historical legacy did not have a lasting effect.

Unlike Sadeq Khalkhali, although Ayatollah Khomeini declared monarchy to be un-Islamic, he rarely attacked the ancient legacy of the kings of Iran. In a rather prudent way, positioning himself as an alternative to the Pahlavi monarch, Khomeini sensed that this legacy did mean something to the masses, and he was concerned mainly with attacking the presumptuous abuse of this legacy by the Pahlavi state. Indeed, in recent years there has been growing interest in Khomeini's relation to the question of Iranian national identity in the Islamic Republic. Rising nationalist sentiments in Iran in the past two decades have sent some Iranian researchers back to Khomeini's writings to locate a source of legitimacy for this trend. Khomeini was vague enough to merit contradictory interpretations of his legacy, giving the Islamic Republic the ideological flexibility that a nation-state as diverse as Iran needs.

Khomeini's utterances regarding national identity at large and its Iranian version in particular leave the hearer (or believer) quite perplexed. At times, he seemed to detest it, as, for example, when he stated, "Those who say, we want to revive nationalism, they are against Islam. . . . Islam opposes nationalism. To say that we want nationalism is tantamount to [saying that] we do not want Islam."[23] On other occasions, he seemed to endorse it. Take, for example, this utterance: "We accept [the concept of] nationhood [*milliyat*], . . . including that of Iranian nationhood, as long as it is within the boundaries of Islam. Islam sanctions Muslim countries [*mamalik-i islami*], and defending them is part of religious commandments [*vajibat*], but not in a way that marginalizes their Islam, and then we hear nationalist tunes of pan-Iranism."[24] As in other spheres of his political philosophy, regarding nationalism Khomeini seems to have left wide room for himself and thence for the next generation of the Islamic Republic's leadership to maneuver.

Moreover, Khomeini was not immune to the somewhat romanticized views regarding a struggle between East and West and Iran's role in it. He shared this dichotomous view with other left-leaning, Third Worldist intellectuals of his time, such as Jalal Al-e Ahmad and Ahmad Fardid (1909–94).[25] The collision between Iran and the West, according to these Iranian observers, was a local case of much greater friction between East and West. On one occasion, Khomeini adopted a rather apologetic tone not easily identified with his thought:

> We need to remind ourselves that we are human beings who also have a place in the world. The East also counts . . . not everything is the West. . . . The East had great treasures and great intellectual weight that surpassed everyone else. . . . Medicine came from the East to the West, civilization went from East to West, but the propaganda is that we are behind the West in everything.[26]

This apologetic tone, rarely attributed to Khomeini, would challenge the Islamic Republic's attempt to overcome the tension between its ambition to represent and export a supranational religious ideal and its need to establish and defend a nation-state, albeit one that is committed to Shi'i values and mores.

Let us now turn to the ways in which the Islamic Republic dealt with the legacy of the regime it came to replace.

Nowruz and *Cheharshanbe Suri*

National festivals are important tools in developing and sustaining national awareness. The rituals that compose a national celebration are the brick and mortar of the socialization of emotions of belonging and sharing a destiny among the members of a nation.[27]

Nowruz, the Iranian New Year, is celebrated in Iran during the week of the vernal equinox, March 20. A reminder of Iran's Zoroastrian past, Nowruz has been celebrated for centuries throughout Asia among various societies, among them Azeris, Kurds, and Afghanis. Yet it has been identified with Iranians and their cultural legacy, mainly thanks to the Sassanids, who founded their rule on the Zoroastrian faith, setting an example of the mutual beneficial services that rulers and priests can lend each other in Iran.[28]

The Pahlavi state cultivated this notion and projected an Iranian-centered image of the holiday so as to establish itself as a modern reincarnation of the pre-Islamic periods. This process included, for instance, an imagined connection between the Achaemenid past, the festival of Nowruz, and the site that symbolized the splendor of that era, Persepolis. Iranians were led to believe in a Gordian knot connecting the three. For instance, Pahlavi writings described a famous relief on the staircase of the Apadana in Persepolis that shows vassals or servants bowing down and bringing gifts to the king (believed to be Darius) as a scene depicting Nowruz, although it is doubtful whether the festival even existed in the time of Darius, let alone that of Cyrus the Great (who, it should be remembered, did not live to see Persepolis).

In its early years, the Islamic Republic tried to discourage pre-Islamic traditions, such as the celebration of Nowruz. Some of the ulema perceived Nowruz as a pagan festival that contradicts the Shi'i values that Iran should stand for.[29] Indeed, its very existence challenged the Islamic opposition's claim to authenticity because it represented traditions that go back to long before Islam's arrival in Iran in the seventh century. As a marker of time, it diminished the break that the coming of Islam was perceived to be and thus also the Islamic historiography of the salvation of pagan Iran. However, with the Islamic Republic's coming of age, there was a shift in the attitude to Nowruz that went hand in hand with the shift regarding other representations of nationalism that the Islamic Republic learned to deal with and eventually appropriate, adding an Islamic coloring along the way.

The evolution of the state clergy's approach to Nowruz is emblematic of the dynamic of leadership–society relations: the clerics were led by the people but later tried to rein in their followers and lend ideological depth to their adjustable attitude. From the mid-1990s, the leadership of the Islamic Republic started to develop the notion that not only is Nowruz *not* repugnant to Islam, but it is also in fact a Muslim festival.[30] This idea was established mainly on the basis of two mutually complementary claims. The first was explicit and depicted Nowruz as expressing Islamic values and hence as essentially Islamic. The second argument was that Nowruz was initially indeed a pagan festival, but with the coming of Islam it was purified and shed its negative elements. Its negative origins have been eradicated, and thus it poses no threat whatsoever. On the contrary, once its pagan components had been stripped away, all the good qualities latent in it were revealed.

This latter strategy, which I refer to as "appropriation of national symbols," characterizes the approach taken by Iranian clergy and lay scholars alike in the past two decades to national symbols from pre-Islamic periods. The Nowruz messages broadcast by Supreme Leader 'Ali Khamenei are filled with patriotic messages in this spirit. Beyond mere patriotism, Khamenei strives to identify the nation with the state. For instance, in his Nowruz speech for 2005, the supreme leader stated: "The state is an agent of the nation, and the nation is the commander of the state."[31] In other speeches, he tried to refute the seeming tension between the national event and the Shi'i faith. His attempts to do so are important in showing both the need to bridge the gap and the theology that emanates from such attempts, which is a stark example of the development of religious nationalism in Iran in the past three decades.

> Islam, when faced with the tradition of Nowruz, was very constructive and creative [in dealing with it]. The enemies of Iran try to spread the false notion that the Islamic Republic is an enemy of Nowruz. But that is obviously not true. To the young people I would like to point out the clever and multifaceted approach of Islam to the various cultures that were prevalent in the countries it entered. Wherever Islam encountered local traditions and rites, it filled them with the right values. Islam did the same to other traditions, like the hajj and the encircling of the Ka'aba [*tawaf*]. It extracted the pagan element within them and filled them with monotheistic elements. The same happened with Nowruz. Islam gave it a human, Islamic, and spiritual dimension and then passed it back to the people.[32]

In this Nowruz message, Khamenei then offered a blessing in which the believer addresses God, asking for a good year ahead. He continued by describing the way different Iranians celebrate Nowruz and tried to set the boundaries of the national in relation to the religious, stating that although many Iranians add a dimension of positive values to their celebrations, for instance by visiting the tombs of Khomeini or other imams, others "adhere to the foreign voices that call them to celebrate *cheharshanbe suri*. Then some go and celebrate Nowruz in Takht-i Jamshid [Persepolis]. It is natural that Iranians would be proud of the great ruins. However, in terms of values, they [the ruins] represent despotism [*taghut*] and [thus are] not something to take pride in. The joy we feel in Nowruz also came from Islam."[33]

According to this narrative, Islam acknowledged the traditions that existed before its coming to Iran and did not wish to wipe them out. It rather strived to purify them and fill them with positive content. Foreigners have emphasized the pilgrimage to Persepolis at Nowruz, Khamenei points out, but in fact most people prefer to visit the tombs of the imams and saints on the Nowruz vacation. In truth, the people choose to celebrate Nowruz in an Islamic way.[34]

Cheharshanbe suri is an ancient rite related to Nowruz. Taking place on the last Wednesday of the year in the Persian calendar, the rite includes the controversial act of jumping over a bonfire lit for that purpose. The rite is probably a remnant of an ancient practice for driving away demons.[35] Another opinion has it that it is a Zoroastrian act of atonement that purifies the soul at the end of the year in preparation for the year that is about to begin.

As noted, the Islamic Republic showed flexibility and adaptability in its relation to Nowruz, as it did regarding other elements of Iranian nationalism. Although in its first years it tried to ban or at least ignore celebrations of the Iranian New Year, it yielded to public sentiment during the 1990s in the aftermath of the war with Iraq and the death of Ayatollah Khomeini. Yet although Nowruz could be accommodated to the republic's Islamo-national weltanshauung, its appendix, *cheharshanbe suri*, was too great an aberration to swallow. Its pagan origin could not be swept under the rug. Between Nowruz and *cheharshanbe suri*, ulema in the Islamic Republic drew the line that distinguishes the legitimate national legacy from provocative pagan ritualism. Among the clerics who expressed their negative view of *cheharshanbe suri* were Ayatollah Makarim Shirazi, Reza Ustadhi (*imam jom'e* [prayer leader] of Qom), and Ahmad Khatami (*imam jom'e* of Tehran). Khatami even tried to attack the foundation of this rite by claiming that "it is not something our nation does," thus dropping the pretense of authenticity adopted by those who practice it.[36]

The accusations leveled at the citizens who participate in *cheharshanbe suri* are reminiscent of the Pahlavi rhetoric toward socialists, Islamists, and pretty much everyone who did not adhere to the Pahlavi story of progress.[37] That narrative praised the authentic but reprimanded chaos and peril to good order. The same arguments are used to throw a negative light on the practice of jumping over the fire. Among the youth, jumping over the fire has become an expression both of maturity and machoism as well as a way to challenge the Revolutionary Guards and the police, who view the rite as a threat to public order. Challenging the state's claim to authenticity, these youths offer an alternative authenticity, one closer to Iran's pre-Islamic past.[38] *Cheharshanbe suri* demonstrates a dynamic of mutual symbolization of the rite on both sides—the state and the masses (especially the youth, who are prone to less-cautious behavior vis-à-vis the state). Both sides have come to perceive the rite as a hallmark of the legitimacy of the Islamic Republic and its cultural agenda. Unlike for Nowruz as a national festival, no Shi'i mantle was used to conceal *cheharshanbe suri*'s pagan origin. It has become another venue for Iranian youth to express their dissatisfaction with the state. In addition to lighting bonfires in the side streets of Iran's cities and towns, some youths throw firecrackers or other easily obtained inflammables to draw police attention.[39] This becomes a cat-and-mouse game that adds yet another dimension to the latent tensions between state and society in the Islamic Republic.

The annual ordeal for the police is far from being a national threat. It is, however, a litmus test of the state's degree of flexibility toward pre-Islamic rites. Moreover, the (repeated) banning of *cheharshanbe suri* by the Islamic Republic has contributed to the rite's emergence as a symbol of resistance to the political order among the youth.

From Khatami to Ahmadinejad: The Return of Pre-Islamic Symbols

The leadership of the Islamic Republic is far from united about the desired way to express Iranian national identity. Although a shift from puritan ultranationalism to a more flexible attitude and finally to religious nationalism is noticeable, this shift did not occur smoothly or with unanimity.

The debate over the desired balance between the different components of Iranian identity came to the fore during Mohammad Khatami's presidency (1997–2005). The tension between the president on one side and the supreme leader and the Revolutionary Guards on the other, which verged on the former's deposition, revolved around more than (just) civil rights and the freedoms of citizens. It also had to do with what Iranian identity the Islamic Republic should espouse and promote. Supreme Leader 'Ali Khamenei began to speak about Iranians' distinctiveness, but he continued to identify that essence with Islamic principles. In the same period, President Khatami, in contrast, criticized the tendency to prioritize the Islamic identity over the Iranian national one. This was yet another sphere of contention between groups often described as "moderates" and "radicals," even though these terms blur the internal Iranian dimension of the conflict. In other words, the question was one of Iranian identity and was reflected in Iran's foreign relations, among other spheres of life, not the other way around.[40] Both discourses of identity in the Islamic Republic, also known as "Islamiyyat" and "Iraniyyat," claimed to represent authentic Iranian existence.[41] The two political leaders, Khamenei and Khatami, continued the struggle that had begun during the Pahlavi period and whose strong repercussions were felt especially in the last decade and a half of its existence.

The tension between the Islamic and the Iranian national identity was not Mohammad Khatami's creation, but he did express it in a manner that had not been voiced previously in the public sphere. Despite Khatami's collision with the conservative elements in the establishment, first and foremost the Revolutionary Guards, his effect was deep and lasting. At least some of his adversaries were convinced of the importance of what he represented for Iranian national aspirations. Ayatollah Khamenei's speeches at national events contained more nationalist messages during Khatami's administration and have done so ever since. This was another proof of the supreme leader's shrewdness and good political sense, true to the legacy of Ayatollah Khomeini, who nominated him to fill that powerful seat. Ayatollah Khamenei defined his worldview on the role of Islam and nationalism in the year 2000. In the treatise he published then, he refers to the uniqueness of every nation that comes to the fore in its culture. Regarding Iran, he states the following: "Islam is the most important pillar of our national culture. Today, the Iranian nation is proud of the fact that after the passage of fourteen centuries its culture, language, and costumes are intermingled with Islam. Islamic culture, costumes, and practices are part of our culture and in this regard are tantamount to being Islamic, and these two aspects never confront each other." The moral revolution that Iranians experienced testifies to the strength of Islam and its inseparability from their lives because "no strong system can create these values and ethical norms in society unless it succeeds in reforming and rectifying the culture and attitude of the people."[42] By "these values," Khamenei obviously refers to Islamic values. Their relevance is explained by their flexibility and adaptability to society.

Interestingly, the notion of civilization, which was so central in the Pahlavi discourse and its vision of the Great Civilization (*tamaddun-i bozorg*), resurfaced rather than being shoveled under and was appropriated by several of the spokesmen on behalf of the state in this period. It was not copied wholesale, though, but rather its emphasis was changed from pre-Islamic elements to Islamic ones, and, more importantly, it tied the latter to Iran's greatness rather than simply raising the banner of Islamic civilization. An important component of this discourse is the notion of a unique kind of Islam—namely, the identification of Twelver Shi'i Islam with Iranian identity. According to this idea, Iran is the cradle of Twelver Shi'ism, if not historically, then in spirit. As we saw in chapter 2, this idea was created by Orientalists during the twentieth century and was embraced by the Shi'i ulema. This national theology paved the way for a more pragmatic and detailed adoption of ideas such as the identification of Cyrus in the Qur'an. Thus, for instance, Ayatollah Khamenei claimed in a speech delivered to faculty of the Qom seminary in 2001: "Without doubt, Islamic civilization is able to enter the arena of mankind with the same method of the great civilizations of history."[43] The supreme leader borrowed the concept of Islamic civilization and contextualized it in a manner reminiscent of the Pahlavi cultural jargon. It might be the feeling of discomfort with his praise of Iranian nationalism that motivated him to offer a distinction between "national identity" and "nationality": "The countries of the world normally stress the concept of nationality [*milliyat*]. Some emphasize ethnicity. What is nationality? It is a collective identity that with its enjoyment, every country is able to use to its own ability for advancement and success. . . . The national and collective identity in our country has an even higher status than nationality."[44]

However, when he wanted to stress the weaknesses of national ties, he preferred to demonstrate it with the example of Arab nationalism. The weakness of national ties among Arabs is apparent. "Arabs stress Arab identity and [Arab] nationalism or Arab ethnicity; first of all, this identity is limited to Arab circles and is not applicable beyond them. Second, being Arab is an existence that does not transcend national ideals that would be relevant to other nations." The authenticity of the Islamic identity is what makes it superior to the monarchial alternative and its historical and cultural content: "The importance of the Islamic system emanates from its roots that were created by the [Iranian] people. . . . [In contrast,] monarchy has one ideology . . . and that is despotism."[45]

In Khamenei's and other clerics' anti-Western rhetoric, one finds echoes of the discourse of authenticity (and criticism because of the lack thereof) from the late Pahlavi period. Consider, for instance, this sentence from a speech by Khamenei: "If the culture, morality, beliefs and convictions of the enemies and aliens are spread among a nation, such a nation, despite independence in political and economic affairs, cannot claim to be independent."[46] Political sovereignty, then, is a prerequisite and a goal of the human pursuit of authenticity.

President Khatami was the first Iranian leader after the establishment of the Islamic Republic to raise the question of Iranian identity and the tensions inherent in it. Although he did this probably in part to serve his political ambitions, he also represented wide sectors of Iranian society, who responded to his call for a reappraisal of Iranian identity and the balance of its components. Branding himself the voice of the younger generation born into the postrevolution reality, Khatami expressed the identity concerns of those who had become culturally lost under the Islamic cloaking of the Iranian public sphere and state ideology.[47] Khatami tried to pave a third way that did not exclude either the Islamic pillar or the Iranian pillar of identity, rejecting the notion that such a separation is even possible: "There is still the wrong image that we have to split between being Iranian and being Islamic. On the one hand, people have said that we must focus on Islam and take away being Iranian; on the other hand, many have

5. President Mohammad Khatami visits Persepolis, January 2001. Photograph by Atta Kenare, AFP, Getty Images.

claimed that to be Iranian we must take away Islam. Both these [options] are a mistake and a digression from the true way."[48] It is no coincidence that this dramatic change in point of view, even if only to make public what was a common opinion when expressed privately, was done by a politician who was also a cleric. Room to maneuver turns out to be greater in this matter, as in others, when the speaker wears a turban.

Khatami's legacy in this respect is coming to terms with Iranian nationalist inclinations on the part of (some of) the leadership of the Islamic Republic. Surprisingly, some of the politicians often labeled "radical," such as Mahmud Ahmadinejad, followed this line.

However, the discourse of Iraniyyat, which was identified with President Khatami and his assistant Mohammad 'Ali Abtahi, should not be regarded as the Islamic Republic's simple succumbing to Iranian nationalism à la Pahlavi. The two political leaders tried in fact to give Islam its due role in the development of Iranian culture and identity. However, what they actually did is to acculturate Islam—in other words, to perceive Islam as a cultural artifact, one of several, of Iranian identity. Put differently, Khatami both shaped and expressed the idea that would become the hallmark of the Islamic Republic: that Islam is part of Iranian culture, of its civilization, much more than it is an entity Iran is to be defined by. The difference, though merely theoretical at first glance, is in fact critical and implies a cohesive Iranian existence outside the framework of Shi'i Islam. Moreover, it touches upon the question Ayatollah Motahhari was grappling with and his conclusion that Iran served Islam more than any other culture had. Here this conclusion was turned on its head to mean that Islam has served Iran more than any other element in its history.

The Iranian national discourse under the Islamic Republic from the late 1990s included another element: the Iranian diaspora. After being immersed in its own affairs for the first two decades following the revolution, the Islamic Republic started to pay attention to this important resource of national empowerment. This happened at the same time that the republic's leadership changed its attitude to Iranian festivals such as Nowruz. This timing is no coincidence; the celebration of such festivals is common to all Iranians, whether living in Iran or living outside the country, whether devout Muslims or religiously unaffiliated, whether belonging to the Shi'i majority or to the religious and ethnic minorities.

It is no wonder, then, that it was Mohammad Khatami who was also the first to bring into the open the need to develop a more nuanced approach to both the Iranian diaspora and Iran's pre-Islamic heritage. Both, the former in particular, are tightly linked to Iran's standing in the world.[49] Because most of the Iranian diaspora live in the United States and Europe, there is a dire need to lessen the tension between Iran and the West in order to awaken the ties between Iranian expatriates and their homeland. Moreover, to keep Iran relevant to expatriates, it is important to cultivate their Persian ethnicity because that is more likely to bridge the differences with Iranians who are not religiously affiliated, let alone devoutly observant. In a rather rare reference to this sensitive topic (after all, expatriates are people who chose to live elsewhere, a fact that challenges the claim to a model society that the Islamic Republic has aspired to present), President Khatami declared in 1997 that "it is our duty to maintain links with those of the same motherland resident outside the country. . . . I hope that this link takes place especially with the Iranian youth who are born and grow up far from the motherland."[50] Coming to terms with a large expatriate community is, indeed, part of the Islamic Republic's realizing the limits of its own promises and claim to religious perfection. It is yet another facet of its coming to terms with its "normal" existence. The Islamic Republic does not speak with one voice in this matter, as in others. Competing historiographical voices offer different points of view, including one that resembles Khomeini's antinationalist worldview in its most extreme form. Thus, for example, the historian Nasser Pourpirar claims that Iranians have nothing to be proud of in the Achaemenid past or in any other pre-Islamic dynasty, for that matter. According to Pourpirar's antinationalist narrative, not only is pride in the pre-Islamic past false, but even the figures in the periods after the coming of Islam that nationalist historiography elevated, such as the canonical poets Ferdowsi and Sa'adi, were nothing but lackeys of corrupt kings.[51] Veneration of them was due to foreign elements who infiltrated Iranian historiography. For Pourpirar, the Jews are to blame for that infiltration, whereas for Amir Ne'mati and Dariush Ahmady it was Communist thought that cultivated such ideas.[52]

Toward the end of 2010 and beginning of 2011, President Mahmud Ahmadinejad faced a wave of criticism from political rivals, this time including some conservative members of the Majles. Mohammad Reza Bahonar warned of the serious consequences of a call made by Isfandiyar Rahim Masha'i, Ahmadinejad's chief of staff, for the recognition of a unique Iranian school within Islam: "The next provocation [*fitna-yi ayanda*] that rises like a wave comes from within the ranks of the conservative camp," warned Bahonar, "yet it receives no support or legitimacy from the madrasas. This provocation is in the making, and the talk about an Iranian school of thought . . . is one step in this direction."[53] Mohammad Tavakoli, another conservative member of the Majles, complained that the president was advocating for a nationalistic Iranian worldview (Irangira'i) in a manner that could call into question the Islamic Republic's devotion to the Islamic ideals of the revolution.[54]

6. President Mahmud Ahmadinejad and his staff inspect the Cyrus cylinder, Tehran, October 2010. Photograph by Atta Kenare, AFP, Getty Images.

Regardless of whether Ahmadinejad had in fact changed his worldview or was merely using the national banner as an asset in his political struggles, the shift in attitude toward pre-Islamic symbols by a politician well aware of public opinion is telling. Two events that occurred at the same time triggered the alarm expressed by conservatives in the Majles and might shed some light on the symbolic expressions of such efforts. The first was the warm and official welcoming ceremony for the Cyrus cylinder, brought to Iran for exhibition from the British Museum on September 11, 2010.[55] The arrival of the cylinder, which was preceded by a long debate and tension between the British Museum and Iranian authorities, was followed by a formal and well-orchestrated ceremony that included a speech by Ahmadinejad in which he referred to Cyrus as the godfather of all *basijis* (young recruits to the auxiliary militia of the Revolutionary Guards) in Iranian history. To add insult to injury, as noted in chapter 3, the president also referred to "twenty-five hundred years of Iranian history" in his visit to the National Museum in Tehran,[56] a reference reminiscent of the

Pahlavi obsession with Cyrus the Great and his founding of the Achaemenid Empire. The second event to alarm conservatives was the Nowruz ceremony at Persepolis in March 2011, the first state-sponsored ceremony at the site since the fall of the Pahlavi state and the establishment of the Islamic Republic.[57] Celebrations of this kind, according to Tavakoli, could distance Iran from its fellow Muslim countries.[58] The harsh criticism with which these ceremonies were received draws attention to the ways in which the use of history to gain state legitimacy in Iran can be a double-edged sword.

The state stands between a rock and a hard place in this regard, between the more conservative elements in the religiopolitical establishment and the nationalistic trends among the public. Whereas the conservatives protest against what they see as a dangerous nationalist trend, the crowd that gathers at Pasargadae every year on Nowruz is a good example of the demand for more national pride. A couple of hundred people perform the Nowruz rites, spread the famous *haft sin* (seven symbols that begin with the letter *sin*) on a mat in front of the tomb of Cyrus, and celebrate by the site that symbolizes the greatness of ancient Iran. Celebrating Nowruz next to the tomb of Cyrus the Great suggests an alternative foundation of affiliation than the one cultivated by the Islamic Republic; namely, Shi'i Islam. What instigated this "invention of tradition," to use Eric Hobsbawm and Terence Ranger's term, was the struggle in 2004 over the building of a dam that endangered the topography of the surroundings of Pasargadae and the tomb of Cyrus the Great (an issue I discuss further later in this chapter).[59]

It is no wonder that demands for a new memorial day in the Iranian calendar in commemoration of Cyrus the Great were heard in Iran at that time. Cyrus Day is another invented tradition that has made its way into the Iranian calendar, though unlike Nowruz it has yet to receive full recognition by the authorities because it lacks the historical depth Nowruz enjoys. Some Iranians celebrate the festival commemorating Cyrus's entrance to Babylon in the aftermath of its conquest on Aban 7 (October 29).

Ruz Korush-i Bozorg (Cyrus the Great Day) was introduced in the early 2000s and has been gaining momentum ever since. It began with a crowd gathering around the tomb to honor the ancient king believed to be buried there.[60] In recent years, it has become a rally of a few thousand people heading toward Pasargadae on the designated date, causing traffic jams on the single-lane road leading to the site. Beginning from a grassroots initiative, the idea of establishing a day in honor of Cyrus was promoted by Isfandiyar Rahim Masha'i, President Ahmadinejad's chief of staff.[61] Masha'i headed the Sazeman-i Miras-i Farhangi, Sanaye Dasti va Gardshegari Iran (Iran Cultural Heritage, Handcrafts, and Tourism Organization), a role he filled in an activist way, promoting controversial initiatives that the ultraconservatives regarded as too nationalistic.[62] Another partner in the promotion of Cyrus the Great Day was the Department of Literature at Tehran University, which launched the exhibit *Cyrus Day around the World* in 2001. The students' association of the same department held another exhibit in 2003, sounding a clear call to establish a day in honor of Cyrus.[63] Archaeologists, historians, and scholars of classical literature who attended these exhibits cum conferences added an intellectual dimension to the demand to allocate a day in honor of the founder of the Iranian state to the calendar.[64]

In hindsight, the Ahmadinejad administration's attempt to promote the gathering at Pasargadae might be seen as a last-ditch attempt to gain control of a national day in the making, knowing that it had the potential to become a day considered hostile to the Islamic Republic. In fact, some of the characteristics of the gathering by Cyrus's tomb, such as the slogans the crowd recites there, reveal its subversive nature. For instance, in 2016 the crowd numbered several thousand, and the police were alert to any signs of disorder the rally might take.[65] And, indeed, such disorder did occur. The chants of the crowd were mostly in favor of freedom as well as against Iran's involvement in the affairs of Arab countries: "Neither to Gaza nor to Lebanon, I dedicate my soul to Iran alone."[66]

The rally held in 2016 draws on the Pahlavi legacy in another way: it brought back to the surface the dual message derived from the figure of Cyrus. While the chanting of Iranian nationalistic slogans, often with an anti-Arab component, occurred, members of minority groups, such as Arabs from Khuzestan and Kurds, came to remind the crowd of the legacy of tolerance that Cyrus endowed the world.[67]

The State of Archaeology in Iran Today

Cyrus and the Achaemenids have been the stuff of both semiacademic and pseudoacademic publications in Iran in recent years. Their rising popularity notwithstanding, the cultural and especially the religious gap between ancient and modern Iranians seems to have posed a challenge to the latter when dealing with the ancient dynasty. Here, too, the Pahlavi period and its efforts at instilling pride, verging on worship of the Achaemenids, left a mixed legacy. On the one hand, the ancient empire's identification with the Pahlavi era, epitomized in the shah's ostentatious proclamation in front of Cyrus's tomb during the celebrations of twenty-five hundred years of Iranian monarchy in October 1971, connected the Achaemenids with self-aggrandizement at the expense of the people. On the other hand, as we have seen in the example of Cyrus and his appearance in the Qur'an, the Pahlavis left a deep imprint, both intellectual and symbolic, that sought to reassert itself beyond what the shah and his repressive state institutions could have wished for regarding Iranians' view of their ancestors.

An important element in this process of familiarization of the Achaemenids is the question of their religious beliefs. As we saw earlier in the case of Cyrus as Dhul-Qarnayn, many modern Iranians want to see the Achaemenids and Cyrus as precursors of Shi'i Iran, glossing over the cataclysm of the Islamic conquest of Iran. To do so, they have adopted the view (which some scholars find disputable) that the Achaemenids were Zoroastrian. To that they add that Zoroastrianism is monotheistic, which brings the desired conclusion, according to them, that the Achaemenids were not pagans. Interestingly, this narrative, which has become popular in recent years, has been part of the quietist appropriation of the religious-national story of the Islamic Republic, together with the acceptance of the pre-Islamic legacy of the Achaemenids. It is yet another aspect of the balance that Iranians seek between what has too often been described, both in Iran and outside its borders, as two mutually exclusive historical narratives.[68]

Indeed, researchers of Zoroastrianism have contributed, often unknowingly, to the Iranian national aspiration to make Zoroastrianism compatible with monotheism. The attempts to delineate Zoroastrianism along Western notions of religious classification include "monotheistic dualism," "dualistic monotheism," or simply "a particular form of monotheism."[69] We thus get a chain of assumptions that bring about the desired conclusion that Cyrus and the Achaemenids were monotheistic. This conclusion bridges over what otherwise would be hard to elude—the watershed event in Iranian history, the coming of Islam. The existence of such a "chasm" between the pre-Islamic and the Islamic eras in Iranian history challenges the presumption that the Islamic Republic represents both Islamic ideals and Iranian authenticity.

The change in attitudes toward the divide between pre-Islamic periods and those that followed the coming of Islam has found expression in contemporary historiography in Iran as well. Publications that challenge the historical narrative of the Islamic Republic are no longer a rare phenomenon. One such publication is *Dar sarashib-i suqut* (The Steep Fall) by Korush Salihi. Salihi analyzes the reasons for the fall of the Sassanids and the conditions that enabled the Arabs to conquer Iran. On the first point, he tends to agree with ʿAli Shariʿati and other Islamist thinkers who wrote about the topic that there were fractures within Sassanid society and as a result a lack of resilience in the face of the Muslim onslaught. However, regarding the other topic, Salihi makes some very bold assertions, and his conclusions are quite different from that of earlier Iranians who wrote about the divide between pre-Islamic and Islamic Iran and who supported the Islamic Revolution: "It seems, at first glance, that the Islamic conquest of Iran ushered in a completely distinct period that has nothing in common with the one that preceded it. Yet a deeper look reveals a more nuanced picture, with a large degree of continuity."[70]

Far from espousing the ideal view of the Muslim conquest being due to religious zeal and purity, Salihi claims that it was a strategy aimed at avoiding internal conflicts and directing the Arabs' violent energy outward against foreign enemies, specifically the nonbelievers. He goes on to challenge the image of early Islam by asserting that many among the first converts to Islam were indeed driven to convert (or to pretend to do so) for political, economic, and social reasons, not out of religious conviction. In a sarcastic way, Salihi points to the clever logic behind the doctrine of jihad: "You end up in one of two ways, either a martyr in heaven or the owner of stock and plunder."[71]

What seemed like Muslim devotion—that of Abu Sufyan (580–650 CE), for instance—was in fact political and social acumen on the part of the converts, who acknowledged the new reality created by the rise of Islam. Salihi challenges the narrative promoted by Islamist ideologues on more than one level. Not only does he question the Muslim conquerors' religious motivation, but he also does so while paying homage to the anti-Arab rhetoric of Iranian nationalists of the nineteenth century. Early Islam, according to him, reflected the Arab mentality and proclivities to a large degree, more so than the Prophet Mohammad's ideas and decrees. To top off his challenge to the standard view, Salihi uses Third Worldist jargon to describe the Islamic takeover of Iran. The movement of Arabs into Iran should thus be considered colonization (*kulunisazi*) and their influence on the territories to which they immigrated as a setting out to "Arabize" ('Arabi kardan) them.[72]

Despite suffering from neglect and even hostility in the wake of the revolution in 1979, archaeology has regained some of its prestige in the past two and a half decades. As noted earlier, during the revolution Ayatollah Sadiq Khalkhali even toyed with the idea of razing Persepolis to the ground. Although one could argue this wish had to do with the identification of the place with the previous regime and its monarch more than with its direct historical association, it was also no doubt a historical statement of disgust and negation of Iran's pre-Islamic past. The ruins of Persepolis symbolized this past and hence were supposed to pay the price for that past's crimes.[73]

Since Khalkhali's attempt to ruin Persepolis, however, there has been a dramatic change in the Islamic Republic's attitude to archaeology and archaeological sites. The Islamic Republic not only has avoided harming pre-Islamic sites but has also encouraged archaeological teams to dig in Iran once more, after about a decade of neglect that followed the events of 1979.[74]

Two incidents in recent years demonstrate the nationalist color the Islamic Republic has taken on in its state policy. Both involve national symbols: one a rather abstract one, the map of the region, and the other a tangible one, an archaeological site.

In his classic work *Imagined Communities*, Benedict Anderson shows the political significance of maps in educating the public to awareness of a territory as a political entity. Firoozeh Kashani-Sabet explores the role of imagery of the Iranian motherland and its embodiment of the nation during the nineteenth century.[75] The political vicissitudes and flux of Iran's borders and the political importance attached to them in modern history have resurfaced in periods of national struggle against a foreign enemy, be it Britain, Russia, or Iraq. The importance and political sensitivity of the map of Iran and the names thereon emerged in December 2004. In an incident that lasted a couple of months, the Islamic Republic of Iran banned the distribution of atlases and expelled all journalists working for the prestigious publication *National Geographic*. The reason for this measure was the magazine's publication of an updated atlas of the region in which under the name "Persian Gulf" there appeared in parentheses its alternative name: "Arabian Gulf."[76] In addition, three islands—Abu Mussa and the Tunb Islands—were labeled as "currently occupied by Iran," to the great dismay of the Iranian authorities and public.

The controversy evoked harsh reactions from Iranians, mainly those in the diaspora. Mohammad Ala, an Iranian-born business professor at California State University, stated: "We have a lot of positive things in Persian culture, and we want to preserve it," adding in a somewhat defensive tone, "Our history is 7,000 years old," and arguing that even the Prophet Mohammad spoke of the Persian Gulf.[77] Internet blogs took a somewhat more violent tone. Apadina Abbaspour, an Iranian blogger, described the renaming of the area as "spitting in us Iranians' faces! This is you people trying to change and alter history and what is written down for generations!"[78] Yet another young Iranian wrote on the same Internet site: "It is a shame to see what once was a respected journal turned into a political backroom wheeler and dealer and an Arab slave." He also offered an explanation for the conspiracy behind renaming the region: "The reason is due to the fact that the Saudi royal family owns a large amount of shares in all US media and journals."[79]

An entity calling itself the Iranian National Front USA published a message that read: "The enemies of Iran should know, so long as there is one Iranian alive with blood pumping through his or her heart, even the thought of taking one grain of Iranian soil, will strongly be opposed and defeated. Long live Iran!"[80] Among Iranian émigrés, resentment and anti-American feelings were mixed with anti-Arab ones, as articulated in the words of Professor Mojtaba Aghamohammadi of Phoenix University: "History is not a commodity you buy at Walmart and discard after your immediate use of it. Iranians identify existentially with the name 'Persian Gulf,' and when you mess with people's identity, that's when war begins."[81]

In response to these outraged reactions, Allen Carrol, chief cartographer of *National Geographic*, explained the dual name given to the gulf: "We did not want to change the name, but we also did not want people to go to our atlas looking for 'Arabian Gulf' and not find it." In another interview, he stated that the policy of *National Geographic* is to name places as they are called de facto, and it is a fact that some countries in the region do call this gulf the "Arabian Gulf."[82] In retaliation, a group of Iranian bloggers created a link that would be the first to come up when someone searched for "Arabian Gulf" in Google and would take the searcher to a page that read, "The gulf you are looking for does not exist, try Persian Gulf."

The Islamic Republic banned both the distribution of the offending atlas and *National Geographic* journalists visiting the country until the "mistake" was corrected. Mohammad Husayn Khushwakht, in charge of public relations at the Iranian Ministry of Foreign Affairs, expressed the hope that *National Geographic* would correct this shameful and embarrassing mistake as quickly as possible. Under pressure, the magazine published a new version of the atlas with the name "corrected" to "Persian Gulf" with no parenthetical addition.[83]

Maps and names of places are one sphere where loyalty to national symbols has been demonstrated in the Islamic Republic. Another is the return to sites that symbolize the grandeur of ancient Iran. One such site is Pasargadae, where the tomb of Cyrus the Great is located. Recent years have seen gatherings of Iranian citizens in Pasargadae by the tomb of Cyrus, both on Nowruz and on the commemorative innovation called Cyrus the Great Day, discussed earlier. These gatherings draw inspiration from the site and carry latent political disaffection with the powers that be in Iran. In 2008 the gathering culminated in a riot, a mixture of anti-American emotions against the backdrop of the rising pressure of sanctions on Iran as well as antigovernment protests against the policies of the Islamic Republic and what it represents. "Cyrus is our father," some cried, while others chanted rather more nationalistic slogans of Iranian superiority. The rallies at Pasargadae are not a confrontation of two camps, then, but rather a debate between different perspectives regarding Iranian identity in contemporary Iran.

In 2004 UNESCO declared Pasargadae, including Cyrus's tomb, a World Heritage Site, a fact that put the site, which had been quite in the shadows since the downfall of the Pahlavi state, in the spotlight.[84] Interest in the site was also increased by the plan made public during the same year to build a dam near the town of Sivand in order to improve irrigation in the area. Yet it was known that the dam, whose building had been planned a decade earlier, could endanger the tomb's very existence because of the chance of accelerated processes of flooding and erosion of the stones at the site.[85] The Iranian media and public were split over the threat the planned dam would pose to the archaeological sites of the tomb and its surroundings. Diaspora Iranians took an active part in the struggle to save the national site. Enjoying more freedom of speech and easier access to the Internet, they were in a position to raise the issue to a higher national priority within Iran. The sensitivity of the Sivand Dam controversy was evident when anyone who tried to allay the fears of the site's destruction was accused of lacking in patriotism.[86] Because the opposition to the building of the dam was reinforced by Iranian expatriates, the issue formed another example of the intricate and multifaceted relationship between the Islamic Republic and the Iranian diaspora. It emphasized to the Iranian leadership the need to keep up a constant dialog with Iranians abroad in order to avoid the embarrassment they could cause Iran's claim to a nationalist agenda. It is no mere coincidence that during the same period President Ahmadinejad and his chief of staff, Masha'i, were seeking ways to tighten relations with diaspora communities and advocating a more nationalist stand in rhetoric and ceremonial activities.[87] It was at this time that Ahmadinejad promoted the idea of a celebration of Nowruz at Persepolis, to be attended by representatives from Iran's neighbors, such as Azerbaijan and Tajikistan.

The thawing of relations between Iran and the West leading to the nuclear deal of July 2015 raised expectations of widening cooperation between the Iranian archaeological authority and its Western counterparts. The fact that archaeological sites have become the venue for official receptions and visits is another indication of their rising importance once again. Besides the dynamic of nationalization of the Islamic Republic, the issue of Iran's foreign relations plays a significant role in the rehabilitation of archaeological sites, even if indirectly. Iran's archaeological sites are ideal for showing to diplomats, whereas Shi'i shrines are more problematic for those kinds of visits because some of them are houses of learning and sites of pilgrimage for ordinary Iranians and hence are harder to guard. The thorny issue of impurity (*nejasat*) complicates things further, and Iranian clerics may not welcome such visits.

One of the signs of growing awareness of pre-Islamic Persian identity was the activity of the Bunyad-i Fars Shinasi (Fars Studies Foundation). In 1996 this organization held a two-day conference titled "Fars: Mahd-i Tamaddun-i Bozorg" (Fars: Cradle of Civilization), an academic platform for debates on the Fars Province's contribution to Iranian civilization. Indeed, many have seen Fars as encapsulating the spirit of ancient Iran. Many cultural events in the Pahlavi period were centered around the province, first and foremost the Shiraz Arts Festival held in that city and at the archaeological sites to its north between 1967 and 1977.[88] Encompassing both the archaeological sites from the Achaemenid era as well as Shiraz, the hometown of two of the most famous Iranian poets, Sa'adi and Hafez, Fars became the showcase of Iranian culture in the Pahlavi period and has returned to this role since the mid-1990s. President Ahmadinejad tried to revive something of Shiraz's official status with his idea of holding an official ceremony there in 2011, a suggestion that alarmed the conservatives in the Majles, who saw it as a desecration of Islamic values and the achievements of the revolution.

One of the revolutionary demands of the Islamist opposition to the Pahlavi state was that the institution of the monarchy be abolished, so it is particularly interesting to examine the ways in which school textbooks of the Islamic Republic deal with Iran's monarchial past. It should be remembered that in no time before the revolution did the ulema demand the removal of the monarchy as an institution. As late as 1921, in fact, they seemed to have been behind the preservation of this institution, when Reza Khan was contemplating the idea of turning Iran into a republic with the removal of the last Qajar king.[89] Interestingly, the historical narrative Iranians have learned in the Islamic Republic, as reflected in Ministry of Education textbooks, has enhanced national pride while rejecting the monarchial system. To accomplish this, these textbooks distinguish between the Iranian nation and the kings who ruled them for centuries. The ulema are designated a special role in this social chasm as representatives of the genuine spirit of the nation, while the kings are characterized as aloof and detached.[90] This depiction of the social dynamic in Iran builds up the ulema as protagonists in the dramatic overthrow of the corrupt institution of the monarchy, which culminated in correcting the monarchs' deficiencies by eliminating the system of government they headed.

History textbooks educate Iranian children to have pride in the Iranian empires, especially the Achaemenids, the Parthians, and the Sassanids. Although not with the same tone taken in textbooks of the Pahlavi era, these textbooks, including maps describing the vastness of the ancient Iranian empires, instill in young Iranian pupils the idea of a large and well-ruled empire. For instance, the Olympic Games, an ancient legacy usually attributed to ancient Greece, are described as having Iranian origins as well. According to a school textbook for fifth graders, at the same time that the Olympic Games were held in Greece, some twenty-five hundred years ago "ancient Iranians taught their children horsemanship, archery, and polo."[91] Beyond the appropriation of what is often perceived as a Western cultural legacy, the importance of this text is in the need it shows to create such a connection between modern Iranian pupils and their ancestors who lived "twenty-five hundred years ago" (a round number also derived from the Pahlavi era).[92] A recurring theme in the teaching of various dynasties that ruled Iran is the search for the reasons of their downfall, which usually stresses the separation of the king and his court from the masses. According to one fourth grade history book, for instance, from the Achaemenid Darius to the Sassanid Yazdgerd III, Iranian kings were not in contact with their people, were not aware of their plight and difficulties, and hence were removed from their thrones with relative ease when a threat from the outside appeared. Iran's weakness in the face of a foreign invader is consistently attributed to the ruler's alienation from the people.[93]

In describing the context of the Arabs' conquest of Persia, one textbook refers to Iran's chaotic conditions toward the end of the Sassanid dynasty and the people's dissatisfaction with oppression and abuse by the state:

> At this time, Muslims who had a strong and firm belief in God and were fighting for the expansion of Islam, fought against the Sassanid military and were able to conquer the capital of the Sassanid government. . . . The people of Iran who had become tired of the Sassanid kings' years of tyranny and oppression, and had heard Islam's message of salvation and justice, began a new era by accepting Islam.[94]

The text describes the Arab invasion as salvation for the Iranian people and the encounter between the two groups as a conflict between the "Sassanid military" and "Muslim soldiers," thus avoiding the alternative view of the war as one between Iranians and Arabs. Based on students' accounts of the encounter, however, it seems that the textbook has failed to convince them. In fact, it appears that its overemphasis on Islam in the encounter has backfired among students.

Indeed, until the Qajar dynasty, when the positive role of religious figures begins to be emphasized, kings dominate the historiography of the textbooks. They receive the largest number of pages allocated to a group, and their names are mentioned more than others. This trend changes when the textbooks begin discussing the Qajar dynasty, at which point the religious elite take up their more prominent role.

Another important aspect of the historical narrative in textbooks that Iranian students study is the early identification between Iranian identity and Shi'ism. Thus, for instance, the revolts against the Abbasids are depicted in one textbook as started by "the Iranian Muslims, who loathed the Abbasid caliphs, who did not adhere to the Islamic creeds. They [the Muslims] strove to free Iran of the Abbasid grip and establish an independent state after that."[95] The dynasties that ruled Iran, or part of it, in the aftermath of the fall of the Abbasids, such as the Tahirids (821–73 CE), the Safarids (873–900), the Ziarids (928–1042), and the Buyids (935–1055), are described as "independent Islamic states in Iran."[96]

This narrative is simplistic in that it overlooks the fact that these dynasties were far from united or that they recognized, at least in principle, the authority of the Abbasid caliph. More important for the purpose of this discussion is the fact that this same textbook overlooks the Sunni identity of all but one of these dynasties (the Buyids). The fact that the text does not differentiate between the Shiʿi dynasty and its Sunni counterparts suggests that the need to describe national continuity overshadows the need to emphasize religious affinity. The subsequent dynasties—the Ghaznavids, Seljuks, and Khwarazmshahs, who ruled Iran between the tenth and thirteenth centuries—were Turkish linguistically and are described as having been deeply influenced by Iranian culture. The book states that "the progress of many of [these dynasties] was due to the wisdom of clever Iranian ministers."[97]

The notion of continuity and the tendency to gloss over discrepancies in the national narrative are also evident in the way both the Turkish origins and the Sufi inclinations of the dynasty that was to a large degree responsible for Iran's Shiʿi identity, the Safavids (1501–1736), are omitted from the narrative. For instance, Shah Ismail is given credit for "[seeing] in this creed [Shiʿism] a means to unite the people throughout the country."[98] This description encapsulates much of what the Islamic Republic sees in Shiʿism: a prerequisite for national unity.

Considering this analysis of the historical narrative in the school textbooks, we see the tightrope the Islamic Republic is walking when it comes to teaching the history of Iran: while negating the monarchy as a system, it tries (at the expense of glossing over and omitting details) to instill a sense of national pride in and awareness of the greatness of the Iranian people and their culture.

Interviews conducted by Maryam Soltan-Zadeh show that Iranian students' accounts of history seem to agree with the school textbooks' representations up to the Pahlavi era. At this point, however, the students seem to hold views quite contradictory to those they are taught in school. Soltan-Zadeh reached the conclusion that

> it is the image many students have internalized as a fact of history and a clear cause of failure. Implicit in this image is also an admonishment of the past generations for failing to remove this recurring cause of defeat. In the absence of a comprehensive sociopolitical and economic analysis of the historical events, the textbooks have reduced national failures to personal incompetence of the kings who have become the sole target of blame for historical drawbacks.[99]

Paradoxically, this view is coherent with the attempt to preserve the myth of a savior, a role that Ayatollah Khomeini plays when we get to the last two decades of the twentieth century.

Interestingly, the Achaemenid Empire retains its positive image in the eyes of the students Soltan-Zadeh interviewed. This is in no small degree thanks to the fact that one of the main criteria for evaluating Iranian leaders of the past is the issue of territory—its expansion or contraction—as a central element in judging the level of Iran's strength. Therefore, the students consider the vast territory of the Achaemenid Empire as proof of Iran's supremacy in the world during that time.[100] Regional expansion was directly linked to Iran's internal power as well as to its international standing. This view of the Achaemenid Empire stands out in contrast to the wider view of Iranian history, which is mainly negative, replete with national calamities.

Many students apparently make the identification of territorial identity and national sovereignty the main yardstick for evaluating Iranian leaders and their contribution to Iran. Thus, the Achaemenids and the Safavids, despite representing two completely different sets of beliefs and historical circumstances, are perceived as emblems of the greatness of Iran. Generally speaking, the Iranian component of generating historical awareness seems to have had more success than the Shi'i one in that many students do not see Islam as an integral part of Iranian culture but rather as a foreign element.[101]

Conclusion

In the wake of the Islamic Revolution and the establishment of the Islamic Republic, there has been a change in emphasis regarding the existence of the state and its role in the realization of the ideals of the revolution. The Pahlavi era brought about a backlash from the Islamic opposition, especially among its more radical members, causing them to reject pre-Islamic symbols as alien to the Iranian people and culture. According to the spokesmen of this worldview, Islam has been the true uniting force and kernel of Iranian identity. Islam is a source of both pride and values, and no pre-Islamic cultural element can overshadow it. During the two decades preceding the revolution, the Islamic opposition, first and foremost Ayatollah Khomeini, used an antinational rhetoric. Even the very existence of the nation-state (i.e., Iran) was perceived as a temporary phase on the road to an Islamic utopia. However, the Islamic opposition also learned from the Pahlavi experience. While rejecting the Pahlavi regime's value system and symbols, it cherished the state structure as a way to bring about the ideal society. The shift in the Islamic Republic's relation to the existence of the state was sharp and decisive, but the shift in its approach toward Iranian nationalism could be better described as spiral, moving toward the end goal but experiencing setbacks, and have turned out rather to be brief episodes between the continuing tendency of appropriating nationalism for the state's Islamic raison d'être. Another difference between the first change and the second goes beyond the question of the Islamic Republic's sharp break from its early ideological line, which touches upon the degree of awareness with which the change happened. Whereas the shift from seeking an Islamic utopia to acknowledging the existence of the state as the best (and only) viable political expression of the Iranian people occurred swiftly, the ideological and political shift in view occurred slowly and with varying degrees of awareness. The political system built on the ruins of the Pahlavi state cherished other symbolic sites and monuments, but the Islamic Republic could not simply discard those sites and monuments that had already entered the national canon. No ministry or institution was busy shaping or monitoring the transformation in the state's ideology, and yet many of these state-controlled institutions participated in a delicate and often tacit debate.

Despite what seems like the Islamist option's victory over its nationalist rival in the early years of the republic, it turns out that the Islamist identity has been Iranianized and is subject to nationalist interpretations. In other words, the Islamic identity preached by the Islamic Republic, especially from the mid-1990s, is a religious national identity of Iranianized Islam. Beyond the question of flexibility versus rigidity or conservative versus reformist political camps in the Islamic Republic, we see both a degree of continuity and the creation of a new religionational culture.

Conclusion

The Islamic Republic and Iranian Symbols—the Taming of the Shrew

The modern Iranian fascination with ancient Iran originally emanated from the need to find an explanation for the country's seemingly weak status in its region and its political system. The feeling of weakness was followed by a comparison to Iran's glorious past, which at times verged on the fantastic, thus allowing a picture of total contradiction between the great power that Iran used to be and its dismal situation beginning at the turn of the twentieth century. In the eyes of the pioneers of Iranian nationalism in the nineteenth century, ancient Iran represented the opposite of everything that was negative in the contemporary Iranian political order. Social and political criticism soon developed into imagining Iran's past as ideal and its symbols as a way to connect with that past.

In this book, I have focused on two national symbols of ancient Iran used by the Pahlavi state to promote its national agenda. The first was a historical figure, Cyrus the Great, founder of the Achaemenid Empire. The second was Persepolis, the Achaemenid capital from the time of Darius the Great until the conquest of Iran by Alexander the Great. Both Cyrus and Persepolis are historical figures (i.e., they are not merely figments of the imagination), yet they were used in ways that were meant to extend their meaning beyond their historical dimension and thus to serve as national myths. This study has traced the paths by which these historical "artifacts" became symbols and the different and at times conflicting ways in which the state and opposition groups used them to present contesting narratives of Iran. In addition, it has examined these symbols in a wider context, considering how Iranian history in general was perceived by the modernizing elite of the Pahlavi state as well as by the opposition contending for power. Central elements in this perception were the "leap in time" the Pahlavi official historiography took to bring these two historical icons together and the uses it tried to make of them once they were endowed with a symbolic aura.

These two symbols in the Pahlavi modernist attempt to educate Iranians about their country's role in history share a few characteristics, which are important from the ethnosymbolic approach. Both Cyrus and Persepolis were, relatively speaking, unknown to many Iranians because they were not heralded in national epics or folklore literature throughout the ages. Their greatness, then, depended on the Pahlavi state's efforts in marketing them to the public. Both fulfilled a deep desire among the Pahlavi elite and hence the state to attach the greatness of ancient Iran, as whose natural heir the Pahlavi regime saw itself, to specific, tangible, and historical objects.

The figure of Cyrus fit well with the need to identify a specific person, a patriarch of the nation, as the progenitor of the Pahlavi shahs. Cyrus was to Iranian history what Muhammad Reza Shah aspired to be for modern Iran, a point of reference, a compass of identity. The patriarchal perception was given chronological depth by Cyrus, who was a father both in time and place, and who, unlike the mythical figures of kings known to many Iranians from folklore, also provided Iranians with a site that was identified with him, Pasargadae. The legacy of Cyrus was far from unilateral because competing and—to a degree—conflicting messages were attributed to this symbol: he was the propagator of law and order, on the one hand, and the tolerant monarch who predated all Western concepts of human rights, on the other; he was a genuine Iranian symbol, a reference point for Iranian nationalist aspirations, while simultaneously a figure universally appreciated in Judeo-Christian civilization. The relevance of Cyrus to the Western world was expected to enhance his popularity in Iran, even though what he symbolized differed for each audience.

Persepolis added a locus around which to rally symbolically as well as a more scientific aura in the guise of archaeology as a body of research that attests to the greatness of the site and the dynasty that ruled Iran at its height. The proof of greatness provided for Cyrus by Greek literature and the scriptures was replaced with the scientific method and a body of evidence at Persepolis. Both symbols were used in various forms to drive home the educational themes that the Pahlavi state wanted modern Iranians to follow, reinforcing the glory of the past and proving that under a powerful crown, modern Iran is destined for greatness.

Like for other modern societies, for Iran one of the recurring elements in the fashioning of its national historiography was the selection of periods of greatness to be emphasized and exhibited to the public as representing the essence of the nation and hence deserving of attention that exceeds their temporal length. In contrast, periods in which Iran submitted to foreign rule or exhibited weakness were considered an embarrassment to the national self-perception, and hence their role was either played down or neglected by the elite, who tried to shape the Iranian past in light of their prescription for modern Iran. The perception of Iran's past involved both selecting the "right" periods to be glorified and playing down other periods suspected of being less glorious and not fitting the Pahlavi perception of authentic Iranianness. The Pahlavi historical self-perception was influenced and served not only by ideological elements on the domestic level but also as a justification for Iran's pro-Western policy in the world arena. This perception was thus propagated as proof that Iran's alliance with the Western world was loyal to its remote past, its origins and true spirit. The myth of Cyrus specifically was useful to the Pahlavi state, although the legitimacy it sought to earn from that myth was by no means the only motivation to resuscitate memory of the ancient monarch. The myth of Cyrus enabled the Pahlavi state to present itself more easily as tolerant and relatively egalitarian to Iranian Jews because those qualities were aspects of Cyrus's policy, exemplified by his freeing of the Jews from Babylonian captivity. Being tolerant toward minorities in general and toward Jews in particular was therefore considered as being authentically Iranian and as having a long tradition behind it. Considering the accusations leveled at the Pahlavi regime by the Islamic opposition, the need to make this claim becomes clearer. Iran's experience in the rupture from the Pahlavi era to that of the Islamic Republic stresses the "dialectic" part of Pierre Nora's "dialectic of memory and forgetfulness."

It shows that success cannot be guaranteed in the effort to repress collective memory, even with powerful measures, and that "historical density" is a dynamic and living body. The masses, it turns out, can prove far more sophisticated than much of the scholarship on nationalism has considered them: they can embrace at least part of the historical narrative encouraged from above while yet choosing which elements to appropriate and without necessarily endowing the political elite that cultivates these symbols with the legitimacy they seek. The state in the form of the Islamic Republic proved versatile and adaptable. "Historical density" turned out to be the fruit of a dialectical process between the state and society and not the result of a trickle-down progression. In place of this dialectic, a new one reveals itself and challenges Jan Assmann's critique of both Maurice Halbwachs and Pierre Nora. The movement between authentic memory and its institutionalized counterpart turns out to occur on a two-way street, where the people embrace institutionalized symbols (from the Pahlavi era) and state institutions appropriate popular symbols (in the Islamic Republic).

Besides analyzing the process through which history became a field of contention regarding Iranian identity and its manifest destiny, this study showed the dynamics of historical awareness from "above" (i.e. the state) versus the awareness cultivated from "below," sectors of society that seemed alienated from the Pahlavi establishment. The dynamics were emphasized in an attempt to "break" the impression one might get from a one-sided account in which the public is fed from above with the elite's "correct" perception of history. Besides the speeches of opposition leaders in exile or their writings circulated clandestinely among their followers, the Pahlavi state left a sizeable record of the voices it silenced over the years. In the voices of the opposition, one finds that the state was not acting in a void and therefore was not omnipresent, as is sometimes implied by instrumentalist discourse on mythmaking, but rather was competing with other narratives of the history of Iran. Underlying this struggle was nothing less than a struggle for the right image and role of modern Iran both at home and in the world arena. Thus, "trivial" ancient historical matters (such as the origins of Cyrus) became a source for heated debate and a point of contention between the Pahlavi regime and its enemies. In this war, symbols were weapons in the hands of the belligerent parties, and the remote past was its battlefield.

Just as the development of awareness of Iran's glorious past did not start with Reza Shah's rise to power, so it did not end abruptly with the swift termination of his son's rule. Continuity and change in ancient Iranian history were a central theme of modern Iranians' historical narrative. They also form one of the main conclusions of this study: harking back to the greatness of ancient Iran is a need that Iranian nationalism cherished during the Pahlavi period and that was sanctified, albeit with alterations, with the coming of age of the Islamic Republic. My aim in following the thread that connects the Pahlavi period with the period following the Islamic Revolution was twofold. First, I wanted to see the development of the symbols and their meanings over time. Shedding light on the period preceding Muhammad Reza Shah's rise to power challenges the tendency to regard his years in power as monolithic. Beginning with the early Pahlavi period, the state stepped into the field of national symbols with an ever-growing degree of intensity. This process was masterminded from above by state officials and institutions and became identified with the political order at the expense of the mediators of knowledge, intellectuals and clerics alike. This exclusion contributed in large measure to the alienation these two groups felt from the state and from its development of these national symbols. It was no longer the state apparatus that upheld the national vision developed by intellectuals, but rather the opposite. Intellectuals were part of the state to the degree that they were willing to serve the Pahlavi official narrative. Those who were not willing either receded into oblivion or went underground, opposing the Pahlavi historical narrative in secret meetings or publications. I have analyzed some of this group's work, too, because they seemed to have at least as much influence as state historians on Iranians and the historical narrative they consumed. Second, I wanted to challenge the depiction of nationalism as a linear process that tends to emanate from the discourse on nationalism in general and on nationalism in the modern Middle East in particular, as if its contour is destined from the start. Far from suggesting a story of national symbols that served a political elite at a certain time and later was rejected, this book offers a picture of spiral development, where at certain moments (the Islamic

Revolution) one might imagine a reversal to supranational (Shi'i) symbols only to realize that there is no turning back. Unlike the Pahlavi state, the Islamic Republic has demonstrated flexibility and adaptability in dealing with the nationalist demand for a balance and appropriation of symbols of diverse ideological leanings.

In the scholarship on nationalism and its relations to symbols, there is a strong tendency to view symbols instrumentally as tools enabling the political elite to assert themselves and rally the masses around them. Symbols seem to endow the masses with a sense of belonging, but thereafter the masses seem to play the role of acquiescent bystanders or to participate in the national pact, having been convinced of the benefits they get from so doing. The story of Iranian national symbols in Iran challenges this instrumentalist approach for two reasons. First, the basic conclusion that arises from the history of the Pahlavi state, without ignoring its end, is that the ruling elite failed to attain legitimacy by promoting national symbols to the Iranian masses. Although not entirely responsible for this outcome, the symbols cannot be ignored when weighing the reasons for the collapse of the Pahlavi order. This is not meant to argue simplistically that the reason for the downfall of the Pahlavi state was wrong choice of symbols or myths or the wrong ways they were conveyed to the people. It is evident, though, that the choice of symbols, instead of obtaining the legitimacy sought for the regime, contributed to the opposite effect. The Pahlavi state's efforts to express its power in space and time proved to aggravate existing sentiments among wide circles of Iranian society, which ultimately turned against the political order that tried to inculcate those expressions and be built by them.

The symbolism used by the state emanated from more profound elements in the perception of the Pahlavi elite that identified with the state than merely the intention to gain legitimacy in the eyes of the people. It ran as deep as this elite's perception of Iranianness and its meaning in the modern age. This perception had far-reaching implications for Iran's internal affairs as well as for its place among the nations and therefore its foreign policy.

The Islamic Republic soon embraced the nation-state as the only viable means to promote its Shi'i political credo. Moreover, its support for

Islamic causes around the globe proved to be subservient to what the new political elite saw as Iran's national interests. The dynamic that brought about the reemergence of national symbols in the Islamic Republic was different from the dynamic of the period preceding the revolution: the political elite of the Islamic Republic were succumbing to what they thought would motivate society in the shadow of the great national threat posed by Iran's Arab neighbor, Iraq. Furthermore, the new nationalist rhetoric was infused with religious meaning as well to dilute the nationalist emotions it was expected to evoke.

With the Islamic Republic's coming of age, the first decade of the new millennium saw the reemergence of an Iranian self-consciousness that has struck root in at least some of the leadership. The tensions between two camps in the elite regarding the question of the right balance between Iranians' ethnic identity and their religious affiliation have been assuaged slowly by the appropriation of national symbols by the more conservative elements of the clerical establishment, including Supreme Leader 'Ali Khamenei. Although the conservative clerics have the upper hand politically, they seem to have recognized the importance of Iranian symbols and their relevance to the lives of the majority of Iranians in the Islamic Republic. Far from suppressing these ethnic elements, they have incorporated them into their religious world, fulfilling the legacy of some of the Islamic critics of the Pahlavi state four decades earlier. Sanctifying Cyrus the Great and lending religious depth and history to the Iranian New Year were innovations, but they relied on a longer attempt to define Iranian uniqueness through Shi'ism. The thought developed through the 1970s as a response to the Pahlavi cultural project and proved useful in that it instigated Islamic clerics and laymen to pose a Shi'i-Iranian answer to the estrangement of many Iranians from the Pahlavi version of Iranian nationalism.

Above all, the role of Iranian nationalism in the Islamic Republic resembles in a metaphysical way the Iranian national adage that Iran was never conquered by foreigners but rather overpowered the peoples who tried to subdue it. Contrary to Shi'ism, which one could argue has been subservient to the political order in Iran rather than running it, Iranian nationalism became a battle cry to which the Islamic Republic found itself drawn.

The contours of national symbols in Iran add a significant and nuanced validity to the criticism of both Pierre Nora and the instrumentalist approach to nationalism: while acknowledging the power of the state to cultivate national symbols, the story I have told here of national symbols in Iran deprives the state of exclusiveness in cultivating them. Moreover, the state seems to follow social changes in this regard, embracing and appropriating symbols cherished by society. This is apparent in the case of Pahlavi Iran, where, despite using the greatest of means to cultivate national symbols in its own image, the state failed completely in gaining the legitimacy it sought from those symbols. In its turn, the Pahlavi state's unintended descendant, the Islamic Republic, learned that the overthrow of the Pahlavis did not mean the eradication of their symbolic legacy, although it would continue on with different emphasis. The new political elite came to terms with the symbol system they inherited, though whether they did so willingly or not is hard to tell. President Khatami's discourse seems to have been a rather more aware step in this direction.

Research on Iranian nationalism has made considerable strides in the past two decades. We have a better understanding of the processes by which national symbols have been interpreted and reinterpreted according to social-political developments. We can also trace the ties that bind the past four decades since the Islamic Revolution in Iran with the legacy of the Pahlavi period. What seemed like a cultural point of no return, the cataclysmic overthrow of the Pahlavi monarchy, is understood today in a more nuanced way that reveals the continuity running through both periods. With hindsight, it seems that as far as national symbols are concerned, the revolution did not seek to purge Iranian national iconography but rather to bridge the gap that seemed to be widening to an alarming degree between two sets of symbols, the Islamic-Shiʿi ones and the Iranian-ethnic ones. Bridging the gap was a goal that, though never declared before President Khatami was in office, was achieved mainly in two ways: making Islam more compatible with Iranian nationalism and causing Iranian nationalism to incorporate Shiʿism as part of its symbolic vocabulary.

Other questions regarding the nexus of Iranian Shiʿi identity remain to be explored. For example, how have forms of worship transformed over time in the Islamic Republic? Has the change in attitude toward Iranian uniqueness left any mark on the way 'Ashura' is commemorated or on the centrality of *Nahj al-balagha* (The Way of Eloquence), the collection of revelations attributed to 'Ali? Is the mainstreaming of the notion that Cyrus is Dhul-Qarnayn a stage in a longer process? Can we speak of the development of an Iranian reading of the Qur'an? If so, what are its characteristics? These questions remain to be studied in order to obtain a more diverse and multidimensional picture of the mosaic of Iranian identity in the twenty-first century.

Iran's coming to terms with its symbols and their meaning is of course not occurring in a vacuum but shares much with the same process occurring in other Middle Eastern societies. Comparing Iranian society with other societies in the region that have experienced the vicissitudes of relations between the religious and the national component of their identity is vital. I can offer here only some preliminary remarks on this topic. The Islamic opposition in Iran during the last two decades of the Pahlavi state developed an attitude reminiscent of the attitude of Islamists in Egypt during the same time (with Nasserism being eclipsed about a decade before the downfall of the Pahlavi state). Each of these Islamic opposition movements was facing a nation-state with a national agenda (mixed with a socialist flavor in the case of Egypt), buttressed by a formidable and notorious security apparatus known to spare no effort at infiltrating and silencing any opposition. However, considering the similarities, one cannot miss the great difference in the relation to nationalism that developed in the two groups. Whereas Sayyid Qutb, the Egyptian liberal-turned-Islamist, rejected nationalism entirely, seeing it as a threat to Islam in its deepest form, Ayatollah Khomeini and 'Ali Shari'ati were more ambiguous in their rejection. It was not necessarily nationalism itself that they rejected, but rather its manifestations in the nation-state that they abhorred. Nationalism presented as superseding Shi'i Islam was what irritated them rather than the national bond propagated by the state, and in turn it assisted them in formulating their ideological alternative. In other words, it was not nationalism per se that they disapproved of but rather a specific rendition of it: its monarchist form.

It seems that the opposition in Iran was better prepared to take over the state and run it in the name of Islam, whereas the opposition in Egypt seemed to have given up all hope of the national agenda during the 1970s. Dreaming of surpassing nationalism, Qutbism had little future, but Khomeini's Islamism spoke in the name of the people and integrated nationalism in its political and social views. Far from presenting Shi'i Islam as a prescription for the creation of a small *tali'a* (avant-garde), Khomeini succeeded in turning it into an ideology that galvanized the Iranian urban masses in the age of nation-states, whether this outcome was achieved by premeditation or just from the realization that this was the only way to offer an alternative to the Pahlavi state. Instead of replacing the nation-state with an Islamist one, the opposition to the Pahlavi regime replaced one form of nation-state with another that has a different emphasis.

The tension inherent between the promise of a model Shi'i society and the national reality in which it is acting is certain to present a challenge in the coming years.

Notes

Bibliography

Index

Notes

Introduction

1. "Khatami Notified of 'National Tragedy' in Persepolis," *Payvand News*, May 13, 2002, at http://www.payvand.com/news/02/may/1053.html.

2. Anthony Smith, *National Identity* (Reno: Univ. of Nevada Press, 1991), 14.

3. Smith, *National Identity*, 14.

4. Smith, *National Identity*, 25.

5. Anthony Smith, *Chosen Peoples: Sacred Sources of National Identity* (Oxford: Oxford Univ. Press, 2004), 169.

6. Smith, *Chosen Peoples*, 190.

7. Smith, *Chosen Peoples*, 172.

8. Matthew Levinger and Paula Franklin Lytle, "Myth and Mobilization: The Triadic Structure of Nationalist Rhetoric," *Nations and Nationalism* 7, no. 2 (Apr. 2001): 178.

9. Maurice Halbwachs, *On Collective Memory* (Chicago: Univ. of Chicago Press, 1992), 38.

10. Patrick H. Hutton, *History as an Art of Memory* (Hanover, NH: Univ. Press of New England, 1993), 73–90.

11. Jan Assmann, "Communicative and Cultural Memory," in *Cultural Memory Studies: An International and Interdisciplinary Handbook*, ed. Astrid Erll and Ansgar Nünning (Berlin: Walter de Gruyter, 2008), 111–12.

12. Pierre Nora, "Between Memory and History: Les Lieux de Mémoire," *Representations* 26 (Spring 1989): 7–24.

13. Jay Winter and Emmanuel Sivan, "Setting the Framework," in *War and Remembrance in the Twentieth Century*, ed. Jay Winter and Emmanuel Sivan (Cambridge: Cambridge Univ. Press, 1999), 15–20.

14. Lisa Maya Knauer and Daniel J. Walkowitz, "Introduction: Memory, Race, and the Nation in Public Spaces," in *Contested Histories in Public Space: Memory, Race, and Nation*, ed. Daniel J. Walkowitz and Lisa Maya Knauer (Durham, NC: Duke Univ. Press, 2009), 9.

15. Philip L. Kohl, Mara Kozelsky, and Nachman Ben-Yehuda, introduction to *Selective Remembrances: Archaeology in the Construction, Commemoration, and Consecration*

of National Pasts, ed. Philip L. Kohl, Mara Kozelsky, and Nachman Ben-Yehuda (Chicago: Univ. of Chicago Press, 2007), 2.

16. Alon Confino, *The Nation as a Local Metaphor: Wurttemberg, Imperial Germany, and National Memory, 1871–1918* (Chapel Hill: Univ. of North Carolina Press, 1997), 4.

17. See Ferdinand Braudel, "Histoire, sciences sociales: La longue durée," *Annales* 4 (Oct.–Dec. 1958): 725–53, and "Histoire et sciences sociales: La longue durée," *Réseaux* 5, no. 27 (1987): 7–37.

18. Smith, *National Identity*, 25.

19. Anthony Smith, *The Ethnic Origins of Nations* (Oxford: Blackwell, 1987), 178.

20. Smith, *Ethnic Origins*, 179.

21. Nader Nasiri-Moghaddam, *L'archéologie français en Perse (1884–1914)* (Paris: Connaissances et Savoirs, 2004).

22. Afshin Marashi, *Nationalizing Iran: Culture, Power, and the State* (Seattle: Univ. of Washington Press, 2008), 54–55.

23. Richard Cottam, *Nationalism in Iran* (Pittsburgh, PA: Univ. of Pittsburgh Press, 1979), 11.

24. Cottam, *Nationalism in Iran*, 26–27.

25. Cottam, *Nationalism in* Iran, 29.

26. Firouzeh Kashani-Sabet, *Frontier Fictions: Shaping the Iranian Nation, 1804–1946* (Princeton, NJ: Princeton Univ. Press, 1999), 4–6.

27. Cottam, *Nationalism in Iran*, 16–17.

28. See, for example, Benedict Anderson, *Imagined Communities: Reflections on the Origin and Spread of Nationalism* (London: Verso, 1991), 177–79.

29. Mostafa Vaziri, *Iran as Imagined Nation: The Construction of National Identity* (New York: Paragon House, 1993), 5, 101.

30. Ahmad Ashraf, "Iranian Identity," in *Encyclopaedia Iranica* (New York: Encyclopaedia Iranica Foundation, 2006), at http://www.iranicaonline.org/articles/iranian-identity-i-perspectives.

31. Vaziri, *Iran as Imagined Nation*, 152.

32. Mohamad Tavakoli-Targhi, *Refashioning Iran: Orientalism, Occidentalism, and Historiography* (New York: Palgrave, 2001), 132–34.

33. Marashi, *Nationalizing Iran*; Talinn Grigor, "Cultivating Modernities: The Society for National Heritage, Political Propaganda, and Public Architecture in 20th Century Iran," PhD diss., MIT, 2005.

34. See, for example, Eckehard Kulke, *The Parsees in India: A Minority as Agent of Social Change* (New Delhi: Vikas, 1978), and Marashi, *Nationalizing Iran*, 57–64.

35. See, for example, Grigor, "Cultivating Modernities."

36. Grigor, "Cultivating Modernities," 5.

37. Cyrus Schayegh, "Seeing Like a State: An Essay on the Historiography of Modern Iran," *International Journal of Middle East Studies* 42, no. 1 (2010): 37.

38. Kamran Scott Aghaie and Afshin Marashi, eds., *Rethinking Iranian Nationalism and Modernity* (Austin: Univ. of Texas Press, 2014).

39. Kamran Scott Aghaie, "Islamic-Iranian Nationalism and Its Implications for the Study of Political Islam and Religious Nationalism," in *Rethinking Iranian Nationalism and Modernity*, ed. Aghaie and Marashi, 182.

40. Ali Mozaffari, *Forming National Identity in Iran: The Idea of Homeland Derived from Ancient Persian and Islamic Imaginations of Place* (London: I. B. Tauris, 2014), 1, 2, 63.

41. Reza Zia Ebrahimi, *The Emergence of Iranian Nationalism: Race and the Politics of Dislocation* (New York: Columbia Univ. Press, 2016), 6–9.

42. Anthony Smith, *Ethno-Symbolism and Nationalism: A Cultural Approach* (London: Routledge, 2009), 25.

43. Smith, *Ethno-Symbolism and Nationalism*, 129.

44. David Kertzer, *Ritual, Politics, and Power* (New Haven, CT: Yale Univ. Press, 1988), 2, 1, 5, 1; my emphasis.

45. Kenneth Burke, *Attitudes toward History* (Berkeley: Univ. of California Press, 1984), 179.

46. Kamran Scott Aghaie, *The Martyrs of Karbala: Shi'i Symbols and Rituals in Modern Iran* (Seattle: Univ. of Washington Press, 2004), 10.

47. Kertzer, *Ritual, Politics, and Power*, 5.

48. Anthony Smith, "The 'Golden Age' and National Renewal," in *Myths and Nationhood*, ed. Geoffrey Hosking and George Schöpflin (New York: Routledge, 1997), 36–59.

49. John Bodnar, *Remaking America: Public Memory, Commemoration, and Patriotism in the Twentieth Century* (Princeton, NJ: Princeton Univ. Press, 1992), 13.

50. See, for example, Smith, *Ethno-symbolism and Nationalism*, 76–77; Anthony Smith, *Nationalism and Modernism: A Critical Survey of Recent Theories of Nations and Nationalism* (New York: Routledge, 1998), 20–22.

51. As discussed in Jan Assmann and John Czaplicka, "Collective Memory and Cultural Identity," *New German Critique* 65 (1995): 125.

52. Assmann, "Communicative and Cultural Memory," 110; Jan Assmann, "Das kulturelle Gedachtnis," *Erwagen, Wissen, Ethik* 13 (2002): 239–47.

53. Smith, *Ethnic Origins*, 154.

54. Sekandar Amanolahi, "A Note on Ethnicity and Ethnic Groups in Iran," *Iran and the Caucasus* 9, no. 1 (2005): 37–41; Hamid Ahmadi, "Unity within Diversity: Foundations and Dynamics of National Identity in Iran," *Critique: Critical Middle Eastern Studies* 14, no. 1 (2005): 127–47. For a rather more militant approach to the difference between Persian and Iranian, see Alam Saleh and James Worrall, "Between Darius and Khomeini: Exploring Iran's National Identity Problematique," *National Identities* 2014, doi:10.1080/14608944.2014.930426.

55. Shahram Akbarzadeh and James Barry, "State Identity in Iranian Foreign Policy," *British Journal of Middle Eastern Studies* 43, no. 2 (2016): 618.

56. Ali Mozaffari, "The Heritage 'NGO': A Case Study on the Role of Grass-Roots Heritage Societies in Iran and Their Perception of Cultural Heritage," *International Journal of Heritage Studies* 21, no. 9 (2015): 851–52, at http://www.tandfonline.com/toc/rjhs20/21/9.

1. Modern Iran Looks to History

1. Henry Tudor, *Political Myth* (London: Macmillan, 1972); Christopher G. Flood, *Political Myth: A Theoretical Introduction* (New York: Garland, 1996).

2. Ali Ansari, "Shah Mohammad Reza Pahlavi and the Myth of Imperial Authority," PhD diss., Univ. of London, 1998, 176; Ervand Abrahamian, *Iran between Two Revolutions* (Princeton, NJ: Princeton Univ. Press, 1982), 61–69.

3. Nikki R. Keddie, *Qajar Iran and the Rise of Reza Khan 1796–1925* (Costa Mesa, CA: Mazda, 1999), 22–23; Abrahamian, *Iran between Two Revolutions*, 51.

4. Cyril Glasse, *The Concise Encyclopaedia of Islam* (London: Stacey International, 2001), 234.

5. Touraj Atabaki, "Agency and Subjectivity in Iranian National Historiography," in *Iran in the 20th Century: Historiography and Political Culture*, ed. Touraj Atabaki (London: I. B. Tauris, 2009), 71.

6. Levinger and Lytle, "Myth and Mobilization," 178, 177.

7. Mirza Fath 'Ali Akhundzadeh, *Alef bay-i jadid va maktubat* (Tabriz, Iran: Nashr-i Ehya', 1357/1978), 206; all translations from Persian and other non-English sources are mine unless otherwise noted in citations. For other examples of such idealization, see Mirza Fath 'Ali Akhundzadeh, *Maktubat Kemal al-Dawla* (Baku, Azerbaijan: Nashriyat-i Ilm, n.d.), 16, and Fereydun Adamiyat, *Andishehay-i Akhundzadeh* (Tehran: Shareqat Sahmi Khorezmi, 1970), 210.

8. Nasiri-Moghaddam, *L'archéologie française en Perse*, 250–52.

9. Kashani-Sabet, *Frontier Fictions*, 41.

10. Kashani-Sabet, *Frontier Fictions*, 41; Marashi, *Nationalizing Iran*, 99.

11. Nasiri-Moghaddam, *L'archéologie française en Perse*, 254–55.

12. Nasiri-Moghaddam, *L'archéologie française en Perse*, 255.

13. Quoted in Juan Cole, "Marking Boundaries, Marking Time: The Iranian Past and the Construction of the Self by Qajar Thinkers," *Iranian Studies* 29, nos. 1–2 (Winter–Spring 1996): 45.

14. Cole, "Marking Boundaries, Marking Time," 45.

15. Eliz Sanasarian, *Religious Minorities in Iran* (Cambridge: Cambridge Univ. Press, 2000), 52; Abbas Amanat, *Resurrection and Renewal: The Making of the Babi Movement in Iran, 1844–1850* (Ithaca, NY: Cornell Univ. Press, 1989), 351–55.

16. Nasiri-Moghaddam, *L'archéologie française en Perse*, 252–57.

17. Ezzat O. Negahban, *Panjah sal-i bastanshenasi dar Iran* (Tehran: Sazman-i Mirath-i Farhang-i Keshvar, Yadigar-i 'Umr, 1376/1997), 28.

18. Kamyar Abdi, "Nationalism, Politics, and the Development of Archeology in Iran," *American Journal of Archeology* 105, no. 1 (Jan. 2001): 53; Abbas Amanat, *Pivot of the Universe: Nasir al-Din Shah Qajar and the Iranian Monarchy, 1831–1896* (London: I. B. Tauris, 1997), 427; Nasiri-Moghaddam, *L'archéologie française en Perse*, 76.

19. Nasiri-Moghaddam, *L'archéologie française en Perse*, 55; James Goode, *Negotiating for the Past: Archaeology, Nationalism, and Diplomacy in the Middle East, 1919–1941* (Austin: Univ. of Texas Press, 2007), 138. For a testimony to the deep effect this visit to the Louvre had on the shah, see a selection from his diary in Nasir al-Din Shah, *The Diary of H.M. the Shah of Persia during His Tour through Europe in A.D. 1873* (Costa Mesa, CA: Mazda, 1995).

20. On the colonial atmosphere and the exoticism attributed to the ethnic groups displayed in these exhibits at museums in Europe, see Zeynep Celik, *Displaying the Orient: Architecture of Islam at Nineteenth-Century World's Fairs* (Berkeley: Univ. of California Press, 1992), 10–13.

21. Marashi, *Nationalizing Iran*, 28.

22. Marashi, *Nationalizing Iran*, 14.

23. Goode, *Negotiating for the Past*, 128; Nasiri-Moghaddam, *L'archéologie française en Perse*, 147.

24. Mohammad Taqi Mustafavi, "Emanat Dari-ye Khak," *Majale-yi Bararsihay-i Tarikhi*, special bulletin, no. 11 (1975): 80–83; Abu-Alqasem Sahab, *Farhang Khavershenasan* (Tehran: Entesharat-i Sahab, 2535/1971), 290–92.

25. Abbas Khalili, *Korush-i Bozorg* (Tehran: Elmi, 1965), 4.

26. Tavakoli-Targhi, *Refashioning Iran*, 96, 31. See also Marashi, *Nationalizing Iran*, 84–86.

27. Quoted in Hasan Taqizadeh, "Hukm az ruye tajribe," *Kaveh*, Nov. 15, 1918, 5.

28. Keivandokht Ghahari, *Nationalismus und Modernismus in Iran in der Periode zwischen dem Zerfall der Qagaren-Dynastie und der Machtfestigung Reza Schahs: Eine Untersuchung über die intellektuellen Kreise um die Zeitschriften "Kaiweh," "Iransahr," und "Ayandeh"* (Berlin: K. Schwarz, 2001), 5.

29. Tim Epkenhans, *Moral und Disziplin: Seyyed Hasan Taqizade und die Konstruktion eines "progressiv Selbst" in der frühen iranischen Moderne* (Berlin: K. Schwarz, 2005), 183.

30. Hasan Taqizadeh, "Aghaz," *Kaveh*, Jan. 24, 1916, 2.

31. Ghahari, *Nationalismus und Modernismus in Iran*, 85–89.

32. For example, see Prof. W. Geiger, "Nowruz," *Kaveh*, Apr. 18, 1916, 4–5.

33. Atabaki, "Agency and Subjectivity," 71.

34. Magnus T. Bernhardsson, *Reclaiming a Plundered Past: Archaeology and Nation Building in Modern Iraq* (Austin: Univ. of Texas Press, 2005), 20.

35. Grigor, "Cultivating Modernities," 27; Marashi, *Nationalizing Iran*, 75.

36. Stephanie Cronin, *The Army and the Creation of the Pahlavi State in Iran, 1910–1926* (London: Tauris Academic Studies, 1997), 108–39, and *Tribal Politics in Iran: Rural*

Conflict and the New State, 1921–1941 (London: Routledge, 2007), 113–32; Rudi Matthee, "Transforming Dangerous Nomads into Useful Artisans, Technicians, Agriculturalists: Education in the Reza Shah Period," in *The Making of Modern Iran: State and Society under Reza Shah 1921–1941*, ed. Stephanie Cronin (London: RoutledgeCurzon, 2003), 128–48.

37. Houchang E. Chehabi, "Staging the Emperor's New Clothes: Dress Code and Nation-Building under Reza Shah," *Iranian Studies* 26, nos. 3–4 (Summer–Fall 1993): 209–29.

38. The expression used for excavation in this period was *talashu'i*, which means "gold washing;" see Nasiri-Moghaddam, *L'archéologie française en Perse*, 262.

39. Husayn Makki, *Tarikh bist saleh*, 6 vols. (Tehran: Nasher, 1362/1983), 6:161.

40. Abbas Milani, *Eminent Persians*, 2 vols. (Syracuse, NY: Syracuse Univ. Press, 2008), 1:152–54.

41. Milani, *Eminent Persians*, 1:152.

42. For more on Hassan Taqizadeh, see Epkenhans, *Moral und Disziplin*, 183; Hasan Taqizadeh, *Zendegi Tufani: Khaterat-i Sayyed Hasan Taqizadeh* (Tehran: Intisharat-i 'Ilmi, 1989), 181–84; Grigor, "Cultivating Modernities," 43.

43. Grigor, "Cultivating Modernities," 11–39; *Asnad-i az bastan shenasi dar Iran* (Tehran: Vezarat-i Farhang va Ershad-i Eslami 1380/2001), 347–50, 441–47.

44. Goode, *Negotiating for the Past*, 138.

45. Goode, *Negotiating for the Past*, 152–56; Abdi, "Nationalism," 51–54.

46. Goode, *Negotiating for the Past*, 129.

47. Goode, *Negotiating for the Past*, 142.

48. Yael Zerubavel, *Recovered Roots: Collective Memory and the Making of Israeli National Tradition* (Chicago: Univ. of Chicago Press, 1997), 8.

49. Nora, "Between Memory and History," 8.

50. Atabaki, "Agency and Subjectivity," 87.

51. Oliver Bast, "Disintegrating the 'Discourse of Disintegration,'" in *Iran in the 20th Century*, ed. Atabaki, 60–63.

52. William A. Wigram, *An Introduction to the History of the Assyrian Church* (Piscataway, NJ: Gorgias Press, 2004), 173.

53. 'Isa Sadiq, *Yadegar-i 'Umr: Khaterat-i az sargozosht*, 2 vols. (Tehran: Dehkhoda, 1975), 2:214–15.

54. Mohammad Hasan Asef, *Mabni ideologic dar hukumat-i Pahlavi* (Tehran: Markaz-i Asnad Enqelab-i Eslami, 2005), 248.

55. Quoted in Makki, *Tarikh-i bist saleh*, 6:40.

56. Quoted in Makki, *Tarikh bist saleh*, 6:41.

57. Sadiq, *Yadegar-i 'Umr*, 2:192.

58. Sadiq, *Yadegar-i 'Umr*, 2:195.

59. Reza Daveri, *Nasyonalism va enqelab* (Tehran: Entesharat-i Daftar Pezhuhashoy-i Eslami 1365/1986), 6.

60. Hasan Taqizadeh, "Ferdowsi," *Kaveh*, Jan. 24, 1916, 4–5.

61. *Iran Bastan*, Tir 1, 1312/June 22, 1933, 3.

62. See also Sadiq, *Yadegar-i 'Umr*, 201–33; David Smith, introduction to *Firdausi Celebration 935–1935*, ed. David Smith (New York: n.p., 1936), 3–7; Shapur Shahbazi, *Ferdowsi: A Critical Biography* (Costa Mesa, CA: Mazda, 1991), 19–20.

2. A Clash of Pasts

1. Mehrzad Boroujerdi, *Iranian Intellectuals and the West: The Tormented Triumph of Nativism* (Syracuse, NY: Syracuse Univ. Press, 1996), 22, 177; Negin Nabavi, *Intellectuals and the State in Iran* (Gainesville: Univ. Press of Florida, 2003), 19–20, 38.

2. Ali Rahnema, *An Islamic Utopian: A Political Biography of 'Ali Shari'ati* (London: I. B. Tauris, 1998); *Shari'ati bi rivayat-i asnad-i Savak* (Tehran: Markaz-e Asnad-i Enqelab-i Eslami, 1378/1999); Mohammad Hakimpur, *Shari'ati dar zindan: Ta'allumat va khaṭirat-i dawran-i zindan: Hamrah ba biyugrafi-i taḥlili va barrasi-yi andishahha* (Tehran: Entisharat-i Naghmah-i Naw'andish, 1383/2004); Reza 'Alijani, *Shari'ati va Savak: Mururi tahlili bar sih jild-i asnad-i Savak dar barah-i duktur Shari'ati* (Tehran: Entisharat-i Kavir, 1382/2003).

3. *Shari'ati bi rivayat-i asnad-i Savak*, 16.

4. Hamid Dabashi, *Theology of Discontent: The Ideological Foundations of the Islamic Revolution in Iran* (New York: New York Univ. Press, 1993), 119–20.

5. Nabavi, *Intellectuals and the State in Iran*, 100–102.

6. On Massignon's unique career, see Mary Louise Gude, *Louis Massignon: The Crucible of Compassion* (Notre Dame, IN: Univ. of Notre Dame Press, 1996), 107–15; see also 'Abd al-Rahim Qanavat, *Shari'ati va tarikh-i Islam: Nigahi bi ruykard va asar-i duktur Shari'ati dar zaminah-i tarikh-i Islam: Bi zamimah-i pasukh bi "Naqdi bar Islamshinasi"* (Mashhad, Iran: Nashr-i Salih, 1377/1998), 14–18.

7. Jalal Al-e Ahmad, *Occidentosis: A Plague from the West*, trans. R. Campbell (Berkeley, CA: Mizan Press, 1984), 34.

8. Etan Kohlberg, "Western Studies of Sh'ia Islam," in *Belief and Law in Imami Shi'ism* (Aldershot, UK: Variorum; Brookfield, VT: Gower, 1991), 35.

9. Kohlberg, "Western Studies of Sh'ia Islam," 35.

10. Henry Corbin, *The Voyage and the Messenger: Iran and Philosophy*, trans. Joseph Rowe (Berkeley, CA: North Atlantic Books, 1998), 101; *The Voyage and Messenger* is a collection of previously unpublished essays and interviews.

11. Corbin, *The Voyage and the Messenger*, 93.

12. Corbin, *The Voyage and the Messenger*, 94.

13. This approach suffered fierce criticism from conservative clerics. See, for example, "Enteqad-i shadid Mesbah Yazdi az Masha'i," Entekhab, n.d., http://www.entekhab.ir/fa/news/23116/, accessed Jan. 30, 2017.

14. A stark example is the once esoteric idea that Cyrus the Great is mentioned in the Qur'an, which has become a commonplace in the past three decades. See Menahem Merhavy, "Religious Appropriation of National Symbols in Iran: Searching for Cyrus the Great," *Iranian Studies* 48, no. 6 (2015): 933–48.

15. Qanavat, *Shari'ati va tarikh-i Islam*, 15; Hasan Yusufi Ishkavari, *Shari'ati va naqd-i sunnat* (Tehran: Nashr-i Yadavaran, 1379/2000), 78.

16. 'Ali Shari'ati, *Islamshinasi, majmu'a-yi asar*, 3 vols. (Tehran: Qalam, 1360–61/1981–82), 3:13–14.

17. Rahnema, *An Islamic Utopian*, 251.

18. 'Ali Shari'ati, *Bazshenasi huviyat-i Irani Islami* (Tehran: Ilhām, 1361/1983), 229.

19. Talinn Grigor, *Building Iran: Modernism, Architecture, and National Heritage under the Pahlavi Monarchs* (New York: Periscope, 2009); Marashi, *Nationalizing Iran*; Touraj Atabaki and Eric J. Zürcher, eds., *Men of Order: Authoritarian Modernization under Atatürk and Reza Shah* (London: I. B. Tauris, 2004).

20. Akhundzadeh, *Alef bay-i jadid va maktubat*, 206. For other examples of such idealization, see Mirza Fath 'Ali Akhundzadeh, *Maktubat Kemal al-Dawla* (Baku, Azerbaijan: Nashriyat-i 'Ilm, n.d.), 16; Adamiyat, *Andishehay-i Akhundzadeh*, 210.

21. See, for example, the report of various activities orchestrated by Shafa' on the cultivation of Cyrus's heritage: Shojaeddin Shafa', *Korush-i Kabir va bunyad-i shahenshahi Iran* (Tehran: Central Committee of Celebrations of the Iranian Monarchy, 1340/1961).

22. See, for example, Gholam'ali Homayun, *Korush-i Kabir dar asar-i hunariy-i Urupa'iyan* (Tehran: Tehran Univ. Press, 1971), 11.

23. Shari'ati, *Bazshenasi huviyat-i Irani Islami*, 318.

24. Shari'ati, *Bazshenasi huviyat-i Irani Islami*, 318.

25. Shari'ati, *Bazshenasi huviyat-i Irani Islami*, 320.

26. Shari'ati was not the first to warn of the danger of worship of the king. See, for example, Hasan Pirniya's warning fifty years earlier in Asef, *Mabni ideologic dar hukumat-i Pahlavi*, 248.

27. Shari'ati, *Bazshenasi huviyat-i Irani Islami*, 323.

28. Shari'ati, *Bazshenasi huviyat-i Irani Islami*, 29.

29. Ghulamriza Ma'sumi, *Bastanshinasi-i Iran: Az 2407 ta 2535 shahin-shahi* (Tehran: Artish, 1976).

30. Shari'ati, *Bazshenasi huviyat-i Irani Islami*, 30.

31. 'Ali Shari'ati, *Red Shiism* (Tehran: Hamdami, 1979), 8.

32. Shari'ati, *Bazshenasi huviyat-i Irani Islami*, 322.

33. Shari'ati, *Bazshenasi huviyat-i Irani Islami*, 322.

34. Shari'ati, *Bazshenasi huviyat-i Irani Islami*, 323.

35. Interestingly, it seems that Shari'ati was up to date with Western scholarship on Iran, where he probably found out that al-Afghani was indeed an Iranian. See Nikki

R. Keddie, *Sayyid Jamal ad-Din "al-Afghani": A Political Biography* (Berkeley: Univ. of California Press, 1972).

36. Shari'ati, *Bazshenasi huviyat-i Irani Islami*, 49, 51, 163.

37. Shari'ati, *Bazshenasi huviyat-i Irani Islami*, 164.

38. Shari'ati, *Bazshenasi huviyat-i Irani Islami*, 53–54.

39. This perception became the title of a book that tried to establish the thesis historically. See 'Abd al-Husayn Zarrinkub, *Do qarn-i sukut: Sarguẕasht-i ḥavadiṯ va aẉza'-i tarikhi-i Iran dar du qarn-i avval-i Islam az hamlah-i 'Arab ta zuhur-i dawlat-i Ṭahiriyan* (Tehran: Mu'assasah-i Entisharat-i Ahmad 'Ali, 1344/1965).

40. Shari'ati, *Bazshenasi huviyat-i Irani Islami*, 32.

41. Shari'ati, *Bazshenasi huviyat-i Irani Islami*, 265–66, 271, 286, 273.

42. Shari'ati, *Bazshenasi huviyat-i Irani Islami*, 271.

43. Shari'ati, *Bazshenasi huviyat-i Irani Islami*, 272.

44. Shari'ati, *Bazshenasi huviyat-i Irani Islami*.

45. Shari'ati, *Bazshenasi huviyat-i Irani Islami*, 285.

46. Shari'ati, *Bazshenasi huviyat-i Irani Islami*, 281–82.

47. Shari'ati, *Bazshenasi huviyat-i Irani Islami*, 317.

48. Shari'ati, *Bazshenasi huviyat-i Irani Islami*, 285.

49. Shari'ati, *Bazshenasi huviyat-i Irani Islami*, 285.

50. *The Quran*, trans. Abd al-Halim Mahmud (New York: Oxford Univ. Press, 2005).

51. Shari'ati, *Bazshenasi huviyat-i Irani Islami*, 150.

52. Ehsan Yarshater, "Cultural Development of Iran," in *Iran—Past, Present, and Future: Aspen Institute, Persepolis Symposium*, ed. Jane W. Jacqz (New York: Aspen Institute for Humanistic Studies, 1976), 408. See also Ashraf, "Iranian Identity."

53. See, for example, Ayatollah Sadeq Khalkhali, *Khatirat-i Ayatollah Sadeq Khalkhali* (Tehran: Saye, 1379/2000), 274–75.

54. Shari'ati, *Bazshenasi huviyat-i Irani Islami*, 319.

55. This distinction, which has won popularity among researchers of nationalism, has been under recent attack by theoretician Bernard Yack. See Bernard Yack, *Nationalism and the Moral Psychology of Community* (Chicago: Univ. of Chicago Press, 2012), 23–25.

56. Shari'ati, *Bazshenasi huviyat-i Irani Islami*, 145–46.

57. Mahmood T. Davari, *The Political Thought of Ayatullah Mortaza Mutahhari: An Iranian Theoretician of the Islamic State* (London: Taylor & Francis, 2005), 10–14.

58. Ori Goldberg, *Shi'i Theology in Iran: The Challenge of Religious Experience* (London: Routledge, 2012), 33–34.

59. Ali Rahnema and Farhad Nomani, *The Secular Miracle: Religion, Politics, and Economic Policy in Iran* (London: Zed Books, 1990), 38.

60. Rahnema and Nomani, *The Secular Miracle*, 40.

61. Rahnema, *An Islamic Utopian*, 251–53.

62. Michael Fischer and Mehdi Abedi, *Debating Muslims: Cultural Dialogues in Postmodernity and Tradition* (Madison: Univ. of Wisconsin Press, 1990), 187.

63. Mortaza Motahhari, *Selections from "The Reciprocal Services between Islam and Iran,"* trans. Idris Tijjani Samari and Maina Bukar (Qom, Iran: International Center for Islamic Studies, 2004), 58.

64. Mahmood Davari, *The Political Thought of Ayatullah Mortaza Mutahhari: An Iranian Theoretician of the Islamic State* (London: Taylor & Francis, 2005), 10–14.

65. Motahhari, *Selections*, 54.

66. Motahhari, *Selections*, 55.

67. Motahhari, *Selections*, 56.

68. Motahhari, *Selections*, 75.

69. Motahhari, *Selections*, 64.

70. Motahhari, *Selections*, 64.

71. Motahhari, *Selections*, 64.

72. Motahhari, *Selections*, 74.

73. Motahhari, *Selections*, 82.

74. Motahhari, *Selections*, 85.

75. Motahhari, *Selections*, 93.

76. Motahhari, *Selections*, 109. See also Werner Ende, *Arabische Nation und Islamische Geschichte: Die Umayyaden im Urteil Arabischer Autoren des 20. Jahrhunderts* (Beirut, Lebanon: Orient-Institut der Deutschen Morgenlaendischer Gesellschaft; Wiesbaden, Germany: F. Steiner, 1977), 147–53. Ende shows the involvement of national awareness as understood by Shi'ite thinkers in Iraq in their assessment of the early period of Islam.

77. Motahhari, *Selections*, 199.

78. Motahhari, *Selections*, 119.

79. Cyrus Kadivar, "We Are Awake: 2,500-Year Celebrations Revisited," *Parsikhabar*, Jan. 25, 2002, at http://parsikhabar.net/culture/2500-years-the-persepolis-celebrations-of-1971/1510/.

80. Shafa', *Korush-i Kabir*, 279.

81. Nasr even dreamed of acting as a bridge between the Islamic opposition and the shah's regime in a sort of "Islamic royal regime." See Seyyed Hossein Nasr and Ramin Jahanbegloo, *In Search of the Sacred: A Conversation with Seyyed Hossein Nasr on His Life and Thought* (Santa Barbara, CA: Praeger, 2010), 130.

82. Shojaeddin Shafa', *Tawazih al-masa'il* (Paris: Imprimérie Herissey à Evreux, 1360/1981). Interestingly, the thesis Shafa' chose for his book is one that clerics are required to explore in their scholarly training.

83. Shafa', *Tawazih al-masa'il*, introduction.

84. Shafa', *Tawazih al-masa'il*, 38, 42.

85. Shafa', *Tawazih al-masa'il*, 105.

86. Shafa', *Tawazih al-masa'il*, 105.

87. Shafa', *Tawazih al-masa'il*, 106.

88. Shafa', *Tawazih al-masa'il*, 106–7.

89. Shafa', *Tawazih al-masa'il*, 109.

90. Shafa', *Tawazih al-masa'il*, 156–57, 166, 172.

91. Shafa', *Tawazih al-masa'il*, 402.

92. Shafa', *Tawazih al-masa'il*, 421, 391, 381.

93. Shafa', *Tawazih al-masa'il*, 391.

94. Mary Boyce, "Bībī Šahrbānu," in *Encyclopaedia Iranica* (New York: Encyclopaedia Iranica Foundation, 2019), http://www.iranicaonline.org/articles/bibi-sahrbanu.

95. Shafa', *Tawazih al-masa'il*, 398–99, 3.

96. Shafa', *Tawazih al-masa'il*, 866.

97. Shafa', *Tawazih al-masa'il*, 923–24, 959.

98. Shafa', *Tawazih al-masa'il*, 388.

99. Shafa', *Tawazih al-masa'il*, 390, 391.

100. Shafa', *Tawazih al-masa'il*, 410, 411.

101. Shojaeddin Shafa', *Tavallud-i digar: Iran-i kuhan dar hazarah'i naw*, 2nd ed. (N.p.: Farzad, 1999), 10, 17.

102. Shafa', *Tavallud-i digar*, 17, 21.

103. Shafa', *Tavallud-i digar*, 32–33.

104. Shafa', *Tavallud-i digar*, 42.

3. A Lost King Rediscovered

1. On Azad, see Abduhu G. Rasool, *The Educational Ideas of Maulana 'Abul Kalam Azad* (New Delhi: Sterling, 1973); Douglas I. Henderson, *Abul Kalam Azad: An Intellectual and Religious Biography* (Delhi: Oxford Univ. Press, 1993).

2. Mohammad Ibrahim Bastani Parizi, introduction to Abul Kalam Azad, *Korush-i Bozorg (Dhul-Qarnayn)*, 6th ed., trans. Mohammad Ibrahim Bastani Parizi (Tehran: Safa, 1992), 1–145.

3. See, for example, Khomeini's speech in Ruhollah Khomeini, *Islam and Revolution: Writings and Declarations of Imam Khomeini*, ed. and trans. Hamid Algar (Berkeley, CA: Mizan Press, 1981), 177, 214; Khalkhali, *Khatirat-i Ayatollah Sadiq Khalkhali*, 228, 230.

4. Cottam, *Nationalism in Iran*, 27–28.

5. Deborah Levine Gera, *Xenophon's "Cyropaedia": Style, Genre, and Literary Technique* (Oxford: Clarendon Press, 1993), 20.

6. Gera, *Xenophon's "Cyropaedia,"* 14. See also Richard Frye, *The History of Ancient Iran* (Munich: C. H. Beck, 1984), 95–96.

7. On the limited potential of the written sources remaining from the Achaemenid period, see Pierre Briant, *From Cyrus to Alexander: A History of the Persian Empire* (Winona Lake, IN: Eisenbrauns, 2002), 2–4.

8. Richard Cottam, *Iran and the United States: A Cold War Case Study* (Pittsburgh, PA: Univ. of Pittsburgh Press, 1988), 27.

9. Eviatar Zerubavel, *Time Maps: Collective Memory and the Social Shape of the Past* (Chicago: Univ. of Chicago Press, 2012), 7.

10. Ali M. Ansari, *Modern Iran since 1921: The Pahlavis and After* (London: Pearson Education, 2003), 33.

11. See the section "Shojaeddin Shafa': The Historian as a Nationalist Ideologue" in chapter 2.

12. Shafa', *Korush-i Kabir,* 58–66.

13. On the tense relations between Iran and Egypt, for instance, see Shahram Chubin and Sepehr Zabih, *The Foreign Relations of Iran: A Developing State in a Zone of Great-Power Conflict* (Berkeley: Univ. of California Press, 1974), 141–43.

14. For some recent research on this topic, see Afshin Matin-Asgari, "The Academic Debate on Iranian Identity," in *Iran Facing Others: Identity Boundaries in a Historical Perspective*, ed. Abbas Amanat and Farzin Vejdani (New York: Palgrave Macmillan, 2012), 173–92; Ali M. Ansari, *The Politics of Nationalism in Modern Iran* (New York: Cambridge Univ. Press 2012).

15. Frederick Talberg, *Az Korush ta Pahlavi* (Shiraz, Iran: Nashriye Daneshgah-i Pahlavi, 1967). See also Peter Chelkowski, "Graphic Arts," in *Encyclopaedia Iranica* (New York: Encyclopaedia Iranica Foundation, 2002), at http://www.Iranica.com/articles/graphic-arts+frederick+talberg&ct=clnk.

16. Talberg, *Az Korush ta Pahlavi*, 8.

17. Talberg, *Az Korush ta Pahlavi*, 7.

18. Talberg, *Az Korush ta Pahlavi*, 9.

19. Mohammed Reza Shah Pahlavi, *Mission for My Country* (London: Hutchinson, 1961), 23–24.

20. Amir Abbas Hoveyda, budget speech, Feb. 23, 1971, quoted in Ansari, "Shah Mohammad Reza Pahlavi," 305.

21. Mahmud Ashrafi, *Korush-i Kabir* (Tehran: n.p., 1971); Fereydoun Badre'i, *Korush-i Kabir dar Qur'an-i majid va ahd-i atiq* (Tehran: Asatir, 1384/2005); Homayun, *Korush-i Kabir-i*; Mohammad Qa'imi, *Hachamenishiyan dar turat* (Isfahan, Iran: Entesharat-i Ta'yid-i Isfahan, 1970); Shafa', *Korush-i Kabir.*

22. Shapur Shahbazi, *Korush-i Bozorg* (Shiraz, Iran: Danishgah-i Pahlavi, 1970).

23. Shahbazi, *Korush-i Bozorg*, 32.

24. Shahbazi, *Korush-i Bozorg*, 37.

25. Shahbazi, *Korush-i Bozorg*, 37.

26. Albert Champdor, *Cyrus* (Paris: Michel, 1952); Harold Lamb, *Cyrus the Great* (Garden City, NY: Doubleday, 1960).

27. Qa'imi, *Hachamenishiyan dar turat.*

28. Unnumbered SAVAK file, Oct. 1966, in *Bazm-i Ahrīman, Jashnha-yi 2500 salah-i shahanshahi bih rivayat-i asnad-i Savak va darbar*, 4 vols. (Tehran: Markaz-i Bararasi Asnad-i Tarikh-i Vizarat-i Iṭṭila'at, 1377/1998), 2:225.

29. *Bazm-i Ahrīman*, 1:24.

30. It should be noted that in addition to the book on Cyrus, Shahbazi is the author of two books on Persepolis and a book on Ferdowsi, the composer of the national epic, the *Shahnameh*.

31. Sa'id Nafisi, introduction to Maulana Abul Kalam Azad, *Korush-i Bozorg (Dhul-Qarnayn)*, 1st ed. (Tehran: Ibn Sina, 1951), 12–148; 'Ali Asgar Mustafavi, *Zaman va Zendegi Ustaz Purdavoud* (Tehran: n.p., 1371/1993), 127–29; Bastani Parizi, introduction to Azad, *Korush-i Bozorg*, 6th ed., 18.

32. Ashrafi, *Korush-i Kabir*, introduction.

33. Ashrafi, *Korush-i Kabir*, 28.

34. Barbara Johnstone, *Discourse Analysis* (Malden, MA: Blackwell, 2001), 10.

35. Ashrafi, *Korush-i Kabir*, 12.

36. Ansari, *Modern Iran since 1921*, 164; Ansari, "Shah Mohammed Reza Pahlavi," 57.

37. Marvin Zonis, interviewed in *The Last Shah*, directed by Tim Kirby (London: BBC, 1996).

38. Ansari, "Shah Mohammed Reza Pahlavi," 27.

39. According to David Menashri, that was the way some professors from Tehran University regarded the shah's situation (*Iran in Revolution* [in Hebrew] [Tel Aviv: HaKibbutz HaMeuhad, 1988], 29; see also Bertrand de Castelbajac, *L'homme qui voulait être Cyrus* [Paris: Éditions Albatros, 1987]).

40. Abbas Nadjm, "2500 Anniversary of the Founding of the Persian Empire," in *Kurus Memorial Volume*, ed. Indo Iran Cultural Society and K. R. Cama Oriental Institute (Bombay: Iran Culture House, 1974), xix. Nadjm was the consul-general of Iran in Bombay at the time.

41. Homayun, *Korush-i Kabir-i*.

42. Gholam'ali Homayun, "Iran in Europaeischen Bildzeugnissen vom Ausgang des Mittelalters bis ins Actzehnte Jahrhundert," PhD diss., Univ. of Cologne, 1967; Gholam'ali Homayun, *Iran in Historisch-Geographischen Werken Europaeischer Gelehrter im 16 Jh* (Berlin: AMI Band 3, 1970); Gholam'ali Homayun, *Erforschung der altiranischen Architektur durch die Europäer* (Tehran: Tehran Univ., 1976), 2–10.

43. Homayun, *Korush-i Kabir-i*, 5.

44. Homayun, *Korush-i Kabir-i*, 6.

45. Liora Hendelman-Baavur, "The Gender of Modernity" [in Hebrew], PhD diss., Tel Aviv Univ., 2006, 203.

46. Delicia Harvey and Lance Strate, "Image Culture and the Supermodel," in *Critical Studies in Media Commercialism*, ed. Robin Anderson and Lance Strate (New York: Oxford Univ. Press, 2000), 203.

47. Hadi Hedayati, *Korush-i Kabir* (Tehran: Tehran Univ. Press, 1956), 188.

48. According to Steven Ward, between 1970 and 1977 the Iranian defense budget surged from around $900 million to $9.4 billion (*Immortal: A Military History of Iran and Its Armed Forces* [Washington, DC: Georgetown Univ. Press, 2009], 194–95).

49. Massoume Price, *Iran's Diverse Peoples: A Reference Sourcebook* (Santa Barbara, CA: ABC-CLIO, 2005), 267; David Yeroushalmi, *The Jews of Iran in the Nineteenth Century: Aspects of History, Community, and Culture* (Leiden: Brill, 2010), 359–60.

50. Sadeq Khalkhali, *Korush-i doroughin* (Tehran: Saye, 1981).

51. Nawab Ali Yavar Jung, foreword to *Kurus Memorial Volume*, ed. Indo Iran Cultural Society and K. R. Cama Oriental Institute, x.

52. Jung, foreword to *Kurus Memorial Volume*, xii.

53. Homayun, *Korush-i Kabir*, 11.

54. Nadjm, "2500 Anniversary of the Founding of the Persian Empire," xviii.

55. Hedayati, *Korush-i Kabir*, 186–88.

56. Hedayati, *Korush-i Kabir*, 190, 194.

57. Ali Akbar Dareini, *The Rise and Fall of the Pahlavi Dynasty: Memoirs of Former General Hosein Fardust* (Delhi, India: Motilal Banarsidass, 1999), 262–64.

58. Shafa', *Korush-i Kabir*, 20–21.

59. See, for example, Amatzia Baram, "Mesopotamian Identity in Ba'athi Iraq," *Middle Eastern Studies* 19, no. 4 (Oct. 1983): 426–55; Amatzia Baram, *Culture, History, and Ideology in the Formation of Ba'athist Iraq 1968–1989* (New York: St. Martin's Press, 1991), introduction.

60. Shafa', *Korush-i Kabir*, 29.

61. Amélie Kuhrt, *The Persian Empire* (Hoboken, NJ: Taylor and Francis, 2013), 6.

62. See, for instance, Homayun, *Korush-i Kabir*, 5–10. Homayun grapples with the fact that no Iranian literature from the time of Cyrus has survived, which left the memory of him to be recorded by other peoples.

63. *The Qur'an*, trans. Thomas B. Irving (Brattleboro, VT: Amana Books, 1985), sura 18:83–98.

64. The assertion that Dhul-Qarnayn was Alexander the Great originates in the commentary of Ibn Hisham (d. 833, Egypt). Other theories have suggested that Dhul-Qarnayn was a Yemenite king or some other ruler in the Arabian Peninsula.

65. Montgomery Watt, "Iskandar," in *Encyclopedia of Islam*, new ed., ed. P. J. Bearman, Bianquis, C. E. Bosworth, E. Van Donzel, and W. P. Heinrichs, vol. 4 (Leiden: Brill, 1990), 127, at http://dx.doi.org/10.1163/1573-3912_islam_SIM_3630. See also Jalal al-Din Mohammad bin Ahmad al-Mahalli and Jalal al-Din Abd al-Rahman ibn Abu-Baker al-Suyyuti, *Tafsir al-Jalalayn* (Cairo: Maktabat al-Jumhuriyya al-'Arabiyya, 1983), 251, Qur'an 18:83.

66. Henry Rawlinson, "Sir Saiyid Ahmed Khan," in *Sir Sayyid Ahmad Khan, 1817–1898: A Prominent Muslim Politician and Educationist*, ed. M. Ikram Chaghatai (Lahore, Pakistan: Sang-i-Meel, 2005), 109.

67. Shan Mohammad, *Sir Syed Ahmad Khan* (Lahore, Pakistan: Mohammad Iqbal, 1986), 189–91.

68. S. M. Taher Rezwi, *The Parsis: A People of the Book* (Calcutta: Taraporewala and Sons, 1928), 26.

69. Rezwi, *The Parsis*, 129. Rezwi supported his argument by referring to the Book of Daniel in the Bible as well as to some biographical details from the life of Darius.

70. Touraj Daryaee, "Religion of Cyrus the Great," in *Cyrus the Great: An Ancient Iranian King*, ed. Touraj Daryaee (Santa Monica, CA: Afshar, 2013), 16–27.

71. On Azad, see Rasool, *Educational Ideas of Maulana 'Abul Kalam Azad*; Henderson, *Abul Kalam Azad*.

72. Abul Kalam Azad, "Archeology and History" (convocation address at Aligrah Univ., Feb. 20, 1949), in *Speeches of Maulana Azad* (Delhi: Publications Division, Ministry of Information and Broadcasting), 69–74.

73. Abul Kalam Azad, "Welcome Address on the Occasion of the Visit of Their Imperial Majesties, the Shahanshah, and the Empress of Iran, New Delhi, February 19, 1956," in *Speeches of Maulana Azad*, 369–71.

74. Azad, "Welcome Address," 370.

75. M. Siddique, "The Work of Maulana Azad," in *Life and Times of Maulana Abul Kalam Azad*, ed. S. B. Singh and Nagendra Mohana Prasad (Patna, India: Kashi Prasad Jayaswal Research Institute, 1993), 221.

76. Quoted in S. G Mohiuddin, "Religious Thoughts of Maulana Azad," in *Life and Works of Maulana Abul Kalam Azad*, ed. Ravindra Kumar (New Delhi: Atlantic, 1991), 67.

77. On Azad's misunderstanding of Wilhelm Schmidt on this topic, see Henderson, *Abul Kalam Azad*, 202.

78. Henri Frankfort, *The Art and Architecture of the Ancient Orient* (New Haven, CT: Yale Univ. Press, 1996), 364. It seems that as early as 1926, Ernest Herzfeld (who excavated Pasargadae) ruled out the possibility that the winged genius found in the gate at Pasargadae is a king. David Stronach calls the notion—cultivated by Azad and others—that the winged figure represents Cyrus "a palpably mistaken belief" ("Cyrus and Pasargadae," in *Cyrus the Great*, ed. Daryaee, 53–77).

79. Bastani Parizi, introduction to Azad, *Korush-i Bozorg*, 6th ed., 5.

80. SAVAK file no. 5448, 30.3.1341 (1963), in *Bazm-i Ahrīman*, 313.

81. Bastani Parizi, introduction to Azad, *Korush-i Bozorg*, 6th ed.

82. Bastani Parizi, introduction to Azad, *Korush-i Bozorg*, 6th ed., 16–17.

83. Bastani Parizi, introduction to Azad, *Korush-i Bozorg*, 16–17.

84. Bastani Parizi, introduction to Azad, *Korush-i Bozorg*, 18.

85. Nafisi, introduction to Azad, *Korush-i Bozorg*, 1st ed., 27.

86. Dabashi, *Theology of Discontent*, 308.

87. ʿAllamah Mohammad Husayn Tabataba'i, *Tafsir al-mizan* (Qom, Iran: Muassasah-i Maṭbuati Ismāʿīliyān, 1981), 386–87, and *Tafsir al-mizan* (Qom, Iran: Muassasah-i Maṭbuati Ismāʿīliyān, 1985).

88. Tabataba'i, *Tafsir al-mizan* (1981), 387.

89. Tabataba'i, *Tafsir al-mizan* (1981), 388, 387.

90. Tabataba'i, *Tafsir al-mizan* (1981), 386.

91. Tabataba'i, *Tafsir al-mizan* (1981), 389.

92. For an early analysis of the antimonarchical components of the revolutionary movement, see Yann Richard, "Le rôle du clergé: Tendances contradictoires du chiisme iranien contemporain," *Archives de Sciences Sociales des Religions 28e Année* 55, no. 1 (Jan.–Mar. 1983): 5–27; Ansari, *The Politics of Nationalism*, 198–200.

93. Cyrus Ghani, *Iran and the Rise of Reza Shah: From Qajar Collapse to Pahlavi Rule* (London: I. B. Tauris, 1998), 307–8, 315–16.

94. Dabashi, *Theology of Discontent*, 273–77.

95. Khomeini, *Islam and Revolution*, 201.

96. Khalkhali would later become famous with the rise of the clerics in the aftermath of the revolution in 1979 and receive the notorious title "Khomeini's hanging judge." For Khalkhali's autobiography, see Khalkhali, *Korush-i doughin*, 9–10, 41–42. For more on Khalkhali, see Amir Taheri, *The Spirit of Allah: Khomeini and the Islamic Revolution* (London: Hutchinson, 1985), 113, 186–87.

97. Khalkhali, *Korush-i dorughin*, 227–29.

98. Khalkhali, *Korush-i dorughin*, 229.

99. On Esther, see Shaul Shaked, "Book of Esther," in *Encyclopaedia Iranica* (New York: Encyclopaedia Iranica Foundation, 2011), at http://www.iranicaonline.org/articles/esther-book-of.

100. Khalkhali, *Korush-i dorughin*, 229.

101. Khalkhali, *Korush-i dorughin*, 274–75. See also Mozaffari, *Forming National Identity in Iran*, 57.

102. Mateo Mohammad Farzaneh, "Shiʿi Ideology, Secular Nationalism, and the Iran-Iraq War (1980–1988)," *Studies in Ethnicity and Nationalism* 7, no. 1 (2007): 86–103.

103. For the gradual yet consistent transition from the first decade following the Islamic Revolution to the early 1990s, see Abdi, "Nationalism, Politics, and the Development of Archaeology in Iran." Abdi points to President Rafsanjani's visit to Persepolis as a turning point that marks the political elite's recognition of the importance of the pre-Islamic past.

104. Setrag Manoukian, *City of Knowledge in Twentieth Century Iran* (Oxford: Routledge, 2012).

105. According to the catalog of the Iranian National Library.

106. A short list of the publications holding this view includes Musa Mir Mudarris, *Korush va Zu al-Qarnayn az didgah-i tarikh va ayin* (Tehran: Markaz-i Nashr-i ʿUlum-i Danishgahi va Maʿarif-i Islam-i Fazil, 1994); Jalil Irfan'manish, *Korush va bazyabi-i huviyat-i*

milli: Taḥqiqi-i ʻilmi darbarah-ʼi pishinah va kisti-i Zu al-Qarnayn (Tehran: Intisharat-i Farhang-i Maktub, 2010); Korush Karamipur, *Raz Korush-i Bozorg* (Tehran: Intisharat-i ʻIlmi, 2011); Nasir Makarim-Shirazi, *Tafsir-i numunah* (Tehran: Dar al-Kutub al-Islamiyah, 2004).

107. See Shabnam J. Holliday, *Defining Iran: Politics of Resistance* (Farnham, UK: Ashgate, 2011), 23–25.

108. Farah Safizadeh, *Az Korush Hakhamenishi ta Mohammad Khatami* (Tehran: Gofteman, 1999), 14–15.

109. Mudarris, *Korush va Zu al-Qarnayn*, 10.

110. Nasir Usku'i, *Korush: Nabighah-ʼi buzurg-i tarikh* (Tehran: Intisharat-i Bu ʻAli, 1998), 21.

111. Karamipur, *Raz Korush-i*, 153–54.

112. "Bazgosht manshur-i Korush pas az 45 sal," *Iran*, Sept. 12, 2010, at http://www.tabnak.ir/fa/pages/?cid=119554.

113. For a description of the exhibition, see John Curtis, "The Cyrus Cylinder: The Creation of an Icon and Its Loan to Tehran," in *The Cyrus Cylinder: The Great Persian Edict from Babylon*, ed. Irving Finkel (London: I. B. Tauris, 2013), 85–103. For the cylinder's reception in Iran, see Neil McGregor, "The Many Meanings of the Cyrus Cylinder," in *The Cyrus Cylinder*, ed. Curtis, 9–17.

114. Jamshid Bozorg, "Hachaminisiyan basiji va jang-i qudrat," BBC Persian, Sept. 11, 2010, at http://www.bbc.co.uk/persian/iran/2010/09/100911_u03_cyrus_basij_rights_charter.shtml.

115. "Name Ruhaniyat-i Shiraz be Ahmadinejad," *Khabar*, Mar. 19, 2011, at http://www.khabaronline.ir/news-138021.aspx; Mitra Shujaʻi, "Az takhrib-i Takht-i Jamshid ta borgozori Nouruz dar an," *Deutsche Welle*, Mar. 10, 2011, at http://www.dw-world.de/dw/article/0,,6465999,00.html.

4. Persepolis Revisited

1. Quoted in Ervand Abrahamian, *Radical Islam: The Iranian Mojahedin* (London: I. B. Tauris, 1989), 116.

2. See, for example, George Lachmann Mosse, *The Nationalization of the Masses: Political Symbolism and Mass Movements in Germany from the Napoleonic Wars through the Third Reich* (New York: Howard Fertig, 1975); Pierre Nora, *Realms of Memory: Rethinking the French Past*, vol. 1: *Conflicts and Divisions* (New York: Columbia Univ. Press, 1996); Smith, *Ethno-symbolism and Nationalism*:; Athena S. Leoussi and Steven Grosby, eds., *Nationalism and Ethnosymbolism: History, Culture, and Ethnicity in the Formation of Nations* (Edinburgh: Edinburgh Univ. Press, 2007).

3. Quoted in Anna Francis, "Ghirshman Laments Neglected Periods," *Tehran Journal*, Apr. 16, 1968, reprinted in *Surveyors of Persian Art*, ed. Jay Gluck and Noel Silver (Costa Mesa: Mazda, 1996), 528.

4. For more on archaeology in Iran in the late 1960s with some general observations, see Raoul Curiel, George Wright, Maxime Siroux, Graeme Shankland, and Roberto La Francesca, *Programme spécial de préservation et de mise en valeur de l'héritage culturel en liaison avec le développement du tourisme: Conclusions d'un groupe de cinq consultants: Iran* (Geneva: UNESCO, Dec. 1967–Apr. 1968).

5. Curiel et al., *Programme spécial de préservation*, 3.

6. Kamal Aldin Niknami, *Methodological Aspects of Iranian Archaeology: Past and Present* (Oxford: British Archeological Reports International Series, 2000), 38, 39.

7. Nora, "Between Memory and History," 8, 12, 7.

8. Clifford Geertz, "Centers, Kings, and Charisma," in *Culture and Its Creators: Essays in Honor of Edward Shils*, ed. Joseph Ben-David and Terry Nichols Clark (Chicago: Univ. of Chicago Press, 1977), 150–71; Sarah Hanley, "Legend, Ritual, and Discourse in the *Lit de Justice* Assembly: French Constitutional Ideology, 1527–1641," in *Rites of Power: Symbolism, Ritual, and Politics since the Middle Ages*, ed. Sean Willanz (Philadelphia: Univ. of Pennsylvania Press, 1985), 85; Richard Wortman, "Moscow and Petersburg: The Problem of the Political Center in Tsarist Russia, 1881–1914," in *Rites of Power*, ed. Willanz, 265–67.

9. Geertz, "Centers, Kings, and Charisma," 152.

10. Smith, *National Identity*, 77.

11. Rodney Barker, *Legitimating Identities: The Self-Presentation of Rulers and Subjects* (Cambridge: Cambridge Univ. Press, 2001), 13.

12. Eric Hobsbawm, "Introduction: Inventing Traditions," in *The Invention of Tradition*, ed. Eric Hobsbawm and Terence Ranger (Cambridge: Cambridge Univ. Press, 1983), 2.

13. Hobsbawm, "Introduction," 2.

14. Richard Handler and Jocelyn Linnekin, "Tradition, Genuine or Spurious," *Journal of American Folklore* 97, no. 385 (July–Sept. 1984): 273.

15. Handler and Linnekin, "Tradition, Genuine or Spurious," 273.

16. Nora, *Realms of Memory*, 1:2.

17. See, for example, Winter and Sivan, "Setting the Framework"; Hutton, *History as an Art of Memory*, 147–53; Confino, *The Nation as a Local Metaphor*, 12–13.

18. Nora, *Realms of Memory*, 1:2.

19. Winter and Sivan, "Setting the Framework," 10; Bodnar, *Remaking America*, 16–20; Kirk Savage, *Standing Soldiers, Kneeling Slaves: Race, War, and Monument in Nineteenth-Century America* (Princeton, NJ: Princeton Univ. Press, 1997), 5–10.

20. See also Israel Gershoni, *Pyramid for the Nation: Commemoration, Memory, and Nationalism in Twentieth-Century Egypt* [in Hebrew] (Tel Aviv: Am Oved, 2006), 34–44.

21. Winter and Sivan, "Setting the Framework," 10.

22. Gershoni, *Pyramid for the Nation*, 40.

23. Briant, *From Cyrus to Alexander*, 85–88; Mohammad Dandamaev, *A Political History of the Achaemenid Empire* (Leiden: Brill, 1989), 20.

24. See, for example, Shafa', *Tawazih al-masa'il*, introduction.

25. Shapur Shahbazi, "Persepolis," in *Encyclopaedia Iranica* (New York: Encyclopaedia Iranica Foundation, 2011), at http://www.iranicaonline.org/articles/persepolis.

26. See, for example, Eugène N. Flandin and Pascal-Xavier Coste, *Voyage en Perse pendant le années 1840 et 1841*, 2 vols. (Paris: Gile et Jules Baudry, 1851), as well as Carl F. Andreas and Franz Stolze, *Persepolis: Die achämenidischen und sasanidischen Denkmäler und Inschriften von Persepolis, Istakhr, Pasargadae, Shahpur*, 2 vols. (Berlin: n.p., 1882).

27. Shahrokh Razmjou has offered such an explanation in recent years as well. See Shahrokh Razmjou, "Persepolis: A Reinterpretation of Palaces and Their Function," in *The World of Achaemenid Persia: History, Art, and Society in Iran and the Ancient Near East*, ed. John Curtis and St. John Simpson (London: I. B. Tauris, 2005), 231–45.

28. 'Ali Sami, "Bargozori-yi jashn-i Nowruz dar Takht-i Jamshid," *Honar-o Mardom* 104 (June 1971): 2. Takht-i Jamshid (Jamshid's Throne) is the popular name of the Persepolis site among Iranians. It derives from the legendary figure of Jamshid, a king considered Iranians' ancestor.

29. John Perry, *Karim Khan Zand* (Oxford: Oneworld, 2006), 10; John Perry, "Karim Khan Zand," in *Encyclopaedia Iranica* (New York: Encyclopaedia Iranica Foundation, 2011), at http://www.iranica.com/articles/karim-khan-zand.

30. Firoozeh Kashani-Sabet, "Fragile Frontiers: The Diminishing Domains of Qajar Iran," *International Journal of Middle East Studies* 29, no. 2 (1997): 206.

31. Nasiri-Moghaddam, *L'archéologie français en Perse*, 254.

32. Goode, *Negotiating for the Past*, 131.

33. Correspondence between Professor Herzfeld and Court Minister Abulhusayn Taymurtash, Sept. 4, 1929, document no. 6/1, in *Bastanshenasidar Iran* (Tehran: Iranian Ministry of Culture, Oct. 28, 1929), 25–28.

34. Donald Newton Wilber, *Persepolis: The Archaeology of Parsa, Seat of the Persian Kings* (London: Cassell, 1969); Ali Mousavi, "Ernst Herzfeld, Politics, and Antiquities Legislation in Iran," in *Ernst Herzfeld and the Development of Near Eastern Studies 1900–1950*, ed. Ann C. Gunter and Stefan R. Hauser (Leiden: Brill, 2005), 445–75.

35. David Stronach and Rudiger Schmitt, "Apadana," in *Encyclopaedia Iranica* (New York: Encyclopaedia Iranica Foundation, 2019), at http://www.iranicaonline.org/articles/apadana.

36. Ali Mousavi, "Persepolis in Retrospect: Histories of Discovery and Archeological Exploration at the Ruins of Ancient Parseh," *Art Orientalis* 32, no. 1 (2002): 239–40.

37. Kashani-Sabet, *Frontier Fictions*, 44.

38. Ezzat O. Negahban, *Karnameh* (Tehran: Sazman-i Mirath-i Farhang-i Keshvar 1997), 6–7.

39. Naqsh-i Rostam is an archaeological site containing the tombs of four Achaemenid kings and inscriptions describing them, located twelve kilometers northwest of Persepolis.

40. Sadiq, *Yadegar-i 'Umr*, 2:197.

41. Abbas Abdi, interviewed in *The Fall of the Shah*, documentary, BBC, Feb. 2009; Richard Frye, *Greater Iran: A 20th-Century Odyssey* (Costa Mesa, CA: Mazda, 2005), 236–37; *Jashn-i honar-i Shiraz bi revayat-i asnad-i Savak* (Tehran: Markaz-i Bararasi Asnad-i Tarikh-i Vizarat-i Ettelaʿat, 1381/2002), 8, 10–11.

42. According to Abbas Abdi, an opposition activist at the time, left-wing students were even more extreme in their criticism of some performances in Shiraz. See the interview of Abdi in the BBC documentary *The Fall of the Shah*.

43. Goode, *Negotiating for the Past*, 232; Abdi, "Nationalism, Politics, and the Development of Archeology in Iran," 72.

44. Robert Gluck, "The Shiraz Arts Festival: Western Avant-Garde Arts in 1970s Iran," *Leonardo* 40, no. 1 (2007): 22.

45. Interviewed for *Shiraz Arts Festival: Sound the Trumpets, Beat the Drums*, video, n.d., at http://www.youtube.com/watch?v=Ui3rw8ApGo8, accessed Dec. 10, 2016, no longer available.

46. James Harley, *Xenakis: His Life in Music* (New York: Routledge, 2004), 68.

47. *Ruznameh-i Jashn-i Shahenshahi*, Sept. 21, 1971, a special bulletin distributed as a supplement to the *Kayhan* and *Ettelaʿat* newspapers for two months before and during the celebrations, describing in minute detail various aspects of the festivities and their impact around the world.

48. See, for example, *Royal Persia: A Commemoration of Cyrus the Great and His Successors on the Occasion of the 2500th Anniversary of the Founding of the Persian Empire*, exhibition catalog (London: British Museum, 1971); SAVAK file no. 2044/7380, Feb. 22, 1970, in *Bazm-i Ahrīman*, 3:149; SAVAK file no. 1078/252, Jan. 22, 1971, in *Bazm-i Ahrīman*, 4:21; SAVAK file no. 201/1351, May 11, 1971, in *Bazm-i Ahrīman*, 4:59.

49. "Rulers Who Were Endowed with the Title 'the Great' (*Kabir*) by History," *Ruznameh-i Jashn-i Shahenshahi*, Aug. 16, 1971.

50. "Iran Aryamehr dar kenar Iran bastani va Iran Korush," *Ruznameh-i Jashn-i Shahanshahi*, Sept. 7, 1971.

51. "Iran Aryamehr dar kenar."

52. David Stronach, interviewed by the author, Berkeley, CA, Nov. 20, 2013.

53. Talinn Grigor, "Of Metamorphosis: Meaning on Iranian Terms," *Third Text* 17, no. 3 (2003): 211.

54. "Tajali inqilab dar mʿimari," *Ruznameh-i Jashn-i Shahenshahi*, Oct. 10, 1971.

55. Talinn, "Of Metamorphosis," 211.

56. Talinn Grigor, "Preserving the Antique Modern: Persepolis '71," *Future Anterior* 2, no. 1 (2005): 23–24.

57. See, for example, A. Aymard, "Hachamenishiha va Yunaniyan," *Ruznameh-i Jashn-i Shahenshahi*, Sept. 9, 1971, and Arnold Toynbee, "The System of Rule of Cyrus

and His Heirs Is the Same One Sought Today by Modern Rulers," *Ruznameh-i Jashn-i Shahenshahi*, Oct. 4, 1971.

58. See, for example, Mohammad Ibrahim Bastani Parizi, *Historical Atlas of Iran* (Tehran: Univ. of Tehran Press, 1971); *Ruznameh-i Jashn-i Shahenshahi*, Oct. 27, 1971; Yahya Shahidi, ed., *Majale-yi bararsiha-yi tarikhi*, Iranian Military no. 5 (Tehran: Artesh-I Iran, 1970–71).

59. See, for example, *Ettela'at*, Oct. 27, 1971; Mohammad 'Ali Imam Shushtari, "Forsat-i jashn-i shahenshahi, falsafeh-yi insani-yi Iran bi dunya mishinasunad," interview, *Ruznameh-i Jashn-i Shahenshahi*, Oct. 10, 1971; "Tajareb-i shahenshahi Iran mitavonad sar meshqe bashariyat boshad," *Ruznameh-i Jashn-i Shahenshahi*, Oct. 4, 1971.

60. Ansari, "Shah Mohammad Reza Pahlavi," 309.

61. Farian Sabahi, "The Literacy Corps in Pahlavi Iran (1963–1979): Political, Social, and Literary Implications," PhD diss., SOAS Univ. of London, 1999, 104.

62. See, for example, Moscow Radio, a report by Javad Bushehri, chairman of the Celebrations Committee, to the Ministry of Foreign Affairs, Aug. 10, 1969, SAVAK file no. 6241, in *Bazm-i Ahrīman*, 3:127; for Switzerland, SAVAK file no. 261/103/8, Oct. 15, 1969, in *Bazm-i Ahrīman*, 3:131.

63. Quoted in Charles J. Adams, introduction to *Iranian Civilization and Culture: Essays in Honour of the 2,500th anniversary of the Founding of the Persian Empire*, ed. Charles J. Adams (Montreal: Institute of Islamic Studies, McGill Univ., 1972), x–xiii.

64. Adams, introduction to *Iranian Civilization and Culture*, xv.

65. Shushtari, "Forsat-i jashn-i shahenshahi."

66. One prominent historian who developed this attitude was Fereydun Adamiyat (1920–2008). See, for example, Fereydun Adamiyat, *Afkar-i siyasi va ejtema'i va-eqtesadi dar montasher-i nashode dowran-i Qajar* (Tehran: Tagah, 2536/1977), 11–13; Hasan Pirniya, *Tarikh-i Iran-i bastan*, 10th ed., 3 vols. (Tehran: Dunya-i Ketab, 2003), 3:2946.

67. Roger Savory, "Iran: A 2500-Year Historical and Cultural Tradition," in *Iranian Civilization and Culture*, ed. Adams, 77.

68. Giuseppe Tucci, introduction to *Studies and Restoration at Persepolis and Other Sites of Fars*, ed. Ann Britt Tilia (Rome: ISMEO, 1972), xiii.

69. Grigor, "Preserving the Antique Modern," 26.

70. "Do gozaresh az rali bozorg Paris–Takht-i Jamshid–Paris," *Ruznameh-i Jashn-i Shahenshahi*, Sept. 4, 1971.

71. Diane Barthel, *Historic Preservation: Collective Memory and Historical Identity* (New Brunswick, NJ: Rutgers Univ. Press, 1996), 3.

72. Pahlavi, *Mission for My Country*, 27.

73. See, for example, "Iran: The Show of Shows" (editorial), *Time*, Oct. 25, 1971; "On That Day in Takht-i Jamshid," *Kayhan International*, Sept. 25, 1971; William A. McWhirter, "The Shah's Princely Party," *Life*, Oct. 29, 1971.

74. Grigor, "Preserving the Antique Modern," 26.

75. See, for example, Terence Ranger, "The Invention of Tradition in Colonial Africa," in *The Invention of Tradition*, ed. Hobsbawm and Ranger, 235.

76. Shahrokh Golestan, dir., *Flames of Persia* (producer unknown, 1971).

77. See, for example, David Beetham, *The Legitimation of Power* (Basingstoke, UK: Macmillan, 1991).

78. Barker, *Legitimating Identities*, 3.

79. Barker, *Legitimating Identities*, 7, 106.

80. Eli Podeh, *The Politics of National Celebrations in the Arab Middle East* (New York: Cambridge Univ. Press, 2011), 51.

81. "Kaveh va derafsha Kawiyani," *Kaveh*, Jan. 24, 1916, 3; "Nowruz," trans. W. Geiger, *Kaveh*, Apr. 18, 1916, 4–5; George Barandes, "Halat-i Iran az noqtay-i nazaryik bitaraf," *Kaveh*, Aug. 15, 1916, 1–2; Oskar Nidermayer, "Afghanistan," *Kaveh*, June 15, 1917, 3–6; Arthur Christensen, "She'r Pahlavi va she'r Farisi qadim," *Kaveh*, May 21, 1920, 24–26.

82. See, for example, for Switzerland, SAVAK file no. 261/103/8, Oct. 15, 1969, in *Bazm-i Ahrīman*, 3:131; see also Javad Bushehri's dispatch to the committee, Dec. 29 1969, SAVAK file no. 6241, in *Bazm-i Ahrīman*, 3:127.

83. Mohammad A. Dandamaev, "Congrès Internationales des Iranistes à Shiraz," in *Commemoration Cyrus: Actes du Congres de Shiraz 1971 et autres études redigées à l'occasion du 2500e anniversaire de la fondation de l'Empire Perse* (Leiden: Brill, 1974), 3.

84. See, for example, Pieter Geyl, "Toynbee's System of Civilizations," in *Toynbee and History: Critical Essays and Reviews*, ed. Montagu Ashley (Boston: P. Sargent, 1956), 39–72.

85. Elie Kedourie, *The Chatham House Version and Other Middle-Eastern Studies* (London: Weidenfeld and Nicolson, 1970), 354–74.

86. "Shive-yi shahenshahi Koroush va janeshinanash heman ruhiye ast," *Ruznameh-i Jashn-i Shahenshahi*, Oct. 4, 1971.

87. *Ruznameh-i Jashn-i Shahenshahi*, Oct. 4, 1971.

88. Arnold Toynbee, "The First Iranian Empire," in *Commemoration Cyrus*, 17.

89. Georgi Tsereteli, "The Achaemenid State and World Civilization," in *Commemoration Cyrus*, 103, 104.

90. *Sukhanraniha-yi nokhustin-i dawra-yi jalasat-i sukhanrani va bahs darbara-yi shahnama-yi Firdusi* (Tehran: Vizarat-i Farhang va Honar, 1971), 1–5.

91. Quoted in Adams, introduction to *Iranian Civilization*, ix.

92. Savory, "Iran," 77.

93. See, for example, SAVAK file no. 10532/20/h.12, May 14, 1971, in *Bazm-i Ahrīman*, 4:142–43, 154–62.

94. Anthony Parsons, *The Pride and the Fall: Iran, 1974–1979* (London: Jonathan Cape, 1984), 23.

95. Parsons, *The Pride and the Fall*, 21.

96. SAVAK file nos. 1044/3 and 204-40-6-48, in *Bazm-i Ahrīman*, 4:193–94, 4:217, 264–65.

97. See, for example, SAVAK file nos. 1044/3 and 204-40-6-48, in *Bazm-i Ahrīman*, 4:193–94, 4:217, 264–65.

98. See, for example, Dariush Homayoun's testimony in the BBC documentary *The Fall of the Shah*. See also Ahmad Khalili, a government official, complaining in the presence of Shapur Bakhtiyar about the shah's personality cult, file no. 12420/20, Oct. 11, 1970, in *Bazm-i Ahrīman*, 3:292.

99. Negin Nabavi, "The Discourse of 'Authentic Culture' in Iran in the 1960s and 1970s," in *Intellectual Trends in Twentieth-Century Iran: A Critical Survey*, ed. Negin Nabavi (Gainesville: Univ. Press of Florida, 2003), 108.

100. Nabavi, "The Discourse of 'Authentic Culture' in Iran," 94–95.

101. Frye, *Greater Iran*, 237; Anthony Parsons, *The Pride and the Fall*, 54.

102. Nabavi, *Intellectuals and the State in Iran*, 123.

103. SAVAK file no. 324, May 23, 1971, in *Bazm-i Ahrīman*, 4:77.

104. Muhin Dawlatishah Firuz, "Khatirat-i Muzaffar Firuz, Avenues, Paris," in *Bazm-i Ahrīman*, 3:21.

105. SAVAK file no. 1191, Sept. 4, 1971, in *Bazm-i Ahrīman*, 4:246.

106. *Bazm-i Ahrīma* 3:21.

107. 'Ali Shari'ati, *'Are barodar inchunin bud*, trans. Mohammad Amini and Alireza Bazargan (Tehran: n.p., 2006); Ruhollah Khomeini, *Islamic Government* (New York: Manor Books, 1979).

108. Khomeini, *Islam and Revolution*, 198.

109. Khomeini, *Islam and Revolution*, 202.

110. Khalkhali, *Korush-i doughin*, in *Khatirat-i Ayatollah Sadeq Khalkhali*, 251 (*Korush-i doughin* was published both separately and as part of Khalkhali's autobiography). Note that Khalkhali uses "the Middle Ages" in a Eurocentric sense as a negative term.

111. Milani, *Eminent Persians*, 2:xiv; Stephen C. Poulson, *Social Movements in Twentieth-Century Iran* (Lanham, MD: Lexington Books, 2005), 129.

112. Quoted in Elaine Sciolino, *Persian Mirrors: The Elusive Face of Iran* (New York: Touchstone, 2000), 168.

113. Rahnema, *An Islamic Utopian*, 237–39; Ali Rahnema, *Pioneers of Islamic Revival* (London: Zed Books, 1994), 231–34; Dabashi, *Theology of Discontent*, 102–9; Milani, *Eminent Persians*, 2:359–76.

114. Shari'ati, *'Are barodar inchunin bud*, 8.

115. Shari'ati, *'Are barodar inchunin bud*, 10.

116. Abrahamian, *Radical Islam*, 108–9, 122; Boroujerdi, *Iranian Intellectuals and the West*, 105.

117. Burke, *Attitudes toward History*, 179.

118. Dariush Ashuri, "Sunnat va pishraft," *Farhang va Zendegi* 1 (Dey 1, 1348/Dec. 1969–Jan. 1970): 72.

119. Al-e Ahmad, *Occidentosis*, 34.

120. Milani, *Eminent Persians*, 2:813–14; Boroujerdi, *Iranian Intellectuals*, 68, 113.

121. Nabavi, *Intellectuals and the State in Iran*, 102.

5. Celebrating Iranianness in the Islamic Republic

1. Mehdi Moslem, *Factional Politics in Post-Khomeini Iran* (Syracuse, NY: Syracuse Univ. Press, 2002), 60; Ervand Abrahamian, *Khomeinism: Essays on the Islamic Republic* (Berkeley: Univ. of California Press, 1993), 133.

2. *Ettela'at*, Nov. 7, 1987.

3. Quoted in *Keyhan*, June 6, 1984.

4. Quoted in *Ettela'at*, July 23, 1988.

5. Quoted in *Ettela'at*, Feb. 12, 1981.

6. Mahdi Fahimi, *Farhang-i Jabha: Sharha va rajzaha* (Kerman, Iran: Surush, 2007), 2:85.

7. See chapter 3.

8. Shahram Chubin and Charles Tripp, *Iran and Iraq at War* (London: I. B. Tauris, 1988), 9.

9. Amatzia Baram, *Saddam Husayn and Islam, 1968–2003: Ba'athi Iraq from Secularism to Faith* (Washington, DC: Woodrow Wilson Center Press, 2014), 187–205.

10. Ansari, *Modern Iran since 1921*, 169, 298.

11. Shireen Hunter, *Iran after Khomeini* (New York: Praeger, 1992), 93.

12. Sciolino, *Persian Mirrors*, 168.

13. Mohsen M. Milani, *The Making of Iran's Islamic Revolution: From Monarchy to Islamic Republic* (Boulder, CO: Westview Press, 1988), 316.

14. Farideh Farhi, "Crafting a National Identity amidst Contentious Politics in Contemporary Iran," in *Iran in the 21st Century: Politics, Economics, and Conflict*, ed. Homa Katouzian and Hossein Shahidi (London: Routledge, 2008), 13.

15. Hamid Ahmadi, *The Dilemma of National Interest in the Islamic Republic of Iran* (New York: Routledge, 2007), 30, 33.

16. David Menashri, *Revolution at a Crossroads: Iran's Domestic Politics and Regional Ambitions* (Washington, DC: Washington Institute for Near East Policy, 1997), 69.

17. James P. Piscatori, *Islam in a World of Nation-States* (Cambridge: Cambridge Univ. Press, 1986), 111.

18. Houchang Chehabi, "Iran and Iraq: Intersocietal Linkages and Secular Nationalisms," in *Iran Facing Others*, ed. Amanat and Vejdani, 192.

19. Farhi, "Crafting a National Identity," 13.

20. Holliday, *Defining Iran*, 45–48, 79–82.

21. Talinn Grigor, *Contemporary Iranian Art: From the Street to the Studio* (London: Reaktion Books, 2014), 12.

22. Khalkhali, *Korush-i doroughin*, in *Khatirat-i Ayatollah Sadeq Khalkhali*, 227–29.

23. Ruhollah Khomeini, *Sahife-yi Imam, Majmuʿe-'ye asar Imam Khomeini*, 22 vols. (Tehran: Mu'assese-yi Tanzim va Nashr-i Asar Imam Khomeini, 1387/2008), 13:78.

24. Khomeini, *Sahife-yi Imam*, 15:123–24.

25. Al-e Ahmad, *Occidentosis*.

26. Ruhollah Khomeini, *Sahife-yi Nur*, 22 vols. (Tehran: Vezarat-i Farhang va Ershad-i Islami, 1361/1982), 11:193.

27. Amitai Etzioni, "Toward a Theory of Public Ritual," *Sociological Theory* 18, no. 1 (Mar. 2000): 44–59; Dennis Zuev and Fabian Virchow, "Performing National-Identity: The Many Logics of Producing National Belongings in Public Rituals and Events," *Nations and Nationalism* 20, no. 2 (2014): 191–99.

28. Ehsan Yarshater, "The Political History of Iran under the Sasanians," in *The Cambridge History of Iran*, vol. 3: *Seleucid, Parthian, and Sasanian Periods*, ed. Ehsan Yarshater (Cambridge: Cambridge Univ. Press, 1983), 134.

29. A. Shapur Shahbazi, "NOWRUZ ii: In the Islamic Period," in *Encyclopaedia Iranica* (New York: Encyclopaedia Iranica Foundation, 2011), at http://www.iranicaonline.org/articles/nowruz-ii.

30. See, for example, Mohammad Larijani, "ʿId-i mobarak," *Ettelaʿat*, Esfand 23, 1377/Mar. 14, 1999.

31. Ayatollah ʿAli Khamenei, Nowruz message, Jumada al-ula 30, 1436/Mar. 21, 2015, at http://farsi.khamenei.ir/print-content?id=29204.

32. Ayatollah ʿAli Khamenei, Nowruz message, Shawwal 10, 1378/Dec. 31, 1999, at http://farsi.khamenei.ir/speech-content?id=2936.

33. Khamenei, Nowruz message, Shawwal 10, 1378/Dec. 31, 1999.

34. Khamenei, Nowruz message, Shawwal 10, 1378/Dec. 31, 1999.

35. Manouchehr Kasheff and ʿAli-Akbar Saʿidi Sirjani, "ČAHĀRŠANBA-SŪRĪ," in *Encyclopedia Iranica* (New York: Encyclopaedia Iranica Foundation, 2019), at http://www.iranicaonline.org/articles/caharsanba-suri.

36. Quoted in "Khatib-i Jomʿe Tehran: Cheharshanbe suri dar shan mellat ma nist," *Daneshju News*, Mar. 4, 2011, at https://www.balatarin.com/permlink/2011/3/4/2397880.

37. Homayun, *Korush-i Kabir*, 6; Shafaʿ, *Korush-i Kabir*, 29.

38. Bina Mahdavi, "Cheharshanbe suri ya cheharshanbe suzi?" *Ettelaʿat*, Esfand 22, 1385/Mar. 13, 2007.

39. Mahdavi, "Cheharshanbe suri ya cheharshanbe suzi?"

40. Wilfried Buchta, *Who Rules Iran? The Structure of Power in the Islamic Republic* (Washington, DC: Washington Institute for Near East Policy, 2000), 139–42; Ansari, *The Politics of Nationalism*, 246–50.

41. For a discussion of these terms, see Holliday, *Defining Iran*, 23–25.

42. Ayatollah 'Ali Hosseini Khamenei, *The Cultural Viewpoints of the Leader of the Islamic Republic* (Tehran: Center for Cultural and International Studies, 2000), 7, 4.

43. Ayatollah 'Ali Hosseini Khamenei, "Bayanat khabar mu'azzam enqilab islami dar ejtima'i tullab," Aban 14, 1379/Nov. 7, 2000, in *Kalam Vilayat Tariq Hidayat* (Tehran: Zafar, 1380/2001), 13–14.

44. Ayatollah 'Ali Hosseini Khamenei, "Khalam vilayyat nurihdayat: Sukhanraniha-yi Maqam-i Mu'azzam rahbar-i dar jam'iyye javan-i Esfahan," Aban 12, 1380/Nov. 3, 2001, in *Kalam Vilayat Tariq Hidayat*, 79.

45. Khamenei, "Khalam vilayyat nurihdayat," 13–14.

46. Khamenei, *Cultural Viewpoints*, 7.

47. Susan Siavoshi, "Construction of Iran's National Identity: Three Discourses," in *Rethinking Iranian Nationalism and Modernity*, ed. Aghaie and Marashi, 266.

48. Sayyid Mohammad Khatami, "Farhang-i Irani Islami, 1376 (1997)," in *Islam, ruhaniyyat va enqelab-i Islami* (Tehran: Tarh-i Nu, 1379/2000), 18.

49. Holliday, *Defining Iran*, 111.

50. Khatami, "Farhang-i Irani Islami," 20; see also Holliday, *Defining Iran*, 110.

51. Nasser Pourpirar, *Davozda qarn sukut: Bar madan-i Hachamenishiyan* (Tehran: Karnak, 1379/2000), 86–71; see also Dariush Ahmady and Amir Ne'maty Lima'iy, *Davozdah qarn shukuh* (Tehran: Omid Mehr, 1383/2004), 8–10, 29–30.

52. Nasser Pourpirar, *Na'al Varune* (Tehran: Pejuhashgah Farhangi va Andishe Eslami, 1383/2004), 30–35.

53. "Bahonar: 'Maktab-i Irani' fetne ayande ast," BBC Persian, Mar. 12, 2011, at http://www.bbc.co.uk/persian/iran/2011/03/110312_l10_iranism_bahonar_ahmadinejad.shtml.

54. "Name sargeshode Ahmad Tavakoli be Ahmadinejad dar enteqad-i az 'Iranigeri' u," BBC Persian, Mar. 1, 2011, at http://www.bbc.co.uk/persian/iran/2011/03/110301_l10_tavakoli_open_letter_ahmadinejad.shtml.

55. "Bazgosht manshur-i Korush pas az 45 sal"; "Manshur huquq-i bashar be keshvarash bazgosht," *Khabar Online*, Sept. 11, 2010, at https://www.khabaronline.ir/news/91526.

56. Bozorg, "Hachaminisiyan basiji va jang-i qudrat."

57. "Name jame'eh ruhaniyyat-i Shiraz be Ahmadinejad," *Khabar Online*, Mar. 19, 2011, at http://www.khabaronline.ir/news-138021.aspx; Shuja'i, "Az takhrib Takht-i Jamshid ta bargozori Nouruz dar an."

58. "Name sargeshode Ahmad Tavakoli."

59. Mozaffari, "The 'Heritage NGO,'" 851.

60. "Ruz-i Korush; yek chahre va chand tasvir az gozashte vahal," *Farda*, Dec. 23, 2007, at http://www.radiofarda.com/a/f1_kourosh_anniversary/418812.html.

61. "Sabt-i Ruz-i Korush dar taqvim-i melliy-i Iran," *Jamejam Online*, Nov. 21, 2008, at http://www1.jamejamonline.ir/newstext.aspx?newsnum=100954965004.

62. "Tazetarin vakenshha' be 'juryan enherafi' dar dowlat-i Iran," BBC Persian, May 16, 2011, at http://www.bbc.com/persian/iran/2011/05/110516_l07_iran_government_critics.shtml.

63. "Taqvim-i Iran," *Iran*, Oct. 21, 2011.

64. "Bastanshenasan khostar sebt-i ruz-i jahani Korush shodand," *Hamshahri Online*, Nov. 22, 2011, at http://hamshahrionline.ir/details/151828/Culture/historynews.

65. "Tajamu' mardom Pasargad be monasebat-i ruz-i Korush," BBC Persian, Oct. 28, 2016, at http://www.bbc.com/persian/interactivity-37805667; "Dadestan-i shiraz az bazdasht 'amelan' va 'sarshachehaye' marasem-i bazargdosht Korush khabar dad," BBC Persian, Oct. 31, 2016, at http://www.bbc.com/persian/iran-37820435.

66. "Pasargad: Sho'ar ne ghazeh ne lobnan janam feda'-yi Iran," *Hambastegimeli*, Oct. 30, 2016, at https://www.hambastegimeli.com/.

67. "Dar aramgah-i Korush che gozosht," BBC Persian, Oct. 29, 2016, at http://www.bbc.com/persian/iran-37813021.

68. Farhi, "Crafting a National Identity," 13.

69. Manfred Krebernik, *Polytheismus und Monotheismus in den Religionen des Vorderen Orients* (Münster, Germany: Ugarit, 2002), 91–111.

70. Korush Salihi, *Dar sarashib suqut* (Mashhad, Iran: Iran Azad, 1378/1999), 11.

71. Salihi, *Dar sarashib suqut*, 102–4.

72. Salihi, *Dar sarashib suqut*, 203.

73. Sciolino, *Persian Mirrors*, 168.

74. Yusuf Hasanzadeh and Sima Miri, introduction to *Majmu'a-yi maqalat-i hasht sal-i bastanshinasi-yi Iran*, ed. Yusuf Hasanzadeh and Sima Miri (Tehran: Pazina, 2012), 10–11.

75. Anderson, *Imagined Communities*; Kashani-Sabet, *Frontier Fictions*, 135–37.

76. Karen Zraick, "Persian (or Arabian) Gulf Is Caught in the Middle of Regional Rivalries," *New York Times*, Jan. 12, 2016, at http://www.nytimes.com/2016/01/13/world/middleeast/persian-gulf-arabian-gulf-iran-saudi-arabia.html?_r=0; Cyrus Alai, "Cartography of Persia," *Encyclopaedia Iranica* (New York: Encyclopaedia Iranica Foundation, 2012), at http://www.iranicaonline.org/articles/geography-iv-cartography-of-persia-.

77. Quoted in Frank D. Roylance, "Another Name for Gulf Sets Off a Wave of Anger," *Baltimore Sun*, Nov. 25, 2004, at http://articles.baltimoresun.com/2004-11-25/news/0411250185_1_iran-atlas-arabian-gulf.

78. Quoted in Roylance, "Another Name for Gulf."

79. Quoted in Roylance, "Another Name for Gulf."

80. Quoted in Roylance, "Another Name for Gulf."

81. Quoted in Roylance, "Another Name for Gulf."

82. "Statement on Persian Gulf/Arabian Gulf," *National Geographic*, press release, Nov. 23, 2004, at http://press.nationalgeographic.com/2004/11/23/statement-on-persian-gulfarabian-gulf/.

83. "Statement on Persian Gulf/Arabian Gulf."

84. "Pasargadae," UNESCO, n.d., at http://whc.unesco.org/en/list/1106, accessed Jan. 1, 2019.

85. Mozaffari, "The 'Heritage NGO,'" 849–50; Ulrich Boser, "Archaeology NEWS," *Archaeology* 58, no. 6 (2005): 10–13.

86. Soudabeh Sadigh, "Iran: First Trial for Sivand Dam's Inundation Held," *Payvand*, July 5, 2007, at http://www.payvand.com/news/07/jul/1061.html. On the somewhat exaggerated tone of the argument among Iranian expatriates, see Kamyar Abdi, "Sensationalism vs. Rationalism," *Iranian*, Sept. 12, 2005, at http://www.iranian.com/History/2005/September/Heritage4/index.html.

87. Ansari, *Politics of Nationalism*, 277.

88. The festival was meant to fuse East and West in music and dance arts and was known to have procured a few controversial performances that offended Shi'ite clerics. See Frye, *Greater Iran*, 237; Parsons, *Pride and the Fall*, 54; and Vali Mahlouji, *Festival of Arts: Shiraz–Persepolis* (London: Black Dog, 2014).

89. Matthew Elliot, "New Iran and the Dissolution of Party Politics under Reza Shah," in *Men of Order*, ed. Atabaki and Zurcher, 58–60.

90. Maryam Soltan-Zadeh, "History Education and the Construction of National Identity in Iran," PhD diss., Florida International Univ., 2012.

91. Nargese Qeraiyan, Zahra Shamaniyan, and Hussein Qassem Pourmuqaddam, *Farsi, panjam-i dabestan* (Tehran: Vizarat-i Amuzesh va Parvaresh, 1368/1980), 172–73.

92. Qeraiyan, Shamaniyan, and Pourmuqaddam, *Farsi, panjam-i dabestan*, 172–73.

93. See, for instance, *Ta'limat-i ejtema'i cheharam-i dabestan* (Tehran: Vizarat-i Amuzesh va Parvaresh, 1375/1996), 126.

94. M. Javadian, A. Kheirandish, and J. Abbasim, *History: The Second Year of Guidance School Period* (Tehran: Iran's Textbook Publishing and Distribution Office, 2007), 68.

95. *Ta'limat-i ejtema'i cheharam-i dabestan*, 119–20.

96. *Ta'limat-i ejtema'i cheharam-i dabestan*, 125.

97. *Ta'limat-i ejtema'i cheharam-i dabestan*, 124.

98. *Ta'limat-i ejtema'i cheharam-i dabestan*, 132.

99. Soltan-Zadeh, "History Education," 145.

100. Soltan-Zadeh, "History Education," 147.

101. Soltan-Zadeh, "History Education," 256.

Bibliography

Abdi, Kamyar. "Nationalism, Politics, and the Development of Archeology in Iran." *American Journal of Archeology* 105, no. 1 (Jan. 2001): 51–76.

———. "Sensationalism vs. Rationalism." *Iranian*, Sept. 12, 2005. At http://www.iranian.com/History/2005/September/Heritage4/index.html.

Abrahamian, Ervand. *Iran between Two Revolutions.* Princeton, NJ: Princeton Univ. Press, 1982.

———. *Khomeinism: Essays on the Islamic Republic.* Berkeley: Univ. of California Press, 1993.

———. *Radical Islam: The Iranian Mojahedin.* London: I. B. Tauris, 1989.

Adamiyat, Fereydun. *Afkar-i siyasi va ejtema'i va eqtesadi dar montasherh-i nashode dowran-i Qajar.* Tehran: Tagah, 2536/1977.

———. *Andishehay-i Akhundzadeh.* Tehran: Shareqat Sahmi Khorezmi, 1970.

Adams, Charles J. Introduction to *Iranian Civilization and Culture: Essays in Honour of the 2,500th Anniversary of the Founding of the Persian Empire,* edited by Charles J. Adams, x–xiii. Montreal: Institute of Islamic Studies, McGill Univ., 1972.

———, ed. *Iranian Civilization and Culture: Essays in Honour of the 2,500th Anniversary of the Founding of the Persian Empire.* Montreal: Institute of Islamic Studies, McGill Univ., 1972.

Aghaie, Kamran Scott. "Islamic-Iranian Nationalism and Its Implications for the Study of Political Islam and Religious Nationalism." In *Rethinking Iranian Nationalism and Modernity,* edited by Kamran Scott Aghaie and Afshin Marashi, 181–204. Austin: Univ. of Texas Press, 2014.

———. *The Martyrs of Karbala: Shi'i Symbols and Rituals in Modern Iran.* Seattle: Univ. of Washington Press, 2004.

Aghaie, Kamran Scott, and Afshin Marashi, eds. *Rethinking Iranian Nationalism and Modernity.* Austin: Univ. of Texas Press, 2014.

Ahmadi, Hamid. *The Dilemma of National Interest in the Islamic Republic of Iran*. New York: Routledge, 2007.

———. "Unity within Diversity: Foundations and Dynamics of National Identity in Iran." *Critique: Critical Middle Eastern Studies* 14, no. 1 (2005): 127–47.

Ahmady, Dariush, and Amir Ne'maty Lima'iy. *Davozdah qarn shukuh*. Tehran: Omid Mehr, 1383/2004.

Akbarzadeh, Shahram, and James Barry. "State Identity in Iranian Foreign Policy." *British Journal of Middle Eastern Studies* 43, no. 2 (2016): 613–29.

Akhundzadeh, Mirza Fath 'Ali. *Alef bay-i jadid va maktubat*. Tabriz, Iran: Nashr-i Ehya', 1357/1978.

———. *Maktubat Kemal al-Dawla*. Baku, Azerbaijan: Nashriyat-i 'Ilm, n.d.

Alai, Cyrus. "Cartography of Persia." In *Encyclopaedia Iranica*. New York: Encyclopaedia Iranica Foundation, 2012. At http://www.iranicaonline.org/articles/geography-iv-cartography-of-persia-.

Al-e Ahmad, Jalal. *Occidentosis: A Plague from the West*. Translated by R. Campbell. Berkeley, CA: Mizan Press, 1984.

'Alijani, Reza. *Shari'ati va Savak: Mururi tahlili bar sih jild-i asnad-i Savak dar barah-i duktur Shari'ati*. Tehran: Entisharat-i Kavir, 1382/2003.

Amanat, Abbas. *Pivot of the Universe: Nasir al-Din Shah Qajar and the Iranian Monarchy, 1831–1896*. London: I. B. Tauris, 1997.

———. *Resurrection and Renewal: The Making of the Babi Movement in Iran, 1844–1850*. Ithaca, NY: Cornell Univ. Press, 1989.

Amanat, Abbas, and Farzin Vejdani, eds. *Iran Facing Others: Identity Boundaries in a Historical Perspective*. New York: Palgrave Macmillan, 2012.

Amanolahi, Sekandar. "A Note on Ethnicity and Ethnic Groups in Iran." *Iran and the Caucasus* 9, no. 1 (2005): 37–41.

Anderson, Benedict. *Imagined Communities: Reflections on the Origin and Spread of Nationalism*. London: Verso, 1991.

Andreas, Carl F., and Franz Stolze. *Persepolis: Die achämenidischen und sasanidischen Denkmäler und Inschriften von Persepolis, Istakhr, Pasargadae, Shahpur*. 2 vols. Berlin: n.p., 1882.

Ansari, Ali M. *Modern Iran since 1921: The Pahlavis and After*. London: Pearson Education, 2003.

———. *The Politics of Nationalism in Modern Iran*. New York: Cambridge Univ. Press, 2012.

———. "Shah Mohammad Reza Pahlavi and the Myth of Imperial Authority." PhD diss., Univ. of London, 1998.

Asef, Mohammad Hasan. *Mabni ideologic dar hukumat-i Pahlavi*. Tehran: Markaz-i Asnad-i Enqelab-i Eslami, 2005.

Ashraf, Ahmad. "Iranian Identity." In *Encyclopaedia Iranica*. New York: Encyclopaedia Iranica Foundation, 2011. At http://www.iranica.com/articles/iranian-identity-i-perspectives.

Ashrafi, Mahmud. *Korush-i Kabir*. Tehran: n.p., 1971.

Ashuri, Dariush. "Sunnat va pishraft." *Farhang va Zendegi* 1 (1 Dey 1348/Dec. 1969–Jan. 1970): 66–72.

Asnad-i az bastan shenasi dar Iran. Tehran: Vizarat-i Farhang va Ershad-i Eslami, 1380/2001.

Assmann, Jan. "Communicative and Cultural Memory." In *Cultural Memory Studies: An International and Interdisciplinary Handbook*, edited by Astrid Erll and Ansgar Nünning, 109–18. Berlin: Walter de Gruyter, 2008.

———. "Das kulturelle Gedachtnis." *Erwagen, Wissen, Ethik* 13 (2002): 239–47.

Assmann, Jan, and John Czaplicka. "Collective Memory and Cultural Identity." *New German Critique* 65 (1995): 125–33.

Atabaki, Touraj. "Agency and Subjectivity in Iranian National Historiography." In *Iran in the 20th Century: Historiography and Political Culture*, edited by Touraj Atabaki, 69–92. London: I. B. Tauris, 2009.

———. "Constitutionalists sans Frontiers: Iranian Constitutionalism and Its Asian Connections." In *Iran's Constitutional Revolution*, edited by H. E. Chehabi and Vanessa Martin, 341–55. London: I. B. Tauris, 2010.

———, ed. *Iran in the 20th Century: Historiography and Political Culture*. London: I. B. Tauris, 2009.

Atabaki, Touraj, and Erik J. Zürcher, eds. *Men of Order: Authoritarian Modernization under Atatürk and Reza Shah*. London: I. B. Tauris, 2004.

Aymard, A. "Hachamenishiha va Yunaniyan." *Ruznameh-i Jashn-i Shahenshahi*, Sept. 9, 1971.

Azad, Abul Kalam. "Archeology and History" (convocation address at Aligrah Univ., Feb. 20, 1949). In *Speeches of Maulana Azad*, 69–74. Delhi: Publications Division, Ministry of Information and Broadcasting, 1956.

———. *Korush-i Bozorg (Dhul-Qarnayn)*. 1st ed. Tehran: Ibn Sina, 1951.

———. *Korush-i Bozorg (Dhul-Qarnayn)*. 6th ed. Translated by Mohammad Ibrahim Bastani Parizi. Tehran: Safa, 1992.

———. "Welcome Address on the Occasion of the Visit of Their Imperial Majesties, the Shahanshah and the Empress of Iran, New Delhi, February 19, 1956." In *Speeches of Maulana Azad*, 369–71. Delhi: Publications Division, Ministry of Information and Broadcasting, 1956.

Badre'i, Fereydoun. *Korush-i Kabir dar Qur'an-i majid va ahd-i atiq*. Tehran: Asatir, 1384/2005.

"Bahonar: 'Maktab-i Irani' fetne ayande ast." BBC Persian, Mar. 12, 2011. At http://www.bbc.co.uk/persian/iran/2011/03/110312_l10_iranism_bahonar_ahmadinejad.shtml.

Baram, Amatzia. *Culture, History, and Ideology in the Formation of Ba'athist Iraq 1968–1989*. New York: St. Martin's Press, 1991.

———. "Mesopotamian Identity in Ba'athi Iraq." *Middle Eastern Studies* 19, no. 4 (Oct. 1983): 426–55.

———. *Saddam Husayn and Islam, 1968–2003: Ba'athi Iraq from Secularism to Faith*. Washington, DC: Woodrow Wilson Center Press, 2014.

Barandes, George. "Halat-i Iran az noqtay-i nazaryik bitaraf." *Kaveh*, Aug. 15, 1916, 1–2

Barker, Rodney. *Legitimating Identities: The Self-Presentation of Rulers and Subjects*. Cambridge: Cambridge Univ. Press, 2001.

Barthel, Diane. *Historic Preservation: Collective Memory and Historical Identity*. New Brunswick, NJ: Rutgers Univ. Press, 1996.

Bast, Oliver. "Disintegrating the 'Discourse of Disintegration.'" In *Iran in the 20th Century: Historiography and Political Culture*, edited by Touraj Atabaki, 55–68. London: I. B. Tauris, 2009.

Bastani Parizi, Mohammad Ibrahim. *Historical Atlas of Iran*. Tehran: Univ. of Tehran Press, 1971.

———. Introduction to Abul Kalam Azad, *Korush-i Bozorg (Dhul-Qarnayn)*, 6th ed., translated by Mohammad Ibrahim Bastani Parizi, 1–145. Tehran: Safa, 1992.

"Bastanshenasan khostar sebt-i ruz-i jahani Korush shodand." *Hamshahri Online*, Nov. 22, 2011. At http://hamshahrionline.ir/details/151828/Culture/historynews.

Bastanshenasi dar Iran. Tehran: Iranian Ministry of Culture, Oct. 28, 1929.

"Bazgosht manshur-i Korush pas az 45 sal." *Iran*, Sept. 12, 2010. At http://www.tabnak.ir/fa/pages/?cid=119554.

Bazm-i Ahrīman, Jashnha-yi 2500 salah-i shahanshahi bih rivayat-i asnad-i Savak va darbar. 4 vols. Tehran: Markaz-i Bararasi Asnad-i Tarikh-i Vizarat-i Ettela'at, 1998.

Beetham, David. *The Legitimation of Power.* Basingstoke, UK: Macmillan, 1991.

Bernhardsson, Magnus T. *Reclaiming a Plundered Past: Archaeology and Nation Building in Modern Iraq.* Austin: Univ. of Texas Press, 2005.

Bodnar, John. *Remaking America: Public Memory, Commemoration, and Patriotism in the Twentieth Century.* Princeton, NJ: Princeton Univ. Press, 1992.

Boroujerdi, Mehrzad. *Iranian Intellectuals and the West: The Tormented Triumph of Nativism.* Syracuse, NY: Syracuse Univ. Press, 1996.

Boser, Ulrich. "Archaeology NEWS." *Archaeology* 58, no. 6 (2005): 10–13.

Boyce, Mary. "Bībī Šahrbanu." In *Encyclopaedia Iranica.* New York: Encyclopaedia Iranica Foundation, 2019. At http://www.iranicaonline.org/articles/bibi-sahrbanu.

Bozorg, Jamshid. "Hachaminisiyan basiji va jang-i qudrat." BBC Persian, Sept. 11, 2010. At http://www.bbc.co.uk/persian/iran/2010/09/100911_u03_cyrus_basij_rights_charter.shtml.

Braudel, Fernand. "Histoire et sciences sociales: La longue durée." *Réseaux* 5, no. 27 (1987): 7–37.

———. "Histoire, sciences sociales: La longue durée." *Annales* 4 (Oct.–Dec. 1958): 725–53.

Briant, Pierre. *From Cyrus to Alexander: A History of the Persian Empire.* Winona Lake, IN: Eisenbrauns, 2002.

Buchta, Wilfried. *Who Rules Iran? The Structure of Power in the Islamic Republic.* Washington, DC: Washington Institute for Near East Policy, 2000.

Burke, Kenneth. *Attitudes toward History.* Berkeley: Univ. of California Press, 1984.

Celik, Zeynep Mustafavi. *Displaying the Orient: Architecture of Islam at Nineteenth-Century World's Fairs.* Berkeley: Univ. of California Press, 1992.

Champdor, Albert. *Cyrus.* Paris: Michel, 1952.

Chehabi, Houchang. "Iran and Iraq: Intersocietal Linkages and Secular Nationalisms." In *Iran Facing Others: Identity Boundaries in a Historical Perspective,* edited by Abbas Amanat and Farzin Vejdani, 191–216. New York: Palgrave Macmillan, 2012.

———. "Staging the Emperor's New Clothes: Dress Code and Nation-Building under Reza Shah." *Iranian Studies* 26, nos. 3–4 (Summer–Fall 1993): 209–29.

Chelkowski, Peter. "Graphic Arts." In *Encyclopaedia Iranica.* New York: Encyclopaedia Iranica, 2011. At http://www.Iranica.com/articles/graphic-arts+frederick+talberg&ct=clnk.

Christensen, Arthur. "She'r Pahlavi va She'r Farisi qadim." *Kaveh,* May 21, 1920, 24–26.

Chubin, Shahram, and Charles Tripp. *Iran and Iraq at War.* London: I. B. Tauris, 1988.

Chubin, Shahram, and Sepehr Zabih. *The Foreign Relations of Iran: A Developing State in a Zone of Great-Power Conflict*. Berkeley: Univ. of California Press, 1974.

Cole, Juan. "Marking Boundaries, Marking Time: The Iranian Past and the Construction of the Self by Qajar Thinkers." *Iranian Studies* 29, nos. 1–2 (Winter–Spring 1996): 35–56.

Commemoration Cyrus: Actes du Congres de Shiraz 1971 et autres études redigées à l'occasion du 2500e anniversaire de la fondation de l'Empire Perse. Leiden: Brill, 1974.

Confino, Alon. *The Nation as a Local Metaphor: Wurttemberg, Imperial Germany, and National Memory, 1871–1918.* Chapel Hill: Univ. of North Carolina Press, 1997.

Corbin, Henry. *The Voyage and the Messenger: Iran and Philosophy.* Translated by Joseph Rowe. Berkeley, CA: North Atlantic Books, 1998.

Cottam, Richard. *Iran and the United States: A Cold War Case Study.* Pittsburg, PA: Univ. of Pittsburg Press, 1988.

———. *Nationalism in Iran.* Pittsburgh, PA: Univ. of Pittsburgh Press, 1979.

Cronin, Stephanie. *The Army and the Creation of the Pahlavi State in Iran, 1910–1926.* London: Tauris Academic Studies, 1997.

———, ed. *The Making of Modern Iran: State and Society under Reza Shah 1921–1941.* London: Routledge Curzon, 2003.

———. *Tribal Politics in Iran: Rural Conflict and the New State, 1921–1941.* London: Routledge, 2007.

Curiel, Raoul, George Wright, Maxime Siroux, Graeme Shankland, and Roberto La Francesca. *Programme spécial de préservation et de mise en valeur de l'héritage culturel en liaison avec le développement du tourisme: Conclusions d'un groupe de cinq consultants: Iran.* Geneva: UNESCO, Dec. 1967–Apr. 1968.

Curtis, John. "The Cyrus Cylinder: The Creation of an Icon and Its Loan to Tehran." In *The Cyrus Cylinder: The Great Persian Edict from Babylon*, edited by Irving Finkel, 85–103. London: I. B. Tauris, 2013.

Dabashi, Hamid. *Theology of Discontent: The Ideological Foundations of the Islamic Revolution in Iran.* New York: New York Univ. Press, 1993.

"Dadestan-i shiraz az bazdasht 'amelan' va 'sarshachehaye' marasem-i bazargdosht Korush khabar dad." BBC Persian, Oct. 31, 2016. At http://www.bbc.com/persian/iran-37820435.

Dandamaev, Mohammad A. "Congrès Internationales des Iranistes à Shiraz." In *Commemoration Cyrus: Actes du Congres de Shiraz 1971 et autres etudes redigees a l'occasion du 2500e anniversaire de la fondation de l'Empire Perse*, 3–12. Leiden: Brill, 1974.

———. *A Political History of the Achaemenid Empire*. Leiden: Brill, 1989.

"Dar aramgah-i Korush che gozosht." BBC Persian, Oct. 29, 2016. At http://www.bbc.com/persian/iran-37813021.

Dareini, Ali Akbar. *The Rise and Fall of the Pahlavi Dynasty: Memoirs of Former General Hosein Fardust*. Delhi, India: Motilal Banarsidass, 1999.

Daryaee, Touraj, ed. *Cyrus the Great: An Ancient Iranian King*. Santa Monica, CA: Afshar, 2013.

———. "Religion of Cyrus the Great." In *Cyrus the Great: An Ancient Iranian King*, edited by Touraj Daryaee, 16–27. Santa Monica, CA: Afshar, 2013.

Davari, Mahmood T. *The Political Thought of Ayatullah Mortaza Mutahhari: An Iranian Theoretician of the Islamic State*. London: Taylor & Francis, 2005.

Daveri, Reza. *Nasyonalism va enqelab*. Tehran: Entesharat-i Daftar Pezhuhashoy-i Eslami, 1365/1986.

De Castelbajac, Bertrand. *L'homme qui voulait être Cyrus*. Paris: Éditions Albatros, 1987.

Ebrahimi, Reza Zia. *The Emergence of Iranian Nationalism: Race and the Politics of Dislocation*. New York: Columbia Univ. Press, 2016.

Elliot, Matthew. "New Iran and the Dissolution of Party Politics under Reza Shah." In *Men of Order: Authoritarian Modernization under Atatürk and Reza Shah*, edited by Touraj Atabaki and Eric J. Zürcher, 58–60. London: I. B. Tauris, 2004.

Ende, Werner. *Arabische Nation und Islamische Geschichte: Die Umayyaden im Urteil Arabischer Autoren des 20. Jahrhunderts*. Beirut, Lebanon: Orient-Institut der Deutschen Morgenlaendischer Gesellschaft; Wiesbaden, Germany: F. Steiner, 1977.

"Enteqad-i shadid Mesbah Yazdi az Masha'i." Entekhab, n.d. At http://www.entekhab.ir/fa/news/23116/. Accessed Jan. 1, 2019.

Epkenhans, Tim. *Moral und Disziplin: Seyyed Hasan Taqizade und die Konstruktion eines "progressiven Selbst" in der frühen iranischen Moderne*. Berlin: K. Schwarz, 2005.

Etzioni, Amitai. "Toward a Theory of Public Ritual." *Sociological Theory* 18, no. 1 (Mar. 2000): 44–59.

Fahimi, Mahdi. *Farhang-i Jabha: Sharha va rajzaha*. Kerman, Iran: Surush, 2007.

The Fall of the Shah. Documentary. BBC, Feb. 2009.

Farhi, Farideh. "Crafting a National Identity amidst Contentious Politics in Contemporary Iran." In *Iran in the 21st Century: Politics, Economics, and Conflict*, edited by Homa Katouzian and Hossein Shahidi, 7–22. London: Routledge, 2008.

Farzaneh, Mateo Mohammad. "Shi'i Ideology, Secular Nationalism, and the Iran-Iraq War (1980–1988)." *Studies in Ethnicity and Nationalism* 7, no. 1 (2007): 86–103.

Finkel, Irving, ed. *The Cyrus Cylinder: The Great Persian Edict from Babylon*. London: I. B. Tauris, 2013.

Fischer, Michael, and Mehdi Abedi. *Debating Muslims: Cultural Dialogues in Postmodernity and Tradition*. Madison: Univ. of Wisconsin Press, 1990.

Flandin, Eugène N., and Pascal-Xavier Coste. *Voyage en Perse pendant le années 1840 et 1841*. 2 vols. Paris: Gile et Jules Baudry, 1851.

Flood, Christopher G. *Political Myth: A Theoretical Introduction*. New York: Garland, 1996.

Francis, Anna. "Ghirshman Laments Neglected Periods." *Tehran Journal*, Apr. 16, 1968. Reprinted in *Surveyors of Persian Art*, edited by Jay Gluck and Noel Silver, 528–29. Costa Mesa, CA: Mazda, 1996.

Frankfort, Henri. *The Art and Architecture of the Ancient Orient*. New Haven, CT: Yale Univ. Press, 1996.

Frye, Richard. *Greater Iran: A 20th-Century Odyssey*. Costa Mesa, CA: Mazda, 2005.

———. *The History of Ancient Iran*. Munich: C. H. Beck, 1984.

———. "The Political History of Iran under the Sasanians." In *The Cambridge History of Iran*, vol. 3: *Seleucid, Parthian, and Sasanian Periods*, edited by Ehsan Yarshater, 116–80. Cambridge: Cambridge Univ. Press, 1983.

Geertz, Clifford. "Centers, Kings, and Charisma." In *Culture and Its Creators: Essays in Honor of Edward Shils*, edited by Joseph Ben-David and Terry Nichols Clark, 150–71. Chicago: Univ. of Chicago Press, 1977.

Geiger, Prof. W. "Nowruz." *Kaveh*, Apr. 18, 1916, 4–5.

Gera, Deborah Levine. *Xenophon's "Cyropaedia": Style, Genre, and Literary Technique*. Oxford: Clarendon Press, 1993.

Gershoni, Israel. *Pyramid for the Nation: Commemoration, Memory, and Nationalism in Twentieth-Century Egypt*. [In Hebrew.] Tel Aviv: Am Oved, 2006.

Geyl, Pieter. "Toynbee's System of Civilizations." In *Toynbee and History: Critical Essays and Reviews*, edited by Montagu Ashley, 39–72. Boston: P. Sargent, 1956.

Ghahari, Keivandokht. *Nationalismus und Modernismus in Iran in der Periode zwischen dem Zerfall der Qagaren-Dynastie und der Machtfestigung Reza Schahs: Eine Untersuchung* über *die intellektuellen Kreise um die Zeitschriften "Kaiweh," "Iransahr," und "Ayandeh."* Berlin: K. Schwarz, 2001.

Ghani, Cyrus. *Iran and the Rise of Reza Shah: From Qajar Collapse to Pahlavi Rule*. London: I. B. Tauris, 1998.

Glasse, Cyril. *The Concise Encyclopaedia of Islam*. London: Stacey International, 2001.

Gluck, Robert. "The Shiraz Arts Festival: Western Avant-Garde Arts in 1970s Iran." *Leonardo* 40, no. 1 (2007): 20–28.

Goldberg, Ori. *Shi'i Theology in Iran: The Challenge of Religious Experience*. London: Routledge, 2012.

Golestan, Shahrokh, dir. *Flames of Persia*. Producer unknown, 1971.

Goode, James. *Negotiating for the Past: Archaeology, Nationalism, and Diplomacy in the Middle East, 1919–1941*. Austin: Univ. of Texas Press, 2007.

Grigor, Talinn. *Building Iran: Modernism, Architecture, and National Heritage under the Pahlavi Monarchs*. New York: Periscope, 2009.

———. *Contemporary Iranian Art: From the Street to the Studio*. London: Reaktion Books, 2014.

———. "Cultivating Modernities: The Society for National Heritage, Political Propaganda, and Public Architecture in 20th Century Iran." PhD diss., MIT, 2005.

———. "Of Metamorphosis: Meaning on Iranian Terms." *Third Text* 17, no. 3 (2003): 207–25.

———. "Preserving the Antique Modern: Persepolis '71." *Future Anterior* 2, no. 1 (2005): 23–29.

———. "Recultivating 'Good Taste': The Early Pahlavi Modernists and Their Society for National Heritage." *Journal of Iranian Studies* 37, no. 1 (Mar. 2004): 17–45.

Gude, Mary Louise. *Louis Massignon: The Crucible of Compassion*. Notre Dame, IN: Univ. of Notre Dame Press, 1996.

Hakimpur, Mohammad. *Shari'ati dar zindan: Ta'allumat va khaṭirat-i dawran-i zindan: Hamrah ba biyugrafi-i taḥlili va barrasi-yi andishahha*. Tehran: Entisharat-i Naghmah-i Naw' Andish, 1383/2004.

Halbwachs, Maurice. *On Collective Memory*. Chicago: Univ. of Chicago Press, 1992.

Handler, Richard, and Jocelyn Linnekin. "Tradition, Genuine or Spurious." *Journal of American Folklore* 97, no. 385 (July–Sept. 1984): 273–90.

Hanley, Sarah. "Legend, Ritual, and Discourse in the *Lit de Justice* Assembly: French Constitutional Ideology, 1527–1641." In *Rites of Power: Symbolism, Ritual, and Politics since the Middle Ages*, edited by Sean Willanz, 65–106. Philadelphia: Univ. of Pennsylvania Press, 1985.

Harley, James. *Xenakis: His Life in Music*. New York: Routledge, 2004.

Harvey, Delicia, and Lance Strate. "Image Culture and the Supermodel." In *Critical Studies in Media Commercialism*, edited by Robin Anderson and Lance Strate, 203–13. New York: Oxford Univ. Press, 2000.

Hasanzadeh, Yusuf, and Sima Miri. Introduction to *Majmuʿa-yi maqalat-i hasht sal-i bastanshinasi-yi Iran*, edited by Yusuf Hasanzadeh and Sima Miri, 10–11. Tehran: Pazina, 2012.

Hedayati, Hadi. *Korush-i Kabir*. Tehran: Tehran Univ. Press, 1956.

Hendelman-Baavur, Liora. "The Gender of Modernity." [In Hebrew.] PhD diss., Tel Aviv Univ., 2006.

Henderson, Douglas I. *Abul Kalam Azad: An Intellectual and Religious Biography*. Delhi: Oxford Univ. Press, 1993.

Hobsbawm, Eric. "Introduction: Inventing Traditions." In *The Invention of Tradition*, edited by Eric Hobsbawm and Terence Ranger, 1–14. Cambridge: Cambridge Univ. Press, 1983.

———. "Mass Producing Traditions: Europe 1870–1914." In *The Invention of Tradition*, edited by Eric Hobsbawm and Terence Ranger, 263–308. Cambridge: Cambridge Univ. Press, 1983.

———. *Nations and Nationalism since 1780: Programme, Myth, Reality*. Cambridge: Cambridge Univ. Press, 1992.

Hobsbawm, Eric, and Terence Ranger, eds. *The Invention of Tradition*. Cambridge: Cambridge Univ. Press, 1983.

Holliday, Shabnam J. *Defining Iran: Politics of Resistance*. Farnham, UK: Ashgate, 2011.

Homayun, Gholamʿali. *Erforschung der altiranischen Architektur durch die Europäer*. Tehran: Tehran Univ., 1976.

———. "Iran in Europaeischen Bildzeugnissen vom Ausgang des Mittelalters bis ins Actzehnte Jahrhundert." PhD diss., Univ. of Cologne, 1967.

———. *Iran in Historisch-Geographischen Werken Europaeischer Gelehrter im 16 Jh*. Berlin: AMI Band 3, 1970.

———. *Korush-i Kabir dar asar-i hunariy-i Urupaʾiyan*. Tehran: Intisharat-i Tehran Univ., 1971.

Hunter, Shireen. *Iran after Khomeini*. New York: Praeger, 1992.

Hutton, Patrick H. *History as an Art of Memory.* Hanover, NH: Univ. Press of New England, 1993.

Indo Iran Cultural Society and K. R. Cama Oriental Institute, eds. *Kurus Memorial Volume.* Bombay: Iran Culture House, 1974.

"Iran Aryamehr dar kenar Iran bastani va Iran Korush." *Ruznameh-i Jashn-i Shahenshahi*, Sept. 7, 1971.

"Iran: The Show of Shows" (editorial). *Time*, Oct. 25, 1971.

Irfan'manish, Jalil. *Korush va bazyabi-i huviyat-i milli: Taḥqiqi-i* ʻilmi *darbarah-'i pishinah va kisti-i Zu al-Qarnayn.* Tehran: Intisharat-i Farhang-i Maktub, 2010.

Ishkavari, Hasan Yusufi. *Shariʻati va naqd-i sunnat.* Tehran: Nashr-i Yadavaran, 1379/2000.

Jashn-i honar-i Shiraz bi revayat-i asnad-i Savak. Tehran: Markaz-i Bararasi Asnad-i Tarikh-i Vizarat-i Ettelaʻat, 1381/2002.

Javadian, M., A. Kheirandish, and J. Abbasim. *History: The Second Year of Guidance School Period.* Tehran: Iran's Textbook Publishing and Distribution Office, 2007.

Johnstone, Barbara. *Discourse Analysis.* Malden, MA: Blackwell, 2001.

Jung, Nawab Ali Yavar. Foreword to *Kurus Memorial Volume*, edited by Indo Iran Cultural Society and K. R. Cama Oriental Institute, xi–xii. Bombay: Iran Culture House, 1974.

Kadivar, Cyrus. "We Are Awake: 2,500-Year Celebrations Revisited." Parsikhabar, Jan. 25, 2002. At http://parsikhabar.net/culture/2500-years-the-persepolis-celebrations-of-1971/1510/.

Karamipur, Korush. *Raz-i Korush-i Bozorg.* Tehran: Intisharat-i ʻIlmi, 2011.

Kashani-Sabet, Firoozeh. "Fragile Frontiers: The Diminishing Domains of Qajar Iran." *International Journal of Middle East Studies* 29, no. 2 (1997): 205–34.

———. *Frontier Fictions: Shaping the Iranian Nation, 1804–1946.* Princeton, NJ: Princeton Univ. Press, 1999.

Kasheff, Manouchehr, and ʻAli-Akbar Saʻidi Sirjani. "ČAHĀRŠANBA-SŪRĪ." In *Encyclopaedia Iranica.* New York: Encyclopaedia Iranica Foundation, 2019. At http://www.iranicaonline.org/articles/caharsanba-suri.

"Kaveh va derafsha Kawiyani." *Kaveh*, Jan. 24, 1916, 3.

Keddie, Nikki R. *Qajar Iran and the Rise of Reza Khan 1796–1925.* Costa Mesa, CA: Mazda, 1999.

———. *Sayyid Jamal ad-Din "al-Afghani": A Political Biography.* Berkeley: Univ. of California Press, 1972.

Kedourie, Elie. *The Chatham House Version and Other Middle-Eastern Studies.* London: Weidenfeld and Nicolson, 1970.

Kertzer, David. *Ritual, Politics, and Power.* New Haven, CT: Yale Univ. Press, 1988.

Khalili, Abbas. *Korush-i Bozorg.* Tehran: Elmi, 1965.

Khalkhali, Ayatollah Sadeq. *Khatirat-i Ayatollah Sadeq Khalkhali*. Tehran: Saye, 1379/2000.

———. *Korush-i dorughin.* Tehran: Saye, 1981.

Khamenei, Ayatollah ʿAli Hosseini. *The Cultural Viewpoints of the Leader of the Islamic Republic.* Tehran: Center for Cultural and International Studies, 2000.

———. *Kalam Vilayat Tariq Hidayat.* Tehran: Zafar, 1380/2001.

———. Nowruz message, Jumada al-ula 30, 1436/Mar. 21, 2005. At http://farsi.khamenei.ir/print-content?id=29204.

———. Nowruz message, Shawwal 10, 1378/Dec. 31, 1999. At http://farsi.khamenei.ir/speech-content?id=2936.

Khatami, Sayyid Mohammad. "Farhang-i Irani Islami, 1376 (1997)." In *Islam, ruhaniyyat va enqelab-i Islami*, 17–20. Tehran: Tarh-i Nu, 1379/2000.

"Khatami Notified of 'National Tragedy' in Persepolis." *Payvand News,* May 13, 2002. At http://www.payvand.com/news/02/may/1053.html.

"Khatib-i Jomʿe Tehran: Cheharshanbe suri dar shan mellat ma nist." *Daneshju News,* Mar. 4, 2011. At https://www.balatarin.com/permlink/2011/3/4/2397880.

Khomeini, Ruhollah. *Islam and Revolution: Writings and Declarations of Imam Khomeini.* Edited and translated by Hamid Algar. Berkeley, CA: Mizan Press, 1981.

———. *Islamic Government.* New York: Manor Books, 1979.

———. *Sahife-yi Imam, Majmuʿe-ʾye asar Imam Khomeini.* 22 vols. Tehran: Mu'assese-yi Tanzim va Nashr-i Asar Imam Khomeini, 1387/2008.

———. *Sahife-yi Nur.* 22 vols. Tehran: Vezarat-i Farhang va Ershad-i Islami, 1361/1982.

Kirby, Tim, dir. *The Last Shah.* BBC, 1996.

Knauer, Lisa Maya, and Daniel J. Walkowitz. "Introduction: Memory, Race, and the Nation in Public Spaces." In *Contested Histories in Public Space: Memory, Race, and Nation*, edited by Daniel J. Walkowitz and Lisa Maya Knauer, 1–28. Durham, NC: Duke Univ. Press, 2009.

Kohl, Philip L., Mara Kozelsky, and Nachman Ben-Yehuda. Introduction to *Selective Remembrances: Archaeology in the Construction, Commemoration, and Consecration of National Pasts*, edited by Philip L. Kohl, Mara Kozelsky, and Nachman Ben-Yehuda, 1–28. Chicago: Univ. of Chicago Press, 2007.

Kohlberg, Etan. "Western Studies of Sh'ia Islam." In *Belief and Law in Imami Shi'ism*, 31–44. Aldershot, UK: Variorum; Brookfield, VT: Gower, 1991.

Krebernik, Manfred. *Polytheismus und Monotheismus in den Religionen des Vorderen Orients*. Münster, Germany: Ugarit, 2002.

Kuhrt, Amélie. *The Persian Empire*. Hoboken, NJ: Taylor and Francis, 2013.

Kulke, Eckehard. *The Parsees in India: A Minority as Agent of Social Change*. New Delhi: Vikas, 1978.

Lamb, Harold. *Cyrus the Great*. Garden City, NY: Doubleday, 1960.

Larijani, Mohammad. "'Id-i mobarak." *Ettela'at*, Esfand 23, 1377/Mar. 14, 1999.

Leoussi, Athena S., and Steven Grosby, eds. *Nationalism and Ethnosymbolism: History, Culture, and Ethnicity in the Formation of Nations*. Edinburgh: Edinburgh Univ. Press, 2007.

Levinger, Matthew, and Paula Franklin Lytle. "Myth and Mobilization: The Triadic Structure of Nationalist Rhetoric." *Nations and Nationalism* 7, no. 2 (Apr. 2001): 175–94.

Al-Mahalli, Jalal al-Din Mohammad bin Ahmad, and Jalal al-Din Abd al-Rahman ibn Abu-Baker al-Suyyuti. *Tafsir al-Jalalayn*. Cairo: Maktabat al-Jumhuriyya al-'Arabiyya, 1983.

Mahdavi, Bina. "Cheharshanbe suri ya cheharshanbe suzi?" *Ettela'at*, Esfand 22, 1385/Mar. 13, 2007.

Mahlouji, Vali. *Festival of Arts: Shiraz–Persepolis*. London: Black Dog, 2014.

Makarim-Shirazi, Nasir. *Tafsir-i numunah*. Tehran: Dar al-Kutub al-Islamiyah, 2004.

Makki, Husayn. *Tarikh bist saleh*. 6 vols. Tehran: Nasher, 1362/1983.

Manoukian, Setrag. *City of Knowledge in Twentieth Century Iran*. Oxford: Routledge, 2012.

"Manshur huquq-i bashar be keshvarash bazgosht." *Khabar Online*, Sept. 11, 2010. At https://www.khabaronline.ir/news/91526.

Marashi, Afshin. *Nationalizing Iran: Culture, Power, and the State*. Seattle: Univ. of Washington Press, 2008.

Ma'sumi, Ghulamriza. *Bastanshinasi-yi Iran: Az 2407 ta 2535 shahin-shahi*. Tehran: Artish, 1976.

Matin-Asgari, Afshin. "The Academic Debate on Iranian Identity." In *Iran Facing Others: Identity Boundaries in a Historical Perspective*, edited by Abbas Amanat and Farzin Vejdani, 173–92. New York: Palgrave Macmillan, 2012.

Matthee, Rudi. "Transforming Dangerous Nomads into Useful Artisans, Technicians, Agriculturalists: Education in the Reza Shah Period." In *The Making of Modern Iran: State and Society under Riza Shah 1921–1941*, edited by Stephanie Cronin, 128–48. London: Routledge Curzon, 2003.

McGregor, Neil. "The Many Meanings of the Cyrus Cylinder." In *The Cyrus Cylinder and Ancient Persia*, edited by John Curtis, 9–17. London: British Museum, 2013.

McWhirter, William A. "The Shah's Princely Party." *Life*, Oct. 29, 1971.

Mehdevi, Anne Sinclair. *Persia Revisited*. New York: Random House, 1964.

Menashri, David. *Iran in Revolution*. [In Hebrew.] Tel Aviv: HaKibbutz HaMeuhad, 1988.

———. *Revolution at a Crossroads: Iran's Domestic Politics and Regional Ambitions*. Washington, DC: Washington Institute for Near East Policy, 1997.

Merhavy, Menahem. "Religious Appropriation of National Symbols in Iran: Searching for Cyrus the Great." *Iranian Studies* 48, no. 6 (2015): 933–48.

Milani, Abbas. *Eminent Persians*. 2 vols. Syracuse, NY: Syracuse Univ. Press, 2008.

Milani, Mohsen M. *The Making of Iran's Islamic Revolution: From Monarchy to Islamic Republic*. Boulder, CO: Westview Press, 1988.

Mohammad, Shan. *Sir Syed Ahmad Khan*. Lahore, Pakistan: Mohammad Iqbal, 1986.

Mohiuddin, S. G. "Religious Thoughts of Maulana Azad." In *Life and Works of Maulana Abul Kalam Azad*, edited by Ravindra Kumar, 65–78. New Delhi: Atlantic, 1991.

Moslem, Mehdi. *Factional Politics in Post-Khomeini Iran*. Syracuse, NY: Syracuse Univ. Press, 2002.

Mosse, George L. *The Nationalization of the Masses: Political Symbolism and Mass Movements in Germany from the Napoleonic Wars through the Third Reich*. New York: Howard Fertig, 1975.

Motahhari, Mortaza. *Selections from "The Reciprocal Services between Islam and Iran."* Translated by Idris Tijjani Samari and Maina Bukar. Qom, Iran: International Center for Islamic Studies, 2004.

Mousavi, Ali. "Ernst Herzfeld, Politics, and Antiquities Legislation in Iran." In *Ernst Herzfeld and the Development of Near Eastern Studies 1900–1950*, edited by Ann C. Gunter and Stefan R. Hauser, 445–75. Leiden: Brill, 2005.

———. "Persepolis in Retrospect: Histories of Discovery and Archeological Exploration at the Ruins of Ancient Parseh." *Art Orientalis* 32, no. 1 (2002): 209–51.

Mozaffari, Ali. *Forming National Identity in Iran: The Idea of Homeland Derived from Ancient Persian and Islamic Imaginations of Place*. London: I. B. Tauris, 2014.

———. "The 'Heritage NGO': A Case Study on the Role of Grass-Roots Heritage Societies in Iran and Their Perception of Cultural Heritage." *International Journal of Heritage Studies* 21, no. 9 (2015): 845–61.

Mudarris, Musa Mir. *Korush va Zu al-Qarnayn az didgah-i tarikh va ayin*. Tehran: Markaz-i Nashr-i 'Ulum-i Danishgahi va Ma'arif-i Islami-yi Fazil, 1994.

Mustafavi, 'Ali Asgar. *Zaman va zendegi ustaz Purdavoud*. Tehran: n.p., 1371/1993.

Mustafavi, Mohammad Taqi. "Emanat dari-yi khak." *Majale-yi Bararsihay-i Tarikhi*, special bulletin, no. 11 (1975): 80–83.

Nabavi, Negin. "The Discourse of 'Authentic Culture' in Iran in the 1960s and 1970s." In *Intellectual Trends in Twentieth-Century Iran: A Critical Survey*, edited by Negin Nabavi, 91–111. Gainesville: Univ. Press of Florida, 2003.

———. *Intellectuals and the State in Iran*. Gainesville: Univ. Press of Florida, 2003.

Nadjm, Abbas. "2500 Anniversary of the Founding of the Persian Empire." In *Kurus Memorial Volume*, edited by Indo Iran Cultural Society and K. R. Cama Oriental Institute, xvi–xx. Bombay: Iran Culture House, 1974.

Nafisi, Sa'id. Introduction to Maulana Abul Kalam Azad, *Korush-i Bozorg (Dhul-Qarnayn)*, 1st ed., 12–148. Tehran: Ibn Sina, 1951.

"Name jame'eh ruhaniyyat-i Shiraz be Ahmadinejad." *Khabar Online*, Mar. 19, 2011. At http://www.khabaronline.ir/news-138021.aspx.

"Name ruhaniyat-i Shiraz be Ahmadinejad." *Khabar*, Mar. 19, 2011. At http://www.khabaronline.ir/news-138021.aspx.

"Name sargeshode Ahmad Tavakoli be Ahmadinejad dar enteqad-i az 'Iranigari' u." BBC Persian, Mar. 1, 2011. At http://www.bbc.co.uk/persian/iran/2011/03/110301_l10_tavakoli_open_letter_ahmadinejad.shtml.

Nasir al-Din Shah. *The Diary of H.M. the Shah of Persia: During His Tour through Europe in A.D. 1873*. Costa Mesa, CA: Mazda, 1995.

Nasiri-Moghaddam, Nader. *L'archéologie français en Perse (1884–1914)*. Paris: Connaissances et Savoirs, 2004.

Nasr, Seyyed Hossein, and Ramin Jahanbegloo. *In Search of the Sacred: A Conversation with Seyyed Hossein Nasr on His Life and Thought*. Santa Barbara, CA: Praeger, 2010.

Negahban, Ezzat O. *Karnameh*. Tehran: Sazman-i Mirath-i Farhang-i Keshvar 1997.

———. *Panjah sal-i bastanshenasi dar Iran*. Tehran: Sazman-i Miras-ie Farhang-ie Leshvar, Yadigar-i 'Umr, 1376/1997.

Nidermayer, Oskar. "Afghanistan." *Kaveh*, June 15, 1917, 3–6.

Niknami, Kamal Aldin. *Methodological Aspects of Iranian Archaeology: Past and Present*. Oxford: British Archeological Reports International Series, 2000.

Nora, Pierre. "Between Memory and History: Les Lieux de Mémoire." *Representations* 26 (Spring 1989): 7–24.

———. *Realms of Memory: Rethinking the French Past*. Vol. 1: *Conflicts and Divisions*. New York: Columbia Univ. Press, 1996.

"Nowruz." Translated by W. Geiger. *Kaveh*, Apr. 18, 1916, 4–5.

"On That Day in Takht-i Jamshid." *Kayhan International*, Sept. 25, 1971.

Pahlavi, Mohammed Reza Shah. *Mission for My Country*. London: Hutchinson, 1961.

Parsons, Anthony. *The Pride and the Fall: Iran, 1974–1979*. London: Jonathan Cape, 1984.

"Pasargad: Sho'ar ne ghazeh ne lobnan janam feda'-yi Iran." *Hambastegimeli*, Oct. 30, 2016. At https://www.hambastegimeli.com/.

"Pasardagae." UNESCO, n.d. At http://whc.unesco.org/en/list/1106. Accessed Jan. 1, 2019.

Perry, John. *Karim Khan Zand*. Oxford: Oneworld, 2006.

———. "Karim Khan Zand." In *Encyclopaedia Iranica*. New York: Encyclopaedia Iranica Foundation, 2011. At http://www.iranica.com/articles/karim-khan-zand.

Pirniya, Hasan. *Tarikh-i Iran-i bastan*. 10th ed. 3 vols. Tehran: Dunya-i Ketab, 2003.

Piscatori, James P. *Islam in a World of Nation-States*. Cambridge: Cambridge Univ. Press, 1986.

Podeh, Eli. *The Politics of National Celebrations in the Arab Middle East*. New York: Cambridge Univ. Press, 2011.

Poulson, Stephen C. *Social Movements in Twentieth-Century Iran*. Lanham, MD: Lexington Books, 2005.

Pourpirar, Nasser. *Davozda qarn sukut: Bar madan-i Hachamenishiyan*. Tehran: Karnak, 1379/2000.

———. *Na'al Varune*. Tehran: Pejuhashgah Farhangi va Andishe Eslami, 1383/2004.

Price, Massoume. *Iran's Diverse Peoples: A Reference Sourcebook*. Santa Barbara, CA: ABC-CLIO, 2005.

Qa'imi, Mohammad. *Hachamenishiyan dar turat*. Isfahan, Iran: Entesharat-i Ta'yid-i Isfahan, 1970.

Qanavat, 'Abd al-Rahim. *Shari'ati va tarikh-i Islam: Nigahi bih ruykard va asar-i duktur Shari'ati dar zaminah-i tarikh-i Islam: Bih zamimah-i pasukh bih "Naqdi bar Islamshinasi."* Mashhad, Iran: Nashr-i Salih, 1377/1998.

Qeraiyan, Nargese, Zahra Shamaniyan, and Hussein Qassem Pourmuqaddam. *Farsi, panjam-i dabestan*. Tehran: Vizarat-i Amuzesh va Parvaresh, 1368/1980.

The Qur'an. Translated by Thomas B. Irving. Brattleboro, VT: Amana Books, 1985.

The Quran. Translated by Abd al-Halim Mahmud. New York: Oxford Univ. Press, 2005.

Rahnema, Ali. *An Islamic Utopian: A Political Biography of 'Ali Shari'ati*. London: I. B. Tauris, 1998.

———. *Pioneers of Islamic Revival*. London: Zed Books, 1994.

Rahnema, Ali, and Farhad Nomani. *The Secular Miracle: Religion, Politics, and Economic Policy in Iran*. London: Zed Books, 1990.

Ranger, Terence. "The Invention of Tradition in Colonial Africa." In *The Invention of Tradition*, edited by Eric Hobsbawm and Terence Ranger, 211–62. Cambridge: Cambridge Univ. Press, 1983.

Rasool, Abduhu G. *The Educational Ideas of Maulana 'Abul Kalam Azad*. New Delhi: Sterling, 1973.

Rawlinson, Henry. "Sir Saiyid Ahmed Khan." In *Sir Sayyid Ahmad Khan, 1817–1898: A Prominent Muslim Politician and Educationist*, edited by M. Ikram Chaghatai, 109–15. Lahore, Pakistan: Sang-i-Meel, 2005.

Razmjou, Shahrokh. "Persepolis: A Reinterpretation of Palaces and Their Function." In *The World of Achaemenid Persia: History, Art, and Society in Iran and the Ancient Near East*, edited by John Curtis and St. John Simpson, 231–45. London: I. B. Tauris, 2005.

Rezwi, Taher. *The Parsis: A People of the Book*. Calcutta: Taraporewala and Sons, 1928.

Richard, Yann. "Le rôle du clergé: Tendances contradictoires du chiisme iranien contemporain." *Archives de Sciences Sociales des Religions 28e Année* 55, no. 1 (Jan.–Mar. 1983): 5–27.

Royal Persia: A Commemoration of Cyrus the Great and His Successors on the Occasion of the 2500th Anniversary of the Founding of the Persian Empire. Exhibition catalog. London: British Museum, 1971.

Roylance, Frank D. "Another Name for Gulf Sets Off a Wave of Anger." *Baltimore Sun*, Nov. 25, 2004. At http://articles.baltimoresun.com/2004-11-25/news/0411250185_1_iran-atlas-arabian-gulf.

"Rulers Who Were Endowed with the Title 'the Great' (*Kabir*) by History." *Ruznameh-i Jashn-i Shahenshahi*, Aug. 16, 1971.

"Ruz-i Korush; yek chahre va chand tasvir az gozashte vahal." *Farda*, Dec. 23, 2007. At http://www.radiofarda.com/a/f1_kourosh_anniversary/418812.html.

Sabahi, Farian. "The Literacy Corps in Pahlavi Iran (1963–1979): Political, Social, and Literary Implications." PhD diss., SOAS Univ. of London, 1999.

"Sabt-i Ruz-i Korush dar taqvim-i melliy-i Iran." *Jamejam Online*, Nov. 21, 2008. At http://www1.jamejamonline.ir/newstext.aspx?newsnum=100954965004.

Sadigh, Soudabeh. "Iran: First Trial for Sivand Dam's Inundation Held." *Payvand*, July 5, 2007. At http://www.payvand.com/news/07/jul/1061.html.

Sadiq, 'Isa. *Yadegar-i 'Umr: Khaterat-i az sargozosht*. 2 vols. Tehran: Dehkhoda, 1975.

Safizadeh, Farah. *Az Korush Hakhamenishi ta Mohammad Khatami*. Tehran: Gofteman, 1999.

Sahab, Abu-Alqasem. *Farhang khavershenasan*. Tehran: Entesharat-i Sahab, 2535/1971.

Saleh, Alam, and James Worrall. "Between Darius and Khomeini: Exploring Iran's National Identity Problematique." *National Identities* 2014. doi:10.1080/14608944.2014.930426.

Salihi, Korush. *Dar sarashib-i suqut*. Mashhad, Iran: Iran Azad, 1378/1999.

Sami, 'Ali. "Bargozori-yi jashn-i Nowruz dar Takht-i Jamshid." *Honar-o Mardom* 104 (June 1971): 2–6.

Sanasarian, Eliz. *Religious Minorities in Iran*. Cambridge: Cambridge Univ. Press, 2000.

Savage, Kirk. *Standing Soldiers, Kneeling Slaves: Race, War, and Monument in Nineteenth-Century America*. Princeton, NJ: Princeton Univ. Press, 1997.

Savory, Roger. "Iran: A 2500-Year Historical and Cultural Tradition." In *Iranian Civilization and Culture: Essays in Honour of the 2,500th Anniversary of the Founding of the Persian Empire*, edited by Charles J. Adams, 77–89. Montreal: Institute of Islamic Studies, McGill Univ., 1972.

Schayegh, Cyrus. "Seeing Like a State: An Essay on the Historiography of Modern Iran." *International Journal of Middle East Studies* 42, no. 1 (2010): 37–61.

Sciolino, Elaine. *Persian Mirrors: The Elusive Face of Iran*. New York: Touchstone, 2000.

Shafa', Shojaeddin. *Korush-i Kabir va bunyad-i shahenshah-i Iran*. Tehran: Central Committee of Celebrations of the Iranian Monarchy, 1340/1961.

———. *Tavallud-i digar: Iran-i kuhan dar hazarah'i naw*. 2nd ed. N.p.: Farzad, 1999.

———. *Tawazih al-masa'il*. 2nd ed. Paris: Imprimérie Herissey à Evreux, 1360/1981.

Shahbazi, Shapur. *Ferdowsi: A Critical Biography*. Costa Mesa, CA: Mazda, 1991.

———. *Korush-i Bozorg*. Shiraz, Iran: Danishgah-i Pahlavi, 1970.

———. "NOWRUZ ii: In the Islamic Period." In *Encyclopaedia Iranica*. New York: Encyclopaedia Iranica Foundation, 2011. At http://www.iranicaonline.org/articles/nowruz-ii.

———. "Persepolis." In *Encyclopaedia Iranica*. New York: Encyclopaedia Iranica Foundation, 2011. At http://www.iranica.com/articles/persepolis.

Shahidi, Yahya, ed. *Majale-yi bararsiha-yi tarikhi*. Iranian Military no. 5. Tehran: Artesh-i Iran, 1970–71.

Shaked, Shaul. "Book of Esther." In *Encyclopaedia Iranica*. New York: Encyclopaedia Iranica Foundation, 2011. At http://www.iranicaonline.org/articles/esther-book-of.

Shari'ati, 'Ali. *'Are barodar inchunin bud*. Translated by Mohammad Amini and Alireza Bazargan. Tehran: n.p., 2006.

———. *Bazshenasi huviyat-i Irani Islami*. Tehran: Ilhām, 1361/1983.

———. *Islamshinasi, majmu'a-yi asar*. 3 vols. Tehran: Qalam, 1360–61/1981–82.

———. *Red Shiism*. Tehran: Hamdami, 1979.

Shari'ati bi rivayat-i asnad-i Savak. Tehran: Markaz-i Asnad-i Enqelab-i Eslami, 1378/1999.

Shiraz Arts Festival: Sound the Trumpets, Beat the Drums. Video, n.d. At http://www.youtube.com/watch?v=Ui3rw8ApGo8. Accessed Dec. 10, 2016, no longer available.

"Shive-yi shahenshahi Koroush va janeshinanash heman ruhiye ast." *Ruznameh-i Jashn-i Shahenshahi*, Oct. 4, 1971.

Shuja'i, Mitra. "Az takhrib-i Takht-i Jamshid ta borgozori Nouruz dar an." *Deutsche Welle*, Mar. 10, 2011. At http://www.dw-world.de/dw/article/0,,6465999,00.html.

Shushtari, Mohammad 'Ali Imam. "Forsat-i jashn-i shahenshahi, falsafeh-yi insani-yi Iran bi dunya mishinasunad." Interview. *Ruznameh-i Jashn-i Shahenshahi*, Oct. 10, 1971.

Siavoshi, Susan. "Construction of Iran's National Identity: Three Discourses." In *Rethinking Iranian Nationalism and Modernity*, edited by Kamran Scot Aghaie and Afshin Marashi, 253–74. Austin: Univ. of Texas Press, 2014.

Siddique, M. "The Work of Maulana Azad." In *Life and Times of Maulana Abul Kalam Azad*, edited by S. B. Singh and Nagendra Mohana Prasad, 213–33. Patna, India: Kashi Prasad Jayaswal Research Institute, 1993.

Smith, Anthony. *Chosen Peoples: Sacred Sources of National Identity*. Oxford: Oxford Univ. Press, 2004.

———. *The Ethnic Origins of Nations*. Oxford: Blackwell, 1987.

———. *Ethno-Symbolism and Nationalism: A Cultural Approach*. London: Routledge, 2009.

———. "The 'Golden Age' and National Renewal." In *Myths and Nationhood*, edited by Geoffrey Hosking and George Schöpflin, 36–59. New York: Routledge, 1997.

———. *National Identity*. Reno: Univ. of Nevada Press, 1991.

———. *Nationalism and Modernism: A Critical Survey of Recent Theories of Nations and Nationalism*. New York: Routledge, 1998.

———. "The Warwick Debate on Nationalism." *Nations and Nationalism* 2, no. 3 (1996): 357–70.

Smith, David. Introduction to *Firdausi Celebration 935–1935*, edited by David Smith, 3–7. New York: n.p., 1936.

Soltan-Zadeh, Maryam. "History Education and the Construction of National Identity in Iran." PhD diss., Florida International Univ., 2012.

"Statement on Persian Gulf/Arabian Gulf." *National Geographic*, press release, Nov. 23, 2004. At http://press.nationalgeographic.com/2004/11/23/statement-on-persian-gulfarabian-gulf.

Stronach, David, and Rudiger Schmitt. "Apadana." In *Encyclopaedia Iranica*. New York: Encyclopaedia Iranica Foundation, 2019. At http://www.iranicaonline.org/articles/apadana.

———. "Cyrus and Pasargadae." In *Cyrus the Great: An Ancient Iranian King*, edited by Touraj Daryaee, 53–77. Santa Monica, CA: Afshar, 2013.

Sukhanraniha-yi nokhustin-i dawra-yi jalasat-i sukhanrani va bahs darbara-yi shahnama-yi Firdusi. Tehran: Vizarat-i Farhang va Honar, 1971.

Tabataba'i, Mohammad Husayn. *Shi'ite Islam*. Albany: State Univ. of New York Press, 1979.

———. *Tafsir al-mizan*. Qom, Iran: Muassasah-i Maṭbuati Ismāʿīliyān, 1981.

———. *Tafsir al-mizan*. Qom, Iran: Muassasah-i Maṭbuʿati Ismāʿīliyān, 1985.

Taheri, Amir. *The Spirit of Allah: Khomeini and the Islamic Revolution*. London: Hutchinson, 1985.

"Tajali inqilab dar m'imari." *Ruznameh-i Jashn-i Shahenshahi*, Oct. 10, 1971.

"Tajamu' mardom Pasargad be monasebat-i ruz-i Korush." BBC Persian, Oct. 28, 2016. At http://www.bbc.com/persian/interactivity-37805667.

"Tajareb-i shahenshahi Iran mitavonad sar meshqe bashariyat boshad." *Ruznameh-i Jashn-i Shahenshahi*, Oct. 4, 1971.

Talberg, Frederick. *Az Korush ta Pahlavi*. Shiraz, Iran: Nashriye Daneshgah-i Pahlavi, 1967.

Ta'limat-i ejtema'i cheharam-i dabestan. Tehran: Vizarat-i Amuzesh va Parvaresh, 1375/1996.

Taqizadeh, Hasan. "Aghaz." *Kaveh*, Jan. 24, 1916, 1–3.

———. "Ferdowsi." *Kaveh*, Jan. 24, 1916, 4–5.

———. "Hukm az ruye tajribe." *Kaveh*, Nov. 15, 1918, 1–5.

———. "Kaveh va derafshe kawiyani." *Kaveh*, Jan. 24, 1916, 3–4.

———. *Zendegi tufani: Khaterat-i Sayyed Hasan Taqizadeh*. Tehran: Intisharat-i 'Ilmi, 1989.

"Taqvim-i Iran." *Iran*, Oct. 21, 2011.

Tavakoli-Targhi, Mohamad. *Refashioning Iran: Orientalism, Occidentalism, and Historiography*. New York: Palgrave, 2001.

"Tazetarin vakenshha' be 'juryan enherafi' dar dowlat-i Iran." BBC Persian, May 16, 2011. At http://www.bbc.com/persian/iran/2011/05/110516_l07_iran_government_critics.shtml.

Tilia, Ann Britt, ed. *Studies and Restoration at Persepolis and Other Sites of Fars*. Rome: ISMEO, 1972.

Toynbee, Arnold. "The First Iranian Empire." In *Commemoration Cyrus: Actes du Congres de Shiraz 1971 et autres etudes redigées a l'occasion du 2500e anniversaire de la fondation de l'Empire Perse*, 15–18. Leiden: Brill, 1974.

———. "The System of Rule of Cyrus and His Heirs Is the Same One Sought Today by Modern Rulers." *Ruznameh-i Jashn-i Shahenshahi*, Oct. 4, 1971.

Tsereteli, Georgi. "The Achaemenid State and World Civilization." In *Commemoration Cyrus: Actes du Congres de Shiraz 1971 et autres etudes redigées a l'occasion du 2500e anniversaire de la fondation de l'Empire Perse*, 102–7. Leiden: Brill, 1974.

Tucci, Giuseppe. Introduction to *Studies and Restoration at Persepolis and Other Sites of Fars*, edited by Ann Britt Tilia, xi–xiii. Rome: ISMEO, 1972.

Tudor, Henry. *Political Myth*. London: Macmillan, 1972.

"Do gozaresh az rali bozorg Paris–Takht-i Jamshid–Paris." *Ruznameh-i Jashn-i Shahenshahi*, Sept. 4, 1971.

Usku'i, Nasir. *Korush: Nabighah-'i buzurg-i tarikh*. Tehran: Intisharat-i Bu 'Ali, 1998.

Vaziri, Mostafa. *Iran as Imagined Nation: The Construction of National Identity*. New York: Paragon House, 1993.

Ward, Steven. *Immortal: A Military History of Iran and Its Armed Forces*. Washington, DC: Georgetown Univ. Press, 2009.

Watt, Montgomery. "al-Iskandar." In *Encyclopaedia of Islam*, new ed., vol. 4, edited by Peri J. Bearman, Bianquis, C. E. Bosworth, E. Van Donzel, and W. P. Heinrichs. Leiden: Brill, 1990. At http://dx.doi.org/10.1163/1573-3912_islam_SIM_3630.

Wigram, William A. *An Introduction to the History of the Assyrian Church*. Piscataway, NJ: Gorgias Press, 2004.

Wilber, Donald. *Persepolis: The Archaeology of Parsa, Seat of the Persian Kings*. London: Cassell, 1969.

Willanz, Sean, ed. *Rites of Power: Symbolism, Ritual, and Politics since the Middle Ages*. Philadelphia: Univ. of Pennsylvania Press, 1985.

Winter, Jay, and Emmanuel Sivan. "Setting the Framework." In *War and Remembrance in the Twentieth Century*, edited by Jay Winter and Emmanuel Sivan, 9–39. Cambridge: Cambridge Univ. Press, 1999.

Wortman, Richard. "Moscow and Petersburg: The Problem of the Political Center in Tsarist Russia, 1881–1914." In *Rites of Power: Symbolism, Ritual, and Politics since the Middle Ages*, edited by Sean Willanz, 244–72. Philadelphia: Univ. of Pennsylvania Press, 1985.

Yack, Bernard. *Nationalism and the Moral Psychology of Community*. Chicago: Univ. of Chicago Press, 2012.

Yarshater, Ehsan. "Cultural Development of Iran." In *Iran—Past, Present, and Future: Aspen Institute, Persepolis Symposium*, edited by Jane W. Jacqz, 407–19. New York: Aspen Institute for Humanistic Studies, 1976.

———. "The Political History of Iran under the Sasanians." In *The Cambridge History of Iran*, vol. 3: *Seleucid, Parthian, and Sasanian Periods*, edited by Ehsan Yarshater, 116–80. Cambridge: Cambridge Univ. Press, 1983.

Yeroushalmi, David. *The Jews of Iran in the Nineteenth Century: Aspects of History, Community, and Culture*. Leiden: Brill, 2010.

Zarrinkub, 'Abd al-Husayn. *Do qarn-i sukut: Sarguẕasht-i ḥavadi̱s va aẉzaʿ-i tarikhi-i Iran dar du qarn-i avval-i Islam az hamlah-i 'Arab ta zuhur-i dawlat-i Ṭahiriyan*. Tehran: Mu'assasah-i Entisharat-i Ahmad 'Ali, 1344/1965.

Zerubavel, Eviatar. *Time Maps: Collective Memory and the Social Shape of the Past.* Chicago: Univ. of Chicago Press, 2012.

Zerubavel, Yael. *Recovered Roots: Collective Memory and the Making of Israeli National Tradition.* Chicago: Univ. of Chicago Press, 1997.

Zraick, Karen. "Persian (or Arabian) Gulf Is Caught in the Middle of Regional Rivalries." *New York Times*, Jan. 12, 2016. At http://www.nytimes.com/2016/01/13/world/middleeast/persian-gulf-arabian-gulf-iran-saudi-arabia.html?_r=0.

Zuev, Dennis, and Fabian Virchow. "Performing National-Identity: The Many Logics of Producing National Belongings in Public Rituals and Events." *Nations and Nationalism* 20, no. 2 (2014): 191–99.

Index

Page numbers in italics refer to illustrative material.

'Abbas, 'Abd al-Baha, 22
'Abbasid caliphate, 60, 67, 131, 174–75
Abbaspour, Apadina, 169
'Abbas the Great, 120
Abdi, Abbas, 210n42
Abedi, Mehdi, 56
Abtahi, Mohammad 'Ali, 160
Abu Sufyan, 59, 168
Academy of the Persian Language (Farhangestan-i Zaban-i Iran), 5, 30
Achaemenid dynasty: architecture of, 5, 31–32, 121; as identity narrative, 10, 33–34; modern archaeology and, 166–77; national myth and, 18–19, 28, 33–34, 44, 46, 78; parallelism with Pahlavi Iran, 84, 104; scholarly interest in, 5–6, 109–10; success of, 22; textbook depictions of, 173–77; writings about, 31, 80–81, 105, 122. *See also* Cyrus the Great; Pasargadae; Persepolis; Persepolis celebrations (1971)
Adamiyat, Fereydun, 211n66
Afghani, Jaml al-Din, 48, 198n35
Afsharids, 128
Aghaie, Kamran Scott, 9, 12
Aghamohammadi, Mojtaba, 170
Ahmadi, Hamid, 148
Ahmadinejad, Mahmud, 106–7, 160, 162–65, *163*, 171–72
Ahmady, Dariush, 162
Ahmed Khan, Sayyed, 95, 99–100
Akbarzadeh, Shahram, 15
Akhundzadeh, Mirza Fath 'Ali, 10, 20, 21, 22, 25, 37, 44
'Ala', Husayn, 82
Ala, Mohammad, 169
'Alam, Asadollah, 79, 120
Al-e Ahmad, Jalal, 13, 41, 142, 145, 151
Alexander the Great, 81, 94, 101, 106, 109, 116, 179, 204n64
alienation, 13, 53, 74, 134–42, 174, 182, 183
Anderson, Benedict, 6–7, 168–70
Anjuman-i Asar-i Melli (Society for National Heritage), 8, 31
Another Birth (Shafa'), 68
Ansari, Ali, 122–23, 147
anthropology, 110
Arab chauvinism, 59
Arab conquest: conditions enabling, 45–46, 53, 64, 167–68; effects of, 5, 19, 20–21, 128, 132–33, 167; Persepolis celebrations and, 128, 166; textbook depictions of, 174; viewpoints regarding, 4, 20, 36–37, 44–46, 49, 53–54, 58–60, 63–64, 67–69, 167

Arab dynasties, 128. *See also specific dynasty*
Arab ethnicity, 9, 159
Arabian Gulf, 169–70
Arabic language, 5, 67–68, 69, 98
Arabic studies, 60
Arab identity, 57, 159, 165
Arab nationalism, 51, 56–61, 143, 159
Arabs, 44–45, 48, 49–52, 174
"Arab-toxication," 49–51
'Ar barodar, inchunin bud (Indeed, Brother, so It Was) (Shari'ati), 136–37, 140–42
Archaeological Institute of Persepolis, 117
archaeology: change in attitude toward, 31–32; dual role of, 24; excavation rights, 24, 26, 32; focus on everyday life, 109; "gold washing," 196n38; growing interest in, 21–33, 34, 72–74, 95, 96, 98, 109–10, 117–19, 180–81; intellectual ideologues vs., 47, 141–42; Iranian professionalization of, 109–10, 118–19; in modern Iran, 166–77; removal of artifacts, 32, 121; scientific objectivity and, 24–25, 26, 28, 29, 32, 180–81; site restoration, 81–82; writings about, 80. *See also* inscriptions (artifacts); *specific site or artifact*
architecture, 5, 31–32, 121
Aresh (publication), 67
art and artists: depictions of Cyrus the Great, 86–87, *97*, 98, 101, 205n78; mistaken appropriation of, 67–68; Shi'ism and, 50, 51–52, 65, 66–67; Shiraz Arts Festival, 119–20, 135, 172, 210n42; westernization and, 141–42. *See also* museums; music; poetry
Aryanism, 10
Asar-i 'ajam (Heritage of the Persians) (al-Dawla), 118
Ashraf (princess), 76
Ashraf, Ahmad, 7
Ashrafi, Mahmud, 83–84
Ashtiyani, Jalal al-Din, 62
Ashuri, Dariush, 141
Assmann, Jan, 182
Assyrians, 93
Atabaki, Touraj, 28
authenticity, 2, 59. *See also* Iranian authenticity
authentic memory, 3, 182
Avesta language, 45
awareness. *See* national awareness
Ayandeh (journal), 27
Aymard, Andre, 122
Azad, Abul Kalam, 71–72, 96–100, 101, 103, 205n78
Az Korush ta Pahlavi (From Cyrus to Pahlavi) (Talberg), 78–79

Ba'ath Party (Iraq), 93
Babylon, 72, 88, 89, 91–93, 146, 164, 181
Bahonar, Mohammad Reza, 162
Balance in Interpretation, The *(Tafsir al-mizan)* (Tabataba'i), 100–102
Bangladesh, 69
Barker, Rodney, 112, 129
Barry, James, 15
Barthel, Diane, 126–27
basijis, 106, 163
Bastani Parizi, Ibrahim, 71–72, 82, 98, 99–100
Bazargan, Mehdi, 148
belonging: alienation and, 13; civic vs. ethnic nationalism and, 54; national

awareness and, 31; rituals as, 152–53; role of maps in, 6–7; symbolism and, 184
Ben-Yahuda, Nachman, 3
Bernhardsson, Magnus T., 29
Bible, 32, 89, 101, 109; life of Cyrus and, 34, 73, 74, 87, 93, 94, 96, 103, 150. *See also* Hebrew Bible
Bodnar, John, 13, 114
Braudel, Fernand, 3–4
British Archeological Institute, 61
British Institute of Persian Studies (Tehran), 120
British Museum, 106, 120, 163
Buddhism, 50
Bunyad-i Fars Shinasi (Fars Studies Foundation), 172
Burke, Kenneth, 12, 141
Burujirdi, Husayn, 103
Buyid dynasty, 175

Canada, 123–25, 126, 132–33
carpet weaving, mistaken appropriation of, 67–68
car racing, 126
Carrol, Allen, 170
caste society, 45, 53, 68–69, 83–84
"Cave, The" (Qur'an), 72, 94–95, 99, 101
celebrations and ceremonies: audience for, 112; change in meaning of, 9–10; coronations, 35–36, 78–79; creating state legitimacy and, 129–30; ethnosymbolism and, 11; Iranian spirit and, 13–14, 32, 131–32, 136–37, 139; monarchal use of, 76; Nasir al-Din and, 24; role of, 11, 14, 24, 31, 44, 111–15, 152. *See also* rituals; *specific celebration*
censorship, 71–72, 98–99, 135, 169–70
Champdor, Albert, 81
"chauvinistic nationalism," 59, 82, 88, 106
cheharshanbe suri, 154–56
children and youth: books for, 83–84, 172–77; religion and, 55–56, 156, 162; scholarships for, 125
Christensen, Arthur, 37, 74, 130
Christianity, 89
Chronicles (book of), 74, 93
Chubin, Shahram, 146–47
civic nationalism, 54
civilizations, reincarnation of, 131–32
Clarification of Questions (*Tawzih al-masa'il*) (Shafa'), 62–63
clothing, dress codes and, 29, 55
Cold War, 77, 88, 91
collective identity, 2, 9–10, 158–59
collective memory, 1–17; concept of *inscription* and, 9–10; monarchy as symbol of, 33–35; repression and, 19, 60–61, 147, 182
colonialism, 52, 53, 56–57, 168
"commemorative density," 33–35, 128
Communism, 162
Constitutional Revolution, 138
Corbin, Henry, 41, 42–43, 58, 64
"cosmopolitan-universal nationalism," 82, 102
Cottam, Richard, 6–7
cultural cohesion, 7, 15–16, 20–21, 28, 44–45, 49, 64, 161
cultural identity, 2, 48, 49, 77
cultural nationalism, 44, 46
cuneiform inscriptions, 24–25, 72, 79, 95, 147
Cyropaedia, 34
Cyrus cylinder, 72, 73, 81–82, 94, 103, 106, *163*

Cyrus the Great, 71–107; academic conferences on, 90–91, 105, 130–34; appropriation of, 72, 75, 78, 94, 101–6, 150, 158, 163–77, 185; archaeology of in modern Iran, 166–77; artistic representations of, 86–87, *97*, 98, 101, 205n78; "the Cyrus Complex," 84; flexible identity of, 76; human rights and, 62, 81, 91, 123–25, 165, 180, 181; lack of sources about, 72–75, 78–79, 87, 94, 180, 204n62; language of, 72, 99; legacy of, 72, 75, 80, 90, 91, 101, 102, 103, 106, 180; marketing of, 72–73, 180–81; monitoring of publications about, 71–72, 98–99; mythmaking and, 33, 75, 76–93, 100, 101–3, 179–80, 181; politicization of, 13, 14, 15, 71–76, 78–81, 102; in Qur'an, 72, 75, 94–106; religious identity and, 71–74, 78–79, 82–87, 89–90, 92–93, 99, 158, 166, 187; tomb of, 61, 108, 121, 125, 164–65, 166, 170–71; writings about, 71–72, 78–86, 91, 92, 98–102, 105–6. *See also* Persepolis celebrations (1971)

Cyrus the Great (*Korush-e Bozorg*) (Shahbazi), 80–81

Cyrus the Great (*Korush-i-Kabir*) (Ashrafi), 83–84

Cyrus the Great (*Korush-i-Kabir*) (Hedayati), 92

Cyrus the Great Day, 164–65, 170

Cyrus the Great in European Art (*Korush-i Kabir dar asar-i hunariy-i Urupa'iyan*) (Homayun), 85–87, 91, 204n62

Daniel (book of), 101, 205n69

Dari language, 45

Darius (king): Arab chauvinism and, 59; inscriptions regarding, 101, 117; Pahlavi promotion of, 120, 127; Persepolis celebrations and, 126, 127; reception hall of, 118, 153; textbook depictions of, 174; Zoroastrianism and, 95

Darmesteter, James, 64

Dar sarashib-i suqut (The Steep Fall) (Salihi), 167–68

Dawla, Mohammad Nasir Fursat al-, 118

de Morgan, Jacques, 21

Development of Iran during the Pahlavi Era (Nafisi), 33

Dhul-Qarnayn, 94–101, 103, 105, 106, 166, 187, 204n64

didactic construction, memory and, 4

Dieulafoy, Marcel, 21

"dislocative nationalism," 10

dramatic construction, memory and, 4

dress codes, 29, 55

dynasties, textbook depictions of, 172–77. *See also specific dynasties*

Ebrahimi, Reza Zia, 10

education, 125, 172–77

Egypt, 50, 56, 59, 65–66, 77, 140, 187–88

Elamite dynasty, 102, 109–10, 118

elites: court patronage and, 22; flexible identity of Cyrus, 76; Islamic Republic and, 148; monarchy as symbolism, 34–35; role of in celebrations, 82, 111–12, 129, 133–34, 180; shift in attitudes of, 3, 46; study of, 9, 10–11, 13, 180; textbook depictions of, 174; themes of, 33, 91, 180–88. *See also* Iranian intellectuals; *specific person*

embroidery, mistaken appropriation of, 67–68

England, 28, 65, 95
Enlightenment, 27
entitlement, ruling class and, 83–84
ethnicity: balance with religious affiliation, 185, 186; cultural elements of, 11, 53, 75; formation of nations and, 2; modern Iran and, 86, 161; terminology of, 15–16. *See also* Arab ethnicity; Persian ethnicity
ethnic nationalism, 52, 54, 158–59
ethnosymbolism, 6, 10–12, 180
Ettela'at (newspaper), 210n47
Europe: archaeological interests of, 21, 23–29, 30, 32, 34, 72–73, 95, 96, 109–10, 117–18; expansion of, 20; Iranian diaspora and, 161; Iranian influence in, 85; Iranian scholarship and, 81, 95; modern historiography and, 7–8. *See also specific country*
Ezekiel (book of), 128–29

Fall of the Shaw (documentary), 210n42, 213n98
False Cyrus (Khalkhali), 89, 103–4, 138–39
Farah Diba (empress): artistic depictions of, 87; coronation of, 78, 79, 96; foundations under, 76; Nasr and, 62; Persepolis celebrations and, 82; Shiraz Arts Festival and, 119, 135
Fardid, Ahmad, 151
Farhangestan-i Zaban-i Iran (Academy of the Persian Language), 5, 30
Farhi, Farideh, 148
Fars Province, 105, 117, 118, 172
Fars Studies Foundation (Bunyad-i Fars Shinasi), 172
Fath 'Ali Shah, 19–20
Ferdowsi, Abul-Qasim, 30, 34, 36–37, 51, 68, 73, 74, 162
festivals. *See* celebrations and ceremonies
Fida'yan-i Islam, 103
Firuzabad, 135–36
Fisher, Michael, 56
folklore, 28–29, 74, 135, 180
forgetfulness, memory and, 33, 181–82
Forming National Identity in Iran (Mozaffari), 9–10
Foroughi, Mohammad 'Ali, 30, 31, 35–36, 37, 118
France: archaeological missions, 21, 24–25, 32, 117–18; excavation rights, 32; literary translations, 62–63; museum exhibits in, 23; nationality of scholars and, 110; Nora's scholarship and, 3; Orientalist scholarship in, 41–42; Persepolis celebrations and, 126, 136
freedom, as theme, 85, 86
From Cyrus to Pahlavi (*Az Korush ta Pahlavi*) (Talberg), 78–79

Gandhi, Mohammad, 50
Geertz, Clifford, 111
Gera, Deborah Levine, 73
Gershoni, Israel, 114
Gharbzadegi (Westoxication), 41, 142
Ghaznavid dynasty, 175
Ghirshman, Roman, 109–10
Ghotbi, Reza, 119
Ghotbi, Sharazad, 119
Gieger, Wilhelm, 130
Gobineau, Arthur de, 42–43
golden age, cultural identity and, 2, 77
Golestan Treaty, 19–20
Goodarzi, Mohammad, 123–25
Google, place name searches and, 170
Great Civilization (*tamaddun-i bozorg*), 158

Greece, 34, 74, 85–86, 91, 92, 96–98, 103, 122, 173
Grigor, Talinn, 8–9, 127

Hafez, 32, 37, 74
Halbwachs, Maurice, 2–3, 182
Handler, Richard, 112–13
Harvey, Delicia, 87
Hebrew Bible, 74, 93, 103
Hebrew language, 72, 99
Hedayati, Hadi, 88, 89, 91–92
Hekmat, ʿAli Asghar, 31
Hermitage Museum, 120
Herzfeld, Ernst, 34, 117–18, 205n78
"historical density," 182
historical preservation, industrialization and, 127
historicist approach, 5–7
History of Ancient Iran (Pirinya), 21
Hobsbawm, Eric, 112, 113, 164
Holliday, Shabnam, 149–50
Holy Defense. *See* Iran-Iraq War (1980–88)
Homayun, Gholamʿali, 85–87, 91, 204n62
Hoveyda, Abbas, 79–80
human rights, 62, 64, 81, 91, 123–25, 165, 180, 181
Hunter, Shireen, 147
Husayniyya Ershad, 40, 43, 56
Hussein, Saddam, 146

Ibn Hisham, 204n64
Ibn Khaldun, 67
"identity narratives," 9–10
Imagined Communities (Anderson), 168–70
imam-i zaman, 50
imperialism: American, 89, 104; challenging, 48, 49; English, 65; Iran as imperialistic power, 5, 19, 27; Western, 6, 48, 57, 88, 145
"Indeed, Brother, so It Was" (*ʿAr barodar, inchunin bud*) (Shariʿati), 136–37, 140–42
India: Cyrus's rule over, 90–91; growth in cultural heritage and, 8, 25; Indian characteristics, 50; Islamic identity and, 69; origins of Iran and, 84, 96–98; scholarship in, 75, 95–98
Indian Advisory Board of Archaeology, 96
Indian Council for Cultural Relations, 96
Indian language, 45, 59
industrialization, 111, 127
inscription (concept), 9–10
inscriptions (artifacts): Babylonian, 93; at Behistun, 21; cuneiform inscriptions, 24–25, 72, 79, 95, 147; Cyrus cylinder, 72, 73, 81–82, 94, 103, 106, *163*; Darius and, 101, 117; describing Cyrus, 86, 101; feelings of people toward, 46–47, 147; modernist discourse and, 24–25; at Naqsh-i Rostam, 209n39; at Persepolis, 22, 79; photographing of, 117; Sassanid dynasty, 116
instrumentalism, 5–6, 7, 11, 182–83, 184, 186
intellectuals. *See* Iranian intellectuals
Internet, 169, 171
invented traditions, defined, 112–13
Iran: continuity vs. change in, 3–4; as cradle of civilization, 21, 158, 172; golden age of, 2, 77; historical dichotomy in, 53, 80–81, 85–86; name change, 29; origins of, 75, 84–85. *See*

also Islamic Republic of Iran; Islamic Revolution (1979); Pahlavi state; *specific empire or dynasty*
Iran as Imagined Nation (Vazari), 7
Iran Bastan (journal), 98–99
Iran Bastan Museum, 117
Irangira'i, 162–63
Iranian Antiquities Authority, 32, 109, 110
Iranian art, 68
Iranian authenticity: challenges to, 14, 126–27, 134, 136, 137, 142, 153, 155–56, 181–82; competition over, 142; deracination vs., 13; "Islamiyyat" and "Iraniyyat" and, 157; nation-state and, 57–61, 144–45; piety vs., 59; political sovereignty and, 159; political vs. historical, 77–78, 81, 142; post-Revolution, 153, 155–56, 157, 159, 167; preservation of, 126–27; redefining, 43–47, 156; technology and, 126–27; as topic of debate, 40–41
Iranian chauvinism, 59, 82, 88, 106
Iranian diaspora, 161–62, 169–70, 171–72
Iranian folklore, 28–29, 74, 135, 180
Iranian identity: components of, 3–4, 43–47, 83–84, 156–57; continuity of, 69–70; Islamic Republic and, 39, 142, 149, 156–61, 185; media promotion and, 77, 82; monarchy as center of, 34–35, 37, 59, 76–78, 125, 137–38, 151, 159, 171–72; "national identity" vs. "nationality," 158–59; pre-Islamic vs. Islamic, 10; textbook depictions of, 172–77; as topic of debate, 40–41
Iranian intellectuals, 18–36; co-opting of, 134–35; historical themes of, 33; Middle Ages and, 67–68; monarchy as symbol, 34–35; post-WWI, 28; role of, 35, 36, 183; scholarly approaches of, 3, 5–17; scientific objectivity and, 24–25, 26, 28, 29, 32, 133, 180–81; secular affiliations of, 24. *See also* elites; Western education and scholarship; *specific person*
Iranian Majles, 1, 106–7, 162–63, 172
Iranian Ministry of Education, 173–77
Iranian Ministry of Foreign Affairs, 170
Iranian Ministry of Information, 71–72, 99
Iranian National Front USA, 169–70
Iranian nationalism, 1–17; acceptance of, 144–45; biological aspects, 10, 58–59, 60; concept of, 15–16, 41, 44–45, 56–57, 158–59; evolution of, 143–52, 185–88; Irano-Islamic consciousness and, 55–61; "national identity" vs. "nationality," 158–59; origins and rise of, 3–4, 29–38, 59, 179, 183; triadic structure of, 20–21
Iranian National Library, 105
Iranianness, 13–14, 181, 184. *See also* Iranian authenticity; Iranian identity
Iranian New Year. *See* Nowruz (Iranian New Year)
Iranian spirit: absence of, 45–46, 53; American spirit vs., 36; celebrations and ceremonies and, 13–14, 32, 131–32, 136–37, 139; representation of, 5, 8–9; revival of, 57; Shi'ite Islam and, 42–43, 51, 145, 158; "spiritual currency," 12, 141; textbook depictions of, 173; timelessness of, 130; Zoroastrianism and, 42–43, 46
Iran in World Literature (Shafa'), 62–63
Iran-Iraq War (1980–88), 142, 143–44, 145–49, 155
Iraniyyat, 149, 157, 160–61
"Irano-Islamic" culture, 52

Iranshahar (journal), 27
Iraq: skirmishes with, 88; symbolic rivalry with, 93, 106; war with (1980–88), 142, 143–44, 145–49, 155
Isaiah (book of), 71
Islam: Arab influence on, 49, 58, 59–60, 64; compatibility of, 95–96; identity with vs. religious conviction, 69; Iranian heritage vs., 15, 161; Irano-Islamic consciousness and, 55–61; notion of monarchy and, 102–3; Nowruz as Muslim festival, 153–56. *See also* Shi'ite Islam; Sunni Islam; Twelver Shi'i Islam
Islamic art, 68
Islamic history, 31, 81
Islamic identity, 69, 149, 157, 159, 177–78
Islamic Republic of Iran, 3, 143–88; appropriation of Cyrus, 72, 75, 78, 94, 101–6, 150, 158, 163–77, 185; appropriation of national symbols, 9, 65–66, 78, 144, 153–56; archaeology in, 166–77; domestic policy, 149; flexibility and adaptability of, 184; foreign policy of, 142, 143–44, 145–49, 155, 157, 172, 181; Iranian diaspora and, 161–62, 169–70, 171; moderates vs. radicals in, 157; national identity and, 39, 142, 143–52, 177–88; Pahlavi influence on, 15, 62, 142, 144, 152–56; publications challenging narrative of, 167–68; relationship with pre-Islamic history and symbols, 15, 16, 119, 150, 152–65, 166–78, 179–88; rise of, 5, 63, 101–4, 142, 143–52, 187–88; Rule of the Jurisprudent and, 69, 136–37
Islamic Revolution (1979): demands of, 172–73, 177, 186; as evolutionary phase, 41, 69, 143–52; nation-state and, 47; plan for destruction of Persepolis, 139, 147, 148; pre-Islamic legacy of Iran and, 10, 15, 75, 183–84; support for, 167–68
Islamic unity, as universalist ideology, 143
Islamiyyat, 149, 157
Ismail, 175
isolationism, 85
Israel, 17, 72, 92

Jahiliyya period, 20
Jamshid, 35, 116, 117, 209n28
Jashn-i Honar-i Shiraz (Shiraz Arts Festival), 119–20, 135, 172, 210n42
Jews, 72, 89–90, 92, 99, 101, 103–4, 162, 181
Johnstone, Barbara, 83
Judaism, 69

Karbala, 12, 65, 67
Kashani-Sabet, Firoozeh, 6–7, 21, 117, 169
Kaveh (journal), 27, 28, 31, 37, 130, 133
Kayhan (newspaper), 210n47
Kazemzadeh-Iranshar, Hosein, 28
Kermani, Agha Khan, 10, 20, 22, 37
Kertzer, David, 11–12
Khalili, Abbas, 25
Khalkhali, Sadeq: on Cyrus the Great, 89, 103–4, 138–39, 150; Iranian authenticity and, 57; Khomeini and, 51; plan to destroy Persepolis, 139, 147, 168; reputation of, 206n96; writings of, 89, 103–4, 138–39
Khamenei, 'Ali, 145, 146, 154–55, 157–59, 185
Khatami, Mohammad, 1, 105–6, 143, 155, 156–65, *160*, 186
Khayyam, 'Umar, 36

Khomeini, Ruhollah: Bazargan and, 148; death of, 155; foreign relations and, 148–49; Khalkhali and, 51; legacy of, 157, 176; lessons learned, 144; Motahhari and, 55; nationalism and, 51, 54, 144, 145, 151–52, 162, 177, 187, 188; Persepolis celebrations and, 134, 136–38; on rejection of monarchy, 102–3; role of historical myth and, 18–19; Rule of the Jurisprudent, 69, 136–37; *taqrib* movement and, 65–66; writings of, 68, 69, 102–3, 138, 151–52
Khushwakht, Mohammad Husayn, 170
Khwarazmshah dynasty, 175
Kohl, Philip L., 3
Korush-e Bozorg (Cyrus the Great) (Shahbazi), 80–81
Korush-i dorughin (False Cyrus) (Khalkhali), 89, 103–4, 138–39
Korush-i-Kabir (Cyrus the Great) (Ashrafi), 83–84
Korush-i-Kabir (Cyrus the Great) (Hedayati), 92
Korush-i Kabir dar asar-i hunariy-i Urupa'iyan (Cyrus the Great in European Art) (Homayun), 85–87, 91, 204n62
Kozelsky, Mara, 3

Lamb, Harold, 81
language, cultural cohesion and, 7, 15–16, 28, 45. *See also specific language*
legitimacy: creating, 14, 35, 109, 111–12, 114–16, 127, 129–30, 133; state ceremonies and, 129–30; symbols as form of, 115–16
Levinger, Matthew, 2, 20–21
lieux de mémoire, 3
Linnekin, Jocelyn, 112–13
Literacy Corps, 77, 123
longue durée, 3–4
Louvre Museum, 120
Lytle, Paula Franklin, 2, 20–21

Mahallati, Majd ad-Din, 139
Malkum Khan, 25
maps, national identity and, 6–7, 168–70
Marashi, Afshin, 8, 9
martyrdom, 65
Marxism, 40, 55
Masha'i, Isfandiyar Rahim, 162, 165, 171–72
Masse, Henry, 37
Massignon, Louis, 41, 42
Medean dynasty, 102, 110
Mehdevi, Anne Sinclair, 71
memory, 1–17, 110–15; "acceleration of history" and, 110–11, 113–14; authentic, 3, 182; civil society and, 114; "commemorative density" and, 33, 128; didactic construction of, 4; dramatic construction of, 4; forgetfulness and, 33, 181–82; institutionalization of, 3, 115; *lieux de mémoire,* 3; mimetic model of, 114–15; modern forms of, 110–11; primary and secondary agents of, 57, 73, 76, 78, 114, 130; social nature of, 2–3, 15, 110–11. *See also* collective memory
Menashri, David, 148–49, 203n39
Metropolitan Museum (New York), 120
Michener, Roland, 132
middle class, 83, 119, 135, 137
Middle East, 21, 144, 183–84, 187. *See also specific country or empire*
Milani, Mohsen, 148
military, 88, 122–23, 128–29
milliyat, 158–59

miniatures, mistaken appropriation of, 67–68
Mission for My Country (Mohammad Reza Shah), 79
modernism, 4, 6–8, 25, 27–29, 180
modernization, 31, 110–11, 112–15, 127, 133
Mohammad Hasan Khan, 21
Mohammad Reza Shah (r. 1941–79): artistic depictions of, 87; coronation of, 78–79, 96; downfall of, 38, 115, 183; legacy of, 38, 109, 134, 183; Persepolis celebrations and, 108, 115, 120–21, 125–26, 138, 144; personality cult of, 76–77, 135; symbolism of Cyrus and, 74, 79–80, 83–84, 87, 100, 120–21, 125–26, 180; use of celebrations, 76; White Revolution and, 46; writings of, 79. *See also* Pahlavi state
monarchy: abolishment of, 172–73, 175; celebrations for, 76; "decline thesis" and, 125–26; Iranian identity and, 34–35, 37, 59, 76–78, 125, 137–38, 151, 159, 171–72; mythmaking and, 101–3, 134; as outdated, 68; reliance on, 45–46, 53; as symbol of collective memory, 34–35; textbook depictions of, 172–77; ulema view of, 102–3. *See also* Persepolis celebrations (1971)
Mongolian Empire, 128
monotheism, 34, 75, 95–96, 98, 101, 166–67
Mossadeq, Mohammad, 76–77, 91, 115
Motahhari, Mortaza, 55–61, *55*; death of, 56; influence of, 39, 55, 69–70; lessons learned, 144, 161; Nasr and, 62; Shafa' and, 64; Shari'ati and, 56, 58, 60, 64, 69–70; writings of, 55
Mozaffari, Ali, 9–10, 15–16
Mu'in, Mohammad, 59
museums: establishment of, 32; exhibits, 106, 120–21, 123, *163*; fascination with, 41, 141–42; growth of, 23–24. *See also specific museum*
music, 65, 119–20
Muzaffar al-Din Shah, 22
myths and mythmaking: cosmopolitan elements of, 82; cultivation of, 11, 18–19, 28, 48, 70, 73, 77, 134, 182, 184; Cyrus the Great and, 18–19, 33, 75, 76–93, 100, 101–3, 179–80, 181; monarchy and, 134; Orientalism and, 134

Nabavi, Negin, 142
Nabonidus, 91–92
Nadir Shah, 128
Nafisi, Sa'id, 20, 31, 33, 82, 100
Naqsh-i Rostam, 119, 209n39
Nasir al-Din Shah, 22, 23–24, 117
Nasr, Seyyed Hossein, 62, 200n81
Nasser, Gamal 'Abdel, 50, 77, 143
Nasserism, 56, 187
national awareness, 18–38; from above vs. from below, 13, 112, 113, 182, 183; cultural revival of, 31; importance of, 6, 10, 15; modernity and, 133; as phase of nationalism, 52–53; political implications of, 15; Qajar dynasty and, 8, 20, 22; rise of, 6, 8, 9, 12–13, 14, 18–29, 31, 36; role of celebrations in, 152
National Geographic (journal), 169–70
National Iranian Radio and Television, 119
nationalism, 1–17; "chauvinistic nationalism," 59, 82, 88, 106; civic vs. ethnic, 54; continuity and, 1–2, 3–4; "cosmopolitan-universal nationalism," 82, 102; "dislocative," 10; historical continuity

and, 1–2; "historical density" and, 182; as linear process, 183–84; mythologies of, 3–4, 18–19, 28; phases of, 52–53; "positive" vs. "negative," 145; religious nationalism, 147, 154, 156–57, 166, 178; Third World and, 56–57, 145; triadic structure of, 2, 20–21. *See also* Arab nationalism; Iranian identity; Iranian nationalism
National Museum of Iran, 106, 117, 163–64
"negative" nationalism, 145
Ne'mati, Amir, 162
Neo-Achaemenid style, 5, 31–32
newspapers/journals, 77, 130, 135, 138, 167–68. *See also specific title*
Niedermayer, Oskar, 130
Niknami, Kamal, 110
Nora, Pierre, 3, 33, 110–11, 113–15, 181–82, 186
nostalgia, 28, 47
Nowruz (Iranian New Year): celebration of, 152–56, 164, 170; *cheharshanbe suri* and, 154–56; Iranian diaspora and, 161, 171–72; Pahlavi self-aggrandizement and, 150, 152–53; Persepolis celebrations and, 106–7, 116–17, 185
nuclear treaties, 172

Olympic Games, 173
opposition movements, influences on, 144
oppression, 85, 86
Oriental Institute (University of Chicago), 118
Orientalism, 9, 42–43, 58, 61, 64, 127, 134, 158
Ottoman Empire, 26

paganism, 57, 75, 76, 143, 152–56, 166
Pahlavi state: "decline thesis" as theme of, 125–26; as evolutionary phase, 143–52, 177–88; foreign policy of, 6, 76–78, 87–91, 93, 204n48; legacy of, 72, 76, 151–56, 165, 166, 177, 186; notion of civilization and, 51, 108, 131, 141, 158; origins of nationalism, 4–5, 8–9, 13; reawakening of Iran imagery, 33, 125, 133, 138–39; self-exoticism of, 126; shift from, 3, 134–42; worldview of, 8–9, 39–41, 60–69
Pahlavi University, 78, 79
Pakistan, 69
parades, 24, 111, 122–23, *124*, 125, 128–29
Parsons, Anthony, 134
Parthian dynasty, 34, 128, 173
Pasargadae: archaeological deterioration in, 1; celebrations at, 61–62, 108, 164–65; Cyrus's tomb, 61, 108, 121, 125, 164–65, 166, 170–71; Sivand Dam proposal, 171–72; winged figure at, *97*, 98, 205n78; World Heritage Site status, 171
patriotism, 8, 28, 110, 154
Pearls of the Crowns in the History of the Parthians (Saltanah), 21–22
Persepolis: archaeological deterioration in, 1, 118; growing fascination with, 119; as historical myth, 18–19, 116–17; Iranian interest in, 109, 117–19; Islamic Republic and, 106–7, 139, 150, 164; Khatmani visits, *160*; marketing of, 180–81; museum exhibitions and, 120–21; national importance of, 109, 116–17; origins of name, 117; razing of ruins at, 139, 147, 168

Persepolis celebrations (1971), 13–14, 108–42; advertising for, 123, 130; audiovisual performance at, 123, 125, 126, 127–29; car racing at, 126; conferences about, 130–34; cost of, 136; criticisms of, 134–42; denial of access to, 136; diplomatic and foreign involvement in, 123–25, 126, 127, 133, 139; as historical myth, 18–19; as invented commemoration, 113; media coverage of, 122, 127, 130; militaristic aspects, 122–23; Mohammad Reza Shah's speech for, 108, 125–26, 128–29; museum exhibits commemorating, 120–21, 123; origins of, 32, 61, 77, 82, 85; Pahlavi legitimacy and, 109, 111–12, 114–16, 127, 129–30, 133; Shafa' and, 61–62, 70, 77, 82, 120, 121; Shari'ati and, 13, 47–48, 136, 140–42; site selection, 112; soldiers' parade, 122–23, *124*, 125, 128–29; spiritual challenges to, 136–37; symbolism of, 108–9, 111–12, 115, 119, 121, 123, 125, 128–29, 134, 137, 139–40; technology and, 126–27; writings for and about, 71–72, 98–99, 116–17, 120, 122, 136–37, 140–42, 210n47

Persian Empire, 123–25. *See also specific dynasty*

Persian ethnicity, 15–16, 59, 63, 69, 75, 144, 161–62

Persian Gulf, 69, 145–47, 169–70

Persian language, 5, 15, 19, 21, 60, 79

Pesce, Luigi, 22, 117

piety, 59

Pirniya, Hasan, 20, 21, 30, 35

poetry: as heritage fostering, 34, 36–37, 74; Shi'ism and, 66–67; tombs of poets, 8, 9, 30, 32, 34, 63. *See also specific poet*

popular culture, 82–83

"positive" nationalism, 145

Pourpirar, Nasser, 162

pre-Islamic Iran, 16–17; collective identity and, 9–10; consecration of, 4, 5; Irano-Islamic consciousness and, 30, 59–61, 108; promotion of, 14–15; redefining, 43–54, 167; as symbol system, 12

propaganda: Cyrus the Great as, 74, 103–4; Khalkhali on, 138–39; Persepolis celebrations and, 116, 120, 127, 134, 138–39; Shari'ati and, 141; war and, 104, 146–47

protests and riots, 165, 171

public opinion, influencing, 8, 163

public space, 3, 8–9, 24

publishing, role of, 19, 27, 31

Purdavud, Ibrahim, 59, 82

Qa'imi, Mohammad, 81

Qajar dynasty: archaeology and, 21–22, 24, 26, 30; national awareness and, 8, 20, 22; Pahlavi characterization of, 33, 37; Persepolis celebrations and, 128; textbook depictions of, 174; treaties signed, 19–20; Zand and, 117

Qawam al-'Ulama-yi Kirmanshahi, 26

Qur'an, 52, 72, 75, 94–106, 158, 166, 187

Qutb, Sayyid, 187–88

race theory, 48–52, 57, 58–59, 60, 63

racism: Arab conquest and, 68–69, 168; deracination and, 13; "dislocative

nationalism" and, 10; human rights and, 62, 64, 81, 91, 123–25, 165, 180, 181; Iranian nationalism as outcome of, 7; Qur'an and, 52; Shu'ubiyya movement and, 60
radio, 77, 138
Rafsanjani, Akbar Hashemi, 105, 146
rallies, 165, 171
Ranger, Terrance, 112, 113, 164
rationalism, 7–8, 27, 95
Rawlinson, Henry, 21, 24–25, 95
Razmjou, Shahrokh, 209n27
Refashioning Iran (Tavakoli-Targhi), 7–8
religious nationalism, 147, 154, 156–57, 166, 178
Rethinking Iranian Nationalism and Modernity (Aghaie and Marashi), 9
Return to the Self (Shari'ati), 108
revolution. *See* Islamic Revolution (1979)
Revolutionary Guards, 106, 156, 157, 163
Reza Shah Pahlavi (r. 1925–41): coronation of, 29, 30, 35–36; Iran as republic, 173; legacy of, 5, 8–9, 29–38, 44, 183; poetic influences on, 30. *See also* Pahlavi state
Rezwi, Taher, 95–96
Richard, Jules, 22, 117
riots and protests, 165, 171
rituals: as belonging, 152–53; change in meaning of, 9–10; as expression of politics, 11–12; against injustice, 65; religious ethics as, 53–54
Rome, 85
Rubaiyat (Khayyam), 36
Rule of the Jurisprudent *(vilayat-i faqih)* (Khomeini), 69, 136–37
Russia, 6, 19–20, 28, 123
Ruz Korush-i Bozorg (Cyrus the Great Day), 164–65
Sa'adi, 32, 162, 172
Sabahi, Farian, 123
Sadiq, 'Isa, 31, 36, 118–19, 133
Safavid dynasty, 22, 64–65, 120, 128, 175, 176
Salihi, Korush, 167–68
Saltanah, I'timad al-, 21–22
Sami, 'Ali, 116–17
Sassanid dynasty: fall of, 37, 42, 44, 53, 64, 167–68; Iranian historical identity and, 34, 49, 59; Motahhari on, 59; Persepolis celebrations and, 128; renewed interest in, 109–10; Rezwi on, 95–96; Shafa' on, 64; Shari'ati on, 45–46, 49, 51, 53, 54; social schisms in, 45, 53, 64, 68–69; textbook depictions of, 173–74; vulnerability of, 45–46
Saudi Arabia, 59, 169
Savage, Kirk, 114
SAVAK, 40, 60–61, 66, 71–72, 86, 134, 135–36
Savory, Roger, 126, 132–33
sayyid, 66
Schayegh, Cyrus, 9
school textbooks, 172–77
scientific methods, use of, 24–25, 26, 28, 29, 32, 133, 180–81
self-image/perception: celebrations and, 13–14, 82, 137; domestic policy and, 149; elite and, 9, 13, 133–34, 182, 184; historical aspects, 19, 26, 32, 35–36, 48, 61–62, 87, 88–89, 131, 181–82; "natural rights" and, 19; reemergence of, 185; Western culture and, 36, 85. *See also* Iranian authenticity; Iranian identity
Seljuk dynasty, 175
Semites, 49–52, 58

Shafa', Shojaeddin, 61–70; as court historian, 39, 77; influence of, 39, 45, 69–70, 77; Motahhari and, 64; Persepolis celebrations and, 61–62, 70, 77, 82, 120, 121; on Sassanid dynasty, 64; Shari'ati and, 64, 69–70; Shi'ite Islam and, 65–69; writings of, 62–63, 64, 66, 82, 93

Shahanshah (King of Kings), 102–3

Shahbazi, Shapur, 80–81, 82

Shahnameh (Ferdowsi), 30, 37, 51, 68, 73

Shahyad (Shah's Monument), 121

Shari'ati, 'Ali, 13, 39–54, *42*; ambivalence toward nationalism, 41, 56, 58, 144, 145, 187; on historical greatness, 46–47; influence of, 39, 69–70; on Iranian Islam, 48–54; lessons learned, 144; Motahhari and, 56, 58, 60, 64, 69–70; national pride of, 51–52; Persepolis celebrations and, 13, 47–48, 136, 140–42; popularity of, 140, 141; on redefining pre-Islamic Iran, 43–54, 167; Salihi and, 167; Semites vs. Aryans, 49–52; Shafa' and, 64, 69–70; state repression and, 60; worldview of, 41, 42–43, 48–49, 58, 198n35; writings of, 108, 136, 140–42

Shi'i identity, evolutionary phases of, 143–52, 158, 161, 185–88

Shi'ite Islam: defining, 40–41, 51; "forged Shi'ism," 67; Iranian spirit and, 42–43, 51, 145, 158; Irano-Islamic consciousness and, 60; redefining pre-Islamic Iran and, 43–54, 185; repression of, 22, 139; rituals of, 65; Shafa's indictment of, 65–69; Sunni Islam vs., 64–65; symbolism and, 12; textbook depictions of, 174–77

Shiraz Arts Festival, 119–20, 135, 172, 210n42

Shirazi, Makarim, 155

Shu'ubiyya movement, 49, 60

Sivan, Emmanuel, 3, 114

Sivand Dam, 171–72

Smith, Anthony, 2, 4–5, 6, 11, 13, 14, 111

Smith, David Eugene, 36

social media, 169, 170

"social memory," 15, 110–11

Society for National Heritage (Anjuman-i Asar-i Melli), 8, 31

Soltan-Zadeh, Maryam, 176

Soviet Union, 132. *See also* Russia

"spiritual currency," 12, 141

state ceremonies, self-legitimization and, 129–30

Steep Fall, The (*Dar sarashib-i suqut*) (Salihi), 167–68

Story of the Virtuous, The (Motahhari), 55

Strate, Lance, 87

Stronach, David, 61, 121, 205n78

Suhrawardi, 43

Sunni Islam, 43, 64, 65–66, 175

surveillance, SAVAK and, 134

Susa, 23

symbols, 1–17, 179–88; appropriation of, 9, 11, 16, 65–66, 78, 108, 144, 153–56, 182, 184, 185, 186; archaeology and, 25; "commemorative density" and, 33–35; ethnosymbolism, 6, 10–12, 180; external, 137; institutionalized, 182; *invented traditions* and, 112–13; mutual symbolism, 156; repression and removal of, 19, 150; return of, 156–66; selection of, 30, 72–73, 74, 87, 93, 108–25, 128–29, 179–80; as "spiritual currency," 12, 141; systems of in Iran, 12, 186; timelines and, 10, 13, 74, 79, 117, 180; war propaganda and, 104, 146–47. *See also* celebrations and ceremonies; ethnosymbolism; rituals; *specific symbol*

Tabataba'i, 'Allamah Mohammad Husayn, 100–102, 103
Taffazuli, Jahangir, 71–72
Tafsir al-mizan (The Balance in Interpretation) (Tabataba'i), 100–102
Tahirid dynasty, 175
Tajwidi, 'Ali Akbar, 118
Takht-i Jamshid, 35, 116, 117, 121, 154, 209n28. *See also* Persepolis
Talberg, Frederick, 78–79
tamaddun (term), 141
tamaddun-i bozorg (Great Civilization), 158
Taqizadeh, Hasan, 27, 28, 29, 31, 37, 133
taqrib movement, 65–66
Tavakoli-Targhi, Mohamad, 7–8, 25, 162, 164
Tawzih al-masa'il (Clarification of Questions) (Shafa'), 62–63, 64, 66
Tawzih al-masa'il (Khomeini), 68
Taymurtash, Abulhusayn, 30, 118
technology, Iranian authenticity and, 126–27
Tehran University, 96, 165, 203n39
television, 77, 130, 134, 138
"temporal depth," 13
textbooks, Islamic Republic and, 150, 172–77
Third Worldism, 56–57, 89, 104, 145, 151–52, 168
timelines, creation of, 10, 13, 74, 79, 117, 180
Timurid dynasty, 128
Tobacco Rebellion, 48
tolerance, as theme, 85, 89–90
tombs: of Cyrus the Great, 61, 108, 121, 125, 164–65, 166, 170–71; of imams, 154–55; of poets, 8, 9, 30, 32, 34, 63
Toynbee, Arnold, 122, 130–32
Traveler's Narrative, A ('Abbas), 22
treaties, 19–20, 172
Tripp, Charles, 146–47
Tsereteli, Georgi, 132
Turkemanchay Treaty, 19–20
Twelver Shi'i Islam, 158

Umayyad dynasty, 12, 59, 67
UNESCO, 171
United Nations, 81–82
United States: imperialistic ambitions of, 89, 104; Iranian diaspora and, 161, 169–70; Islamic Republic and, 145; as materialistic, 36; Persepolis celebrations and, 61, 82, 132
University of Chicago, 118
Ustadhi, Reza, 155

Vaziri, Mustafa, 6–8
vilayat-i faqih (Rule of the Jurisprudent), 69, 136–37

Warburg, Aby, 15
war propaganda, 104, 146–47
Welles, Orson, 128
Western culture: dress codes, 29, 55; influence of, 25–26, 30–31, 44, 87–88, 119, 135, 141–42; Iranian influence on, 62, 85, 91, 122; popular culture and, 82–83
Western education and scholarship: conferences, 90–91, 105, 130–34; Cyrus cylinder and, 73, 94; influence of on Iranian intellectuals, 5, 7–8, 24–29, 31, 32, 36, 122; modernization and, 31; Third Worldist thought and, 104; White Revolution and, 46. *See also* Orientalism; *specific scholar*

westernization, 31, 77, 111, 141–42
Western nationalism, 54, 145
Western values, 73, 77, 91
Westoxication ("Gharbzadegi"), 41, 142
White Revolution, 46, 77, 115, 123
Winter, Jay, 3, 114
World War I, 26, 28

Xenakis, Iannis, 119–20
xenophobia, 65, 82–83
Xenophon's "Cyropedia" (Gera), 73

Yack, Bernard, 199n55
Yarshater, Ehsan, 53
Yazid ibn Mu'awiyah, 59
youth: books for, 83–84, 172–77; religion and, 55–56, 156, 162

Zand, Karim Khan, 117, 128
Zerubavel, Eviatar, 74
Zerubavel, Yael, 33
Ziarids dynasty, 175
Zoroastrianism: *cheharshanbe suri* and, 155–56; Cyrus and, 73–74; Iranian intellectuals and, 8; Iranian spirit and, 42–43, 46; in modern Iran, 57–58; as monotheistic, 95–96, 166–67; Motahhari and, 57–58; origins of Iran and, 84; Saoshyant, 50; Shafa' and, 64, 66; Shari'ati and, 54; treatment of, 89, 90–91. *See also* Nowruz (Iranian New Year)

Menahem Merhavy earned his PhD from the Department of Middle Eastern and African History at Tel Aviv University in 2012. Formerly a researcher at the Leonard Davis Institute for International Relations at the Hebrew University and a Fulbright postdoctoral fellow at the University of Texas at Austin, Merhavy is currently a fellow at the Harry S. Truman Institute for the Advancement of Peace at the Hebrew University, Jerusalem. He lectures at Rothberg International School of the Hebrew University and Bar Ilan University.